OTHER BOOKS BY THE AUTHORS

Dancing with the Wheel: The Medicine Wheel Workbook
by Sun Bear, Wabun Wind, and Crysalis Mulligan

Black Dawn, Bright Day
by Sun Bear with Wabun Wind

Woman of the Dawn
by Wabun Wind

Walk in Balance
by Sun Bear, Crysalis Mulligan, Peter Nufer, and Wabun

The Bear Tribe's Self-Reliance Book
by Sun Bear, Wabun, and Nimimosha

The Path of Power
by Sun Bear, Wabun, and Barry Weinstock

The Medicine Wheel: Earth Astrology
by Sun Bear and Wabun

*Lightseeds: A Compendium of Ancient and Contemporary
Crystal Knowledge*
by Wabun Wind and Anderson Reed

Buffalo Hearts
by Sun Bear

At Home in the Wilderness
by Sun Bear

The People's Lawyers
by Marlise James, aka Wabun

Sun Bear, Wabun Wind, and Shawnodese

A FIRESIDE BOOK

PUBLISHED BY SIMON & SCHUSTER

New York London Toronto

Sydney Tokyo Singapore

DREAMING
WITH THE
WHEEL

How to Interpret

and Work

with your Dreams

Using the

Medicine Wheel

FIRESIDE
Rockefeller Center
1230 Avenue of the Americas
New York, New York 10020

Designed by Bonni Leon-Berman
Manufactured in the United States of America

10   9   8   7   6   5   4

Library of Congress Cataloging-in-Publication Data
Sun Bear, 1929–
 Dreaming with the wheel : how to interpret and work with your dreams using
the medicine wheel / Sun Bear, Wabun Wind, and Shawnodese.
  p. cm.
 "A Fireside Book."
 Includes bibliographical references and index.
  1. Dream interpretation. 2. Medicine wheels—Miscellanea. 3. Indians of North
America—Religion and mythology. 4. Dreams—Dictionaries. I. Wabun Wind.
II. Shawnodese. III. Title.
 BF1901.S83   1994
 154.6'3—dc20   93-38972
                           CIP

ISBN: 0-671-78416-1

The authors of this book are not your physicians, and the ideas, procedures, and
suggestions in this book are intended to supplement, not replace, the medical and
legal advice of trained professionals. All matters regarding your health require
medical supervision. Consult your health care practitioner before adopting any
suggestions in this book, as well as about any condition that may require diagnosis
or medical attention.

The authors and publishers disclaim any liability arising directly or indirectly from
the use of this book.

To Sun Bear,
who dared to dream,
and by his visions
brought the gift of
dreaming to
so many others.

Acknowledgments

I wish to acknowledge here each person who has made the Medicine Wheel a part of their life. I wish to thank all the people who, over the last several decades, have generously shared their dream life with me, Sun Bear, and Shawnodese. It is from our work with you that the inspiration for this book came.

A special thanks to Sheila Curry, our editor at Simon & Schuster, who originally suggested that we take the material we had gained from working with people's dreams and make it into a book that would help to guide others in their dream life.

This book has had more stops and starts than many of our other publications because of the circumstances surrounding Sun Bear's illness and death. I would like to acknowledge here all the people who gave Sun Bear help, friendship, love, and support of all kinds during his illness. He really appreciated knowing that the love and inspiration he had given to others was being returned to him. It made a difficult time much easier. I thank all of you who took the time to write or call or pray, or in other ways send back to this man some of what you gained from his inspiration and example.

I particularly thank Jaya Bear, whose devotion to Sun Bear and his care was unstinting. I also thank all of the people who were living on Vision Mountain during Sun Bear's illness for the things they did that made life easier for him.

My gratitude to the many people who have come since Sun Bear's passing to help make the work of the Bear Tribe continue. Special thanks to all those who now work in the Bear Tribe offices, and to those who are teachers for the Tribe, regional coordinators, local coordinators, and affiliates. It's a big vision we're fulfilling, part Sun Bear's, part each of ours who work with the foundation he gave. It will take the help of all of us for this vision to grow and continue bringing help to the earth and all her children.

Personal thanks to those who have made writing possible for me with all of the other responsibilities I have had for the Bear Tribe. Special thanks to Kyla Wind, Jeannette Ritter, Marty Kovach, Judith Trustone, Diane Duggan, Margie White, Susan and David James, Jim Caola, Robert James, Dawn Songfeather, Patty Elvey, Beth Davis, Barbara d'Andrea, Moon Deer, Dixie Wind Daughter Carlson, Elisabeth Robinson, Joe Walling, Hanna Mondry, Jaya Bear, Page Bryant, Mary Thorn Gabrielle, Julia Brown, Sue King, Hemetra Crecraft, James Hunter, Scott Guynup, and all the other good people who have helped. Deep appreciation to Howard and Sue Lamb for making everything much easier, clearer, and more loving.

A special thanks to Susan James for her help with research, to Laure Washington and Sara Hetznecker-Sheehan for their help with typing, and to Dorrie Sellers and Arthur and Laure Washington for reading, editing, and commenting upon the manuscript. Thanks also to Thunderbird Woman for her beautiful artwork, which graces these pages.

Thanks to Brant Secunda, Luke Blue Eagle, Steven Foster, Twylah Nitsch, Page Bryant, and Brooke Medicine Eagle for taking the time to talk with me, and for agreeing to let some of their material be utilized in this book.

As always, thanks to all of my relations in all of the kingdoms of creation for their compassion, their understanding, their humor, and their constant reminder that humans are not the universal big cheeses we sometimes take ourselves to be.

—Wabun
Spring 1993

I would like to acknowledge the following dreamers, wise people, and friends who contributed inspiration or material to my understanding of dreams: Sun Bear, Betty Bethards, Dorothy Bryant, Edgar Cayce, Sigmund Freud, Mildred Huber, Carl Jung, Elsie Sechrist, and T. L. Rampa.

—Shawnodese
1993

Authors' Note

We ask those of you thinking of building a Medicine Wheel to only do so on your own land. There has been some inadvertent mistreatment of national park land by people who take stones to build Medicine Wheels without realizing that disturbing the stones sometimes disturbs a very fragile ecosystem.

The Medicine Wheel is designed to be a tool of earth healing. It takes great consciousness of the environment to make sure that each step you take leaves no footprint. Until you have that consciousness, it's best to work in an area where you will cause little damage if you step incorrectly. It is our wish that all Medicine Wheels being built be done in such a way that they help the healing of the Earth Mother. We want to acknowledge here all of you who build Wheels in this way.

Contents

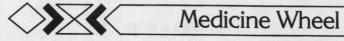

Medicine Wheel

THE CENTER

Name of Stone	Element	Mineral
Creator	All or Any	All or Any
Earth Mother	Earth	Clay
Father Sun	Fire & Air	Geode
Grandmother Moon	Water	Moonstone
Turtle Clan	Earth	Petrified Wood
Frog Clan	Water	River Rock
Thunderbird Clan	Fire	Lava Rock
Butterfly Clan	Air	Azurite

THE SPIRIT

Name of Stone	Element	Mineral
Waboose (North)	Earth	Alabaster
Wabun (East)	Air	Pipestone
Shawnodese (South)	Water	Serpentine
Mudjekeewis (West)	Fire	Soapstone

THE MOONS

	Dates	Name of Moon	Mineral
North	Dec. 22-Jan. 19	Earth Renewal	Quartz
North	Jan. 20-Feb. 18	Rest & Cleansing	Silver
North	Feb. 19-March 20	Big Winds	Turquoise
East	March 21-April 19	Budding Trees	Fire Opal
East	April 20-May 20	Frogs Return	Chrysocolla
East	May 21-June 20	Cornplanting	Moss Agate
South	June 21-July 22	Strong Sun	Carnelian Agate
South	July 23-Aug. 22	Ripe Berries	Garnet & Iron
South	Aug. 23-Sept. 22	Harvest	Amethyst
West	Sept. 23-Oct. 23	Ducks Fly	Jasper
West	Oct. 24-Nov. 21	Freeze Up	Copper & Malachite
West	Nov. 22-Dec. 21	Long Snows	Obsidian

THE SPIRIT

Name of Quality	Position	Mineral
Cleansing	Outer North	Sodalite
Renewal	Middle North	Peridote
Purity	Inner North	Herkimer Diamond
Clarity	Outer East	Mica
Wisdom	Middle East	Jade
Illumination	Inner East	Calcite
Growth	Outer South	Fluorite
Trust	Middle South	Lapidilite
Love	Inner South	Rose Quartz
Experience	Outer West	Hematite
Introspection	Middle West	Lapis Lazuli
Strength	Inner West	Amber

Reference Chart

CIRCLE

Plant	Animal	Color
All or Any	All or Any	All or Any
Corn, Beans, Squash	Tortoise	Forest Green
Sunflower	Lizard	Sky Blue
Mugwort	Loon	Silver/White
Cattails	Turtle	Green/Brown
Algae	Frog	Blue/Green
Fireweed	Thunderbird	Red
Butterfly Weed	Butterfly	Translucent w/Blue

KEEPERS

Plant	Animal	Color
Sweetgrass	White Buffalo	White
Tobacco	Golden Eagle	Gold & Red
Sagebrush	Coyote	Yellow & Green
Cedar	Grizzly Bear	Blue & Black

AND TOTEMS

Plant	Animal	Color	
Birch	Snow Goose	White	✿
Quaking Aspen	Otter	Silver	✾
Plantain	Cougar	Turquoise	✵
Dandelion	Red Hawk	Yellow	✽
Blue Camas	Beaver	Blue	✿
Yarrow	Deer	White & Green	✾
Wild Rose	Flicker	Pink	✵
Raspberry	Sturgeon	Red	✽
Violet	Brown Bear	Purple	✿
Mullein	Raven	Brown	✾
Thistle	Snake	Orange	✵
Black Spruce	Elk	Black	✽

PATHS

Plant	Animal	Color
Echinacea	Raccoon	Pale Green
Red Clover	Earthworm	Dark Green
Trillium	Dolphin	Translucent White
Rosemary	Hummingbird	Clear
Sage	Owl	Jade Green
Wild American Ginseng	Firefly	Fluorescent Blue
Comfrey	Rabbit	Violet
Borage	Salmon	Lavender
Hawthorne	Wolf	Rose
Olive	Whale	Steel Grey
Chamomile	Mouse	Royal Blue
Nettle	Ant	Golden Yellow

THE VISION OF A MAN; THE BIRTH OF A VISION

The vision of the Medicine Wheel continues to unfold. Sun Bear was the visionary who originally brought the concept of the Medicine Wheel back to the people. Over the years, many others have added to his original vision. All of those who read *The Medicine Wheel: Earth Astrology* and then built a Medicine Wheel in their own home or on their land have become a part of that vision. *The Medicine Wheel* is now available in over ten languages and the book has been read worldwide by well over half a million people. An untold number of Medicine Wheels have been built as a result of Sun Bear's original vision.

The vision has been further helped by all those who have attended a Medicine Wheel Gathering. Thus far there have been close to sixty gatherings, each attended by an average of five hundred people. There have also been many who have participated in workshops given by Sun Bear, Wabun, or their many students about the Medicine Wheel.

The idea for *Dreaming with the Wheel* came in part from the people who have come to Sun Bear, Wabun, and Shawnodese over the years and told them their dreams about symbols from the Medicine Wheel. Often these people had the dreams before they had ever heard about the vision of the Medicine Wheel, and then were very surprised that someone could tell them that their dream of an eagle going from east to west was simply the spirit force moving in its usual manner.

Over time, Sun Bear, Wabun, and Shawnodese began to conclude that the symbols of the Medicine Wheel were forming a whole new language in the collective unconscious. That made sense, since the spirit of a place helps to form the people. Once people of European heritage came to the Americas, it was inevitable that they would be affected by the symbolic life that had been on the American continent for untold thousands of years, and that this symbolic life would begin to enter their consciousness in ways they might not have guessed. Undoubtedly, this process was helped by the fact that so many symbols of the Americas were similar to the forbidden and thus repressed earth symbols of the rest of the planet.

As Sun Bear, Wabun, and Shawnodese traveled outside the United States, they received reports from people who were dreaming of the Medicine Wheel symbols, again before they had any prior knowledge of it. This phenomena mystified them for a time. Then they began to wonder: Is it possible that if the collective consciousness shifts in one part of the world, this affects the stream of collective consciousness that helps mold the dream life of people all around the globe? Are we that connected in some parts of our being?

Just as animals brought to the North American continent from Europe changed somewhat in both appearance and habits, so did humans. Central to the belief system of any Earth people is a great respect for the spirits that walk upon the land, the spirits that protect and guard the land. When any beings come into a new area, they become affected by the spirits, the energies, of that land, and they are never the same. When Europeans first came here, hoping to practice their religion in the way they had been denied in Europe, it was inevitable that their philosophies, their concepts, and their very being would be changed over time through their encounters with the energies of the new world. And this has been the case. Much of the culture of the Americas today is a beautiful hybrid of the cultures of the many people who came here and, willingly or not, became affected by the energies of this great land.

To take one small, specific example, the eagle, which to Native people of this country represented the messenger of the Creator, became the symbol of the new federation of states that became the United States. The eagle became as important to the newcomers who adopted this symbol as it had been to the Native people; this magnificent raptor became one symbol with two meanings. Yet freedom, and the power to understand the different realms of reality, is inherent in both meanings.

One day, several years after people began reporting to them their Medicine Wheel dreams, Sun Bear and Wabun were having lunch with Sheila Curry, their editor at what was then Prentice Hall Press. Sheila began to talk about the possibility of doing a book on dreams that would incorporate some of the wisdom of the Medicine Wheel. It seemed a natural unfolding of the vision, and so they agreed.

They invited Shawnodese, who has a great deal of training both in Western psychology and in working with dreams, to become a coauthor of this book. He has been responsible for contributing a good deal of the dream material that has been used in all of the Bear Tribe educational programs, and they wished to add his expertise.

In the interim between discussing and actually undertaking the book, Sun Bear was diagnosed as having cancer. Shortly thereafter, he provided Wabun with tapes and notes he had made on the subject of dreaming, and also reminded both her and Shawnodese of the many times they had been with him when he both lectured and talked about dreams and his dream life. He felt certain the book should go ahead, no matter the outcome of his illness. Sun Bear then launched a program of treatment for the cancer; tragically, the treatment did not succeed. In June 1992, Sun Bear passed into spirit.

Sun Bear lived a life based upon vision. What better way to honor him than to complete a book about dreaming and vision? Above all else, in this visionless society, that's what set Sun Bear apart. Not only was he given the gift of vision, which we all are given, but he was also given the courage that allowed him to live by his visions, and he did not have easy visions to live by.

Sun Bear saw in his visions that his work was to teach Earth healing to people of all races, of all nationalities. He knew that he could not limit this teaching only to his own people, the Ojibwas, or to the other Native people. That would have made his life much easier, but his visions told him early on that he must give away what he knew to all the people in order for life to continue in a good way.

Sun Bear followed his vision, despite much disapproval and criticism from people who felt that the knowledge of one race should remain only with that race. Sun Bear's visions told him that we are living now in a time of change upon the Mother Earth, and part of this change must come within the heart of humankind. Again and again, Sun Bear saw in his visions that all of life followed the natural law, with the exception of human beings. In all of his teachings, he tried to bring humans back into the sacred web of life, to teach them how important they were to the continuation of life on the planet.

Sun Bear often spoke about his visions. He told of how they were what got him up every morning and carried him forward. His visions were the guiding force in his life, and this was true up until the very end. Sun Bear was concerned about the Bear Tribe until he drew his last breath. While most men want their children to carry on their names and their work, Sun Bear knew it was his vision child, the Bear Tribe, that would carry on the message the Creator had given to him.

Sun Bear often spoke about dreams and the power of dreams. Frequently, he would dream of a person or a place before he actually encountered that person or place on the Earth Mother. His dreams gave his guidance and help. They also gave him knowledge of things that cannot be known in the waking state. Sun Bear was a dream master, one who could teach through the dream state, one who could bring messages to others as they dreamed, one who could receive information in dreams that were being sent by others. According to letters that we have received from people around the planet, Sun Bear still continues his work.

To make this book as comprehensive as possible, Wabun chose to speak with some people whom she and Shawnodese consider to be expert in different aspects of dreaming. Among these people are Luke Blue Eagle, Twylah Nitsch, Page Bryant, Steven Foster, and Brooke Medicine Eagle. In the first section of this book, Wabun and Shawnodese bring the words of these teachers together through a five-day teaching dream council on Vision Mountain, the Bear Tribe's retreat center in Washington State. While this dream council never actually happened, it proved a good method to weave the teaching material together.

Dreaming is an unknown territory to many people. Historically, the dreamtime was as important to people as the waking hours. One of the reasons for the imbalance on the earth today is that so many people can't even remember, let alone work with, the material that comes to them in their dreams. This book provides the reader with an easy-to-follow guide to dreamtime.

In the beginning of the book are different views of the dreamtime, both historical and contemporary; an exploration of the difference between dreams and visions, if there is one; and stories of some dreams and visions that have come to the dream council teachers. Later in the book, these teachers give ways to prepare to dream, methods to help you in dreamtime, and a variety of ways to interpret and work with your dreams.

In the second section of the book is the "Dream Language of the Earth," a glossary of the symbols Wabun, Shawnodese, and Sun Bear encountered in their own dreams and in talking with people about dreams. Each entry in this section has key words, a natural description, common dream meanings, trick dream meanings, and transcendent meanings.

The best way to use the "Dream Language of the Earth" is to read it through entirely before you begin to work with your dreams. By doing so, you will begin to incorporate even more of this dream language into your own dreamtime. Then, when you go back to this section as you dream, you will have gained the ability to understand more specifically what each of these symbols means in your own dream life.

Part One

The Dream Council

THE DREAM COUNCIL

Welcome, friend. Come and sit with us in a dream circle. Let's imagine we can all sit together in the longhouse at Vision Mountain. We have a talking stick* we can pass, a pine branch Sun Bear picked up from the earth outside. As one of us speaks, the rest of us listen as attentively as we can. We're here to learn how to make the dreamtime a more active part of our lives. Through this learning, we will be able to bring about a much better balance in our lives, and on our planet.

People who lived close to the earth all around the world had a great respect for the dreamtime. They knew what we call waking reality is only one of the many realities open to us two-leggeds.

The sun is preparing to set, the twilight to come. Some say this is the

---

*See Appendix, exercise one.

time of day when you can most easily find a "crack" between the realms of reality. We hear our brothers the thunder beings in the distance. They add their good medicine to the dream circle.

This is the first night of the dream circle, so it is time now to share the medicine of dreaming. With Sun Bear are two of his medicine helpers, Wabun and Shawnodese. Wabun has been with him since 1970, growing into her power and understanding. She has helped guide hundreds of people on vision quests. She has worked hard to understand the language of dreams, and she has a powerful gift for bringing dreams into reality. Some of Sun Bear's most important medicine dreams have become reality through her gift.

Shawnodese has worked with Sun Bear since 1979. Understanding and working with dreams has been part of his medicine since childhood. Through his dreams, he helped to create Sun Bear's apprentice program and has taught many workshops on dreams in that program and elsewhere. Shawnodese is also a healer of both mind and body.

Sun Bear, Wabun, and Shawnodese have invited other teachers to join the dream circle and share their experiences of the dreamtime. Luke Blue Eagle, a young man who has studied with Sun Bear for over a decade, sits in the dream circle. He is one of Sun Bear's apprentices who now has apprentices of his own. He comes from the north country, from Canada, and has a good understanding of the dream world. He'll be teaching for most of the five days, although he has some friends in Spokane to visit sometime during the circle.

Steven Foster is here tonight and tomorrow. Steven is the director of the School of Lost Borders, where people learn about wilderness rites and ceremonies of initiation. Steven has guided a large number of people in such rites, and is the author of several books about this process. He has to do some visiting, too, but will be back later to help.

Grandmother Twylah Nitsch of the Wolf Clan Teaching Lodge has shared some of her teachings with Wabun via a taped interview, and Wabun will present this interview as the council proceeds. In Twylah's eighty years of earth walk, she has had the opportunity to dream many dreams and see them come into being on earth. She has helped many people to understand the dreams that have come to them.

Brooke Medicine Eagle has also shared teachings with Wabun through a taped interview. This sister is an Earthkeeper and healer who knows how to be guided by her dreams, and knows how to inspire others to dream.

Page Bryant, Sun Bear's first apprentice, an author and teacher of twenty-five years, spoke on tape with Wabun earlier about a couple of stories that come from her studies about the dream life of people.

Waiting to hear from these teachers, both those in the circle and those who will speak via tape, is an international group of students who have come to learn how to better experience the dreamtime. Of the thirty people here, eighteen have been out to fast in the wilderness; of these, five guide others in this wilderness initiation process. Eleven participants are from Europe, two from Canada, the rest from the United States. Two participants are doctors, seven are therapists or counselors, and one is a minister.

It's a good circle of people. All of the teachers have taken the time to both dream and go out into the wilderness themselves to seek vision. So have many of the participants.

But the teachers and the students aren't the only ones in this circle. The spirit forces, the keepers of the dreams, are here, too. They'll tell stories between the words you might hear, stories that might guide you into living a dream life.

Wabun takes the talking stick and begins to speak. "In a time so long ago most people forget it ever existed, we all lived in the dreamtime. It did not matter whether we were awake or asleep. We all remembered where we came from, who we were, and where we were going. With our eyes open, we could see and feel as much beauty as most people only feel today when they shut their eyes in sleep.

"We could fly. We could talk to the animals. We could hear what they said back to us. We could go to the gods; we could part the waters. We could love wholly and completely. We could gather, we could chant, we could dance, we could drum. We could build, we could birth. We could feel the beauty of the Earth Mother. We lived within the sacred web of life.

"There were only two things we could not do: We could not think, and we could not speak. But there was no need for speech. What I felt, you knew. And what you knew, I felt within me. We could communicate so completely that if one of us had a need, others of us would give whatever help was required. If the need was to be alone, we could withdraw. If the need was to be supported, we would draw closer. If the need was for ecstasy, we would share joy. If the need came from one of our animal brothers or sisters, we would give whatever they needed. If a plant encountered problems, we would try to remedy them. If the balance of the earth was threatened, we would draw together and bring that balance back into place.

"And then time passed. With its passage, change occurred. We began to realize we were singular. We felt the difference between yours and mine. Within a short period of time, we began to think. Our thoughts drove even more distance between us. When that happened we drew apart in a way we never had before. We started to categorize, to measure. Thoughts were different from the communications we had before. They were singular in such a way that our unity was never quite the same. While we could feel together, dream together, we could not quite think together. Unity seemed not within the nature of thought.

"More time passed. The sounds we had made in the past to honor the Earth Mother, to honor all of the Creation, began to change. Instead of the tones of unity, we uttered the words of singularity. As we spoke them, we put even more distance between us. While these words sounded alike, they were not. All of them held the feeling meaning of the person speaking them. While we thought we spoke the same language, we never did.

"As we began to speak, we began to understand more clearly the changes that had occurred. We realized the difference between being awake and being asleep. We lost our ability to speak to the animals, or to hear what they said to us. We could no longer feel the plants, or the minerals, or the elementals in quite the same way, except when we closed our eyes. A part of us yearned for the former unity we held between us. Yet only with our eyes closed could we approach that state of unity.

"One day a young one did something with her words that no one had ever done before. She used them to try to describe the feeling of unity she had experienced with her eyes closed. She used them to tell others about her dream.

" 'What is this?' all the other people said, at first with disbelief. 'How could this young one fly like a bird? How could she speak to the stars and know the hearts of the animals?'

"She said to her people, 'Just close your eyes for a moment and remember.' And they did. They remembered the times when in sleep they had talked to the animals, when they had been one with what they now called the gods. They remembered what it was to feel the ecstatic joy of unity, the wonder of true community, the passion beyond passion of complete love. They remembered, and they spoke. As they spoke, they wove that other reality into the reality that had become their everyday life. And they knew this was good.

"Time went on. Some people remembered to speak of their dreams, others forgot. Some cultures respected the power of dreams, others feared it. That young girl was born many times more—sometimes as a young man, sometimes as a young woman. Always it was her destiny to speak of the wonder of dreams. Always her speech was met with many negative feelings by the people who denied the dreamtime. But those who remembered what their hearts had felt in the reality of the dream heard her with happiness. These people found more joy in life and had less fear of death. Sometimes the rememberers were the prophets. Sometimes they were the truth-speakers. Sometimes they were the persecuted. But always they spoke their truth, and by so doing they helped the people to remember and helped the people to live.

"Perhaps that young woman, wearing either a male or female body, is someone you know today. Perhaps she is your teacher, your grandmother, your husband, your child. That young woman, and her brother from the dreamtime, is very present today, trying to teach us that for life to continue we have to weave back the broken cords. We have to remember not only our individuality but also our unified core. We have to learn again that we can and must listen to the animals, the plants, and all parts of the sacred web of life.

"Come now, brothers and sisters, and allow this dream circle to help you remember," Wabun concludes, and passes the stick back to Sun Bear.

"It's good, sister, ho!" he says. "Now let's all go to bed and see what dreams come to us."

DREAM WISDOM

People awaken with a sense of anticipation to begin this first full day of meeting in dream circle. It is a bright, clear, and crisp autumn day, washed clean by the rains that came with the thunder beings last night. The magic of the mountain begins to work on the participants new to the area, as it always has. Many find themselves rising earlier than usual and going out to take a walk and feel the energy both of the place and of the pine trees that seem to guard the location where the longhouse is built.

Some people walk as far as the pond where the Tribe's original sweat lodge was built. Others walk a little farther to see the first Medicine Wheel built as a result of Sun Bear's vision. More hardy souls go beyond, up to the area known as the Moon Rocks. Others climb still farther to the Air Mound, which gives a beautiful view of Long Lake in the distance and much of the surrounding countryside.

The teachers have agreed that there will be no firm time constraints on the beginnings and endings of the dream council. Since this is a time of contemplating the dreamtime, and since dreamtime has no sense of clock time, the teachers agree that the material will best be served by allowing participants to walk, talk, and interact both with one another and with the magic of the mountain. An additional benefit to the teachers is that it will give them time also to enjoy being on Vision Mountain.

When people are done with breakfast, Sun Bear suggests that the morning circle take place outdoors, so as to take advantage of the light and warmth of Father Sun before he climbs too high in the sky. It isn't a terribly warm day, yet people seem to feel just fine sitting in the sun wearing light jackets.

Sun Bear takes the talking stick and reminds people that the person holding the talking stick has the right to speak, while everyone else has the right to listen. Then he begins: "I am a dreamer. Dreaming is one of my strong medicines, and much of my medicine comes to me through dreams. I delight in this, as I always feel good with the spirits. I always keep a notebook close to my bed so I can write down the good ideas that come to me from my dreams. You can do this, too. When people ask me where I get some of my super ideas, I tell them very honestly, 'I dreamed it up!'

"To me, dreaming is a time when we get in touch with the spirits. It's a time we set aside when we are not being bothered with all the rush and run of everyday life. We are able to go to our bed at night and pray for strong dreams, dreams that will tell us things about what is happening in the world, dreams that will take us off into different parts of the universe so we can learn through things that we hadn't brought into our lives and our minds before.

"In the Native way, we always feel we have certain spirits that come to us. These are guardian spirits and protector spirits. Sometimes the best time they can come to us is when we are in our dreams. So we pray for them to come, and when they do they give us very powerful direction and teaching.

"There are many dreamer societies among the Western Indian people. Chief Joseph was a member of a very powerful dreamer society. Among the other Natives, Wovoka was the Paiute prophet and a great dreamer. Like many Native people, he relied very much on his dreams to teach him and give him knowledge.

"The Australian Aborigines say their life history consists of over forty thousand years in the dreamtime. They even dream their children before they are born. They dream whether they will be boys or girls. They dream what they will look like, and what their behavior patterns will be. The Aborigines feel that all the rest of creation can dream. Sometime back there was a movie called *Where the Green Ants Dream*. In it, many Australian Aborigines were protesting a uranium mining company going into an area to mine because they believed that was the area where the green ants dream. They knew that to disturb that area was to disturb the whole of nature.

"When Aboriginal youth reach a certain age, they go out on a special voyage called a walkabout. It is done at a sacred area, such as Ayers Rock, which used to be a favorite location. At this time, they live off the land completely in the old way. They live off what they call bush tucker, which is the food they can get off the bushes. They hunt for their own food. In their travels, they go from one dreamer place to another. They go to each place and pray. As I've mentioned, Ayers Rock is a very powerful dreamer rock for many of the Aboriginal people. As they go along across the country, they have all kinds of sacred places. The young men pray that the spirits come to them there and give them new knowledge.

"The Aborigines are very powerful in their knowledge of how to dream about something or someone, and change the events or improve the health of the person they are dreaming about. Some of the Aborigine people I met told me there was one man who was going to build a supermarket in an area. He found out that part of the area was the place where old men come to dream. So he set that aside for them so they could continue to pray and dream there. This is a very strong and respected part of the Australian culture."

When Sun Bear puts down the stick, indicating that he is done speaking for now, Luke Blue Eagle asks whether he can have the stick next. When it comes to him he begins to speak.

"The dream world and the dream work was a part of the training of all the medicine people, of all the shamans, and it's a part also of teaching. Like the Australian Aborigines, many Native people teach the history of their nations through the dreamtime. What I'd like to add about the Walkabout . . . is that they're taught directly from the ancestors in the dream world about their heritage. This is also a part of the American Indian way of looking at things. Dreaming was a part of everyday life; when you woke up in the morning, you'd discuss your dreams with the family. And people would know that there were different types of dreams and qualities of dreams, that there are serious dreams and dreams that don't mean anything. Unfortunately, society today has lost this kind of knowledge. But everybody in Native societies had access to this body of knowledge that's in the dream world. So everybody was considered as some kind of an authority on life and spiritual matters, because everybody could dream.

"Dreaming was considered to be the real world, as opposed to awakened, everyday life, which was an illusion for many peoples. Natives used to look at the dream world as the real world that was actually the creative aspect of our being. They believed that what we did in the dream world had direct influence over what we would do in the awakened world. They believed that the dream world or the dreamtime had physical consequences, that what you were doing in the dream world was creating what was happening in the physical. They believed that actually we are all in one big dream that is the Creator's dream, and that's what's creating the world we're in.

"Consequently, they believed that if you had things you're not sure about, you could ask the dream world to tell you if it's true or not. And that you can trust what the dream world says, where you can't always trust your awakened perceptions. I believe this is also true today.

"When people talk to me about dreams that they've had, the symbols that come up most frequently are animals. I think that's because animals are the closest to humans as far as our relationship with the various kingdoms is concerned. They speak to people in a way that is very refreshing and important for them. The animals have a way of life that is very simple, and very, very in the moment. This is something that we have lost, and we are estranged from our true nature by not being able to be with ourselves in the present moment. The teachings that come from the different animals are relevant to understanding who we are on a much more basic and fundamental level, which people need to come back to today. So, as I work with people and their dreams, I often find a lot of animals coming up in the dreams. Often these are very helpful in getting the person to come back to a more basic and simple way of understanding who they are."

Wabun asks if she can have the talking stick next. "When people have come to me with their dream symbols, animals often appear. Sometimes plant and mineral beings, particularly those associated with the Medicine Wheel, also appear in people's dreams. I always think that it's really good when someone from the other kingdoms of creation comes to visit a human in the dream state. It's so important for people today to recognize the necessity for them to come back into harmony with the sacred circle of life, to realize that humans aren't the only beings that exist on the planet. I always like to remind people when I'm teaching that to most of the Earth peoples I've studied, humans are only one of many kingdoms of being on the Earth Mother. Kingdoms isn't a good word, but I've yet to find one that's better.

"Native people around the world seem to have all believed that the first beings on the earth were the elements: earth, water, fire, and air. The elements were considered to be the most independent because they could exist apart from any of the other kingdoms of creation on the earth. Native people considered the plant beings to also be relatively independent, because they could exist with only the help of the elements. They considered the animal beings to be more dependent than the elements or plants because the animals could not survive without the help of both. And they considered the two-leggeds, the humans, to be the most dependent of all, because we can't survive without the help of the other three—the elements, the plants, and the animals. That's one of the things I like best about the Medicine Wheel system: It teaches people to respect those other three kingdoms upon the Earth Mother.

"When I talked to our good sister Page Bryant, who was not able to be with us but wanted to share some words with the dream council, she had a good story about the animal beings."

"Wabun," says Page's tape-recorded voice, "I wanted to tell you a story I heard when I studied about the Skidi Pawnee. *Skidi* means wolf, so they were the Wolf Clan people of the Pawnee Nation of the Great Plains. For all practical purposes, they are now extinct. I think of them most often as the star cult of the Great Plains because of their star lore as well as their ceremonials that were related to the stars. All of their cosmology was related to the stars, more so than with any other Native people I have read about. The Skidi Pawnee people believed that the earth, when it was first born from a union between the Morning Star and the Evening Star, was without life. Then animals, who were actually stars, came down to the earth, and they were given all of the original teachings by the Creator. When humans came, the animals had been here first; so the animals were the teachers of the humans.

"One of their sacred villages, called Pa'huk—which meant Pumpkin Vine Village—was located where the Platte, Loop, and Republican rivers meet. The Skidi Pawnee believed that deep inside the bluff of the Republican River, underneath the water, was the Animal Lodge. Here lived one of each of the animals and one human. The only way you could get into the Animal Lodge as a human was through dreams. If you succeeded, you were taught the traditional teachings, and you might also be given prophecies and ceremonies. There is one very famous story in the Skidi Pawnee tradition about a little boy who dreamed his way into the Animal Lodge. He came back and told the people of his tribe a lot of the wisdom that had been given to him in that way by the animals.

"Pa'huk is right outside of what is now called Omaha. It is said that in the place that marked the spot where the Animal Lodge was, there was a great cedar tree. This tree was said to be always filled with birds of all different kinds—hawks and crows and wrens, all different kinds of birds. To this day, the older people in the area say that there is a very unusual tree there, one that is always filled with birds."

On the tape, Wabun asks Page whether she feels there is a difference between dreamtime and waking reality.

"Yes, and no," Page replied. "There is obviously a difference in terms of the state of consciousness one is in. But I believe that the information and guidance we receive in the dream state is the same as what we receive awake in the so-called intuitive or alpha state. But I would also say, personally, that the dream state is more real to me simply because it's in that state that the ego's out of the way. So to me, it's a truth arena within my consciousness."

Wabun turns off the tape, adding that she would like to emphasize that to her the dream state is a very special time in that it is when people can see the truth about themselves as well as the truth about the universe. She continues by saying that she feels it is important that people see the truth about themselves so that what they first believe to be universal truths are not colored by their own misconceptions.

Shawnodese asks whether he can add something to that point, and the talking stick is passed to him. "Most of the dream seminars I've taught," he says, "have been within the context of studying Native American philosophy and approaches to life. I often have a very psychological bent to the material I present. Not surprisingly, participants will sometimes ask me, 'What's all this psychological stuff got to do with shamanic dreaming, medicine dreams, vision dreams? I want you to teach me how to have power dreams that will bring me spirit allies to work with my own personal medicine and my development of personal power.' I suspect many of you in the dream circle might have just the same question.

"In general, the attitude of people who are seeking to understand spiritual truths, to learn spiritual practices that will allow them to become more aware of themselves and their connections to the earth, has an element in it that I find totally amazing. One does not expect a newborn baby to run the Boston Marathon. First the baby has to learn how to roll over, then how to scoot, then how to crawl. Finally, it stands up and begins to take its first few, tentative steps, with many falls along the way. Later, it begins to walk freely. Much later, it learns to run, skip, and jump. This ever-increasing freedom over the force of gravity only comes as a result of the development of both strength and skill. Yet the spiritual seeker often suffers from the mistaken expectation that he or she should have fantastic, miraculous results instantly.

"Except for the truly gifted and lucky individual, it just isn't so. Even the most gifted individual must be trained—muscles must be strengthened, skills must be honed. As it is on any quest for development. Before you run, jump, and dance, learn first how to walk solidly on two feet.

"This is why I present information that may be considered 'psychological' as the first step in working with your dreams. Unless you are a psychologically well-balanced person, your emotional garbage will continually color and pollute your dreaming process. This can make it almost impossible to sort out delusional, egotistical wish fulfillment from the true medicine dream. The phrase 'know thyself' applies perhaps more directly to the study of dreamtime than to any other aspect of your life. If you truly know yourself, it then becomes easy to sort out the extraordinary, the spirit gift aspect of a dream, from the bizarre and conflicted psychological aspects of a dream. It really is quite possible for a dream to contain powerful elements both of a psychological and of a spiritual nature. But it is only through knowledge of yourself that you will be able to isolate and act upon the elements of a dream correctly.

"If you wish to dream powerful dreams, clean up your emotional garbage. You cannot escape who you are, not even in your dreams. But through your dreams, and through work with your dreams, you can enhance and expand who you are."

When the circle comes together again after a brief break, Shawnodese takes the talking stick and says, "During this interlude, all of us thought it would be good if we also took a few minutes now and went around the circle to introduce ourselves. We got so carried away with the material this morning that we didn't make time for introductions, so we'd like you to tell us your name, where you come from, what you do to make a living, what you really do if how you make your living has nothing to do with that, and your beginning Medicine Wheel totem if you know it."

Shawnodese then hands the talking stick to the person sitting to his right, and it passes from person to person around the circle, with everyone giving the information that has been requested. There are a preponderance of people from the helping professions; seven therapists and/or counselors, five people who guide vision quests, two doctors, and one minister. There are also four students, two homemakers, a retired couple, two business consultants, three secretaries, one accountant, and one person who is unemployed. There are nine people in the group who were born in Butterfly or Air Clan positions, eight in Thunderbird Clan positions, seven in Frog Clan positions, and six in Turtle Clan positions. Wabun comments that it should be a group very anxious to talk, very inspired, excited, and with the need both to be willing to open up emotionally and to learn to ground themselves. Wabun says she anticipates there might be more information to cover than time will allow, and that there will be a desire on each person's part to make sure the material they most want to hear about will be covered.

"Since I have the talking stick," Wabun says, "I'd like to take a few minutes to touch upon the dream work done by the Senoi people of Malaysia.

"Now, I realize there is some controversy as to the validity of the studies done of the Senoi dream work, but whatever the truth of the matter, it is a fascinating theory, and one that has helped many people to understand and work with their dreams in a better way.

"Like the aboriginal people of Australia, the Senoi believe that dreams are very real, and that the dreams a person has can and should both be continued and completed, so that the dreamer will get some knowledge that will be useful both to him and to his people, to the rest of the tribe.

"The Senoi, according to anthropologists, are a very peaceful tribe with very little anxiety or illness and no violent crimes reported for the past several hundred years. Anthropologists attribute some of this to the dream work the Senoi do.* They say their dream work allows them to get rid of fears that would otherwise cause them to act in disharmonious ways. The Senoi also believe that all pleasant dreams can give something that is beautiful or useful to the group.

"It is said that the Senoi actively work with their children to make sure they will know how to conduct themselves in their dreams. First they encourage children to remember dreams, mainly by the example they set discussing their dreams every morning. They also teach their children to complete whatever happens in their dreams. For example, if a child has a dream of falling that scares them and makes them wake up, the Senoi would encourage the child to relax and enjoy the fall, knowing that there was a gift for them or their people whenever they came to the bottom. Another way they would deal with dreams of falling is to encourage the child to start flying at some point during the fall, and to fly until they came to someone or something that had a gift for the child or for the tribe.

"If a child dreams of a monster or something else that frightens him, the Senoi would tell the child that, rather than running away, he should stand there, look at the monster, and ask the monster what gift the monster has for him or his people. They also encourage the children to see a continuity between the waking state and the dreaming state by acting out gifts that come in the dream state. For example, if a child hears a song in a dream, the Senoi will encourage the child to sing that song for the whole

*See Appendix, exercise two.

group. Or if they learn a dance, they will be encouraged to show every-one how to do that dance.

"Because of this work with children and dreams, dreams do not become a fearful part of life, but rather a wondrous part of life, something to look forward to. I often wonder how many of the sleep problems adults in this society report could be conquered by using some of the same techniques for dream work that the Senoi are said to have used.

"Over the years I've read a lot on and talked to various Native people about the dream state. One thing that stands out from these conversations and readings is just how much Native people consider dreaming to be an essential part of life. In listening to you, Sun Bear, I realize how much dreams guide your life, and I also realize how different this is from the things we're taught in the mainstream culture. When I grew up there was no attention given to my dreams, and I don't ever remember receiving support or help for the nightmares I had from time to time. Consequently, I began to ignore my dreams, and it took me quite a while to recognize that dreams could be a very helpful aspect of my life. I think that my ex-perience is quite common, and sad.

"When I started to pay attention to my dreams and visions, it opened up a whole new world for me. It made me realize that what I had been taught as defining the world was very narrow compared to what the world really is."

When Wabun is finished, Steven Foster indicates that he would like the talking stick, so it is passed around the circle to him.

"Meredith and I also have been doing a lot of research on the Aborig-ines," Steven says. "They say that in the beginning was the dream, and all of their ceremonies are attempts to get back to that dream world, to that dreaming. It seems to me that this sort of thing is still real today, not only with Native peoples but with so-called civilized people as well.

"Meredith and I and a few friends recently went on our yearly vision fast. During the time of the fast, we were in a dream. Whenever you cross the threshold in a rite of passage, you enter the dream, and the dream lasts however long you stay in that state. A lot of material comes up from the unconscious during that time, from the darkness and the shadows of inwardness. The dream is what is born from the unmanifested, from that fertile source of imagination and creation. The dream is original, yet it also comes from our DNA.

"I've been studying the relationship between what the Native people call the dream and what biologists call DNA. I think that the dream or the voices of the ancestors are certainly in some way or another connected with the DNA drama, the dancing of the genes in the consciousness. We all share in this original DNA; we can call it mother if we want to. So the dream comes from the mother DNA; it comes from that original life, and we continue to dream that original life. In that sense we share dreaming with all the other creatures. We share the dream of life, and death, the dream of the seasons.

"I believe that not only are other animals conscious, but they have emotions, a psychological life, and what you might call a rational life—not perhaps rational in the sense that humans call rational. And they live a life of wholly natural praise and illumination. I would say that we share, on many levels, life and death with all the other creatures, including the dream, the original dream, the Mother dream.

"I identify dreaming with the Mother, the great giver, with the feminine, with the tides, the menstrual flow. Psychoanalysts, particularly those of a Jungian bent, often identify dreaming with the anima, the receptive. In Chinese thought it's identified with the yin, the breathing in. Dream is the prefantasy that gives birth to fantasy. Dream is also daydreaming. So also are the chaotic, the irrational, and the oceanic aspects of human experience. So the dream is primordial. It is a dawning at the place where the sun goes down.

"A lot of things go on while in the dream state, and much of it is little understood. Dreams teach feeling and self-consciousness; they teach us about initiation. The dream is the middle phase of the rite of passage—first severance from a former life, then the threshold or the dream threshold, and finally incorporation. Incorporation, the third phase, involves 'vision' as opposed to 'dream.' The vision is what people do with their dream.

"Vision, then, is that which is manifested by the dream. Vision is conscious. It comes up from the unconscious in the form of dreams. It becomes vision when it becomes conscious, when it is performed, demonstrated, enacted, carried forth with order, purpose, and self-discipline. We have heard many people describe visions that they never did anything about. Vision must have an active element. As a matter of fact, we've begun to define vision in terms of 'What are you doing?' Because otherwise people just talk forever about their visions.

"Vision comes from dreaming what needs to be done. Vision is doing it.

"What was important to me about Black Elk's vision," Steven continued, referring to the famous Lakota visionary who shared his dreams in the book *Black Elk Speaks* by John G. Neihardt, "was not the fact that he had dreams, because we all have dreams, but that he demonstrated for the people what the dreams meant. And the people were blessed. So the vision always has a component that goes along with it, an enabling of the people to survive. The vision is good for the people in a very practical sense, then. It's a way of taking the chaos of the dream and making it into order, taking the randomness and finding a plan. The way through the dream labyrinth. That's what I would call vision."

Wabun asks for the talking stick for a moment. "Steven, I know you've done a lot of wilderness quests with people from both the United States and Europe, and I know that you have done the actual quests both in this country and in Europe. I wonder whether you find any difference. It seems to me that part of the dream for people is based on place.

"For example, Vision Mountain here, from what we've found out, was a place used by Native people for vision quests for hundreds or thousands of years. When people go out now to quest for their vision, they often report encounters with spirits that seem to be spirits of the land. There is one female spirit that appears in the dreams of many people who have come to quest here, and most often she is portrayed as a Native American woman. There also seem to be some other constantly present spirits that seem a part of the land.

"So, from that and from my own experiences, I've begun to think that the place is part of the dream, that the spirits of the land are the keepers who bring the dream to the people who go there to dream. To me, this accounts for part of the reason why today so many Americans of European heritage are so interested in the Native American lifestyle and way. The ancestors of many of these people have been in this country for the past two or three or four generations, and so somehow the dream of this land has entered into their genes as much as the dream that their ancestors brought from Europe. It's difficult for me to explain—again, it's one of those areas where English words seem to be lacking—but I have a strong feeling that the place affects the dream, and I wonder whether your experience would corroborate this feeling."

"The Aborigines would definitely say that, wouldn't they?" Steven says when the stick returns to him. "I would tend to agree. Each land has its own character, its own unique character. So the plants and animals take on the character of the place in which they are born and grow up.

"I think we've seen that also in the German people. When we worked with German people over in Germany, they had dreams that were different from the dreams we worked with here in America. Their dreams tended to be more like Grimm's fairy tales. They involved the little house in the dark woods, the little passages in the forest, sunny glens, the wicked witch, talking animals, and things that you often find in fables or fairy tales. Whereas the people in America don't dream so much in fairy-tale settings. They tend to dream in a less metaphorical form. I'm speaking off-the-cuff here, but it seems to be that the symbols are more concrete in America.

"It is probably true that the spirits of place and time also contribute to the dream. In which case, Europe is just crowded and tingling with all the spirits of those who have gone before. I don't know how many thousands of years that goes back. I guess they say at least hundreds of thousands of years. Whereas here in America, a newer continent, the spirits are essentially and only those spirits that have been here since the Ice Age, at least according to what a lot of scientists would say. Which would make the dreams here a little bit more utilitarian, more naked, less jammed.

"In Europe, for thousands and thousands of years, all kinds of people came together. People were conquered by other people, who in turn were conquered. In essence, what happened in Europe a long time ago has recently happened to the Indians on this continent. The white Europeans were now and then overrun by Asian and barbarian hordes. By the same token, here on our continent, the Native peoples were overrun by white invaders.

"It happened to us Europeans a long time ago—a lot of inbreeding, a lot of being conquered and conquering. Hence, a dream matrix that is choked with spirits, with a deeper sense of pain and the dark side. I think the European continent also tends to engender dreams that are more universal in the sense that you see a fuller ethnicity. In America, you don't see this so much. The spirits of the dream of human life in America seem more recent."

After a brief break, Sun Bear takes the talking stick for a moment. "I want to be sure all of you realize that part of the medicine I see both in dreaming and having visions is that it is one way that new ceremonies come to the people," he says. These ceremonies are very important because they help to heal the Earth Mother, and they help to keep everything on the Earth Mother going in a good way. I really appreciate how brother Steven emphasized the necessity of doing something with your vision, and that's very important to me, too. As you all know, I always try and live my life by my visions.

"When people get a song or a prayer or a dance that comes to them in a dream or in a vision, I feel that it's very important that they actually pray that prayer or sing that song or do that dance, because they have received a gift from Spirit, and they need to give that gift out to all their relations on the earth."

ENVISIONING THE WORLD

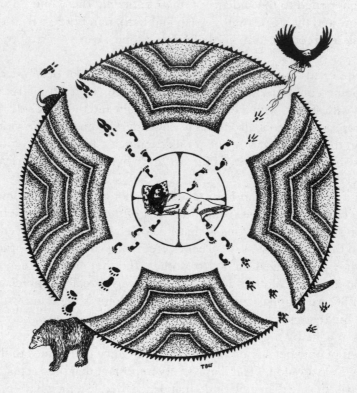

The lightning casts its erratic glow throughout the longhouse as the thunder rumbles overhead. It's the second night of the dream council, and the thunder beings have returned to counsel with the circle. Steven has left to visit some of his family near Seattle. Everyone else remains. The sound of the rain pounding on the tin roof could almost overwhelm a soft-spoken voice. Shawnodese puts a few more logs into the woodstove, making sure to keep at bay the chill that has come with the rain. Wabun adds some water to the pot of herb tea, refills empty cups, and then takes the talking stick.

"One of the most important things to me" says Wabun, "is for people to understand that what we're talking about isn't just something that happened long ago, or in far-off lands. I want people here to know they can have dreams and visions that are powerful and important today, and that they can live according to what they have learned in these visions. I believe one of the most effective things we can do to let people know that, is to tell them about the visions we've had ourselves.

"Sun Bear, I know that people around the world are familiar with the powerful visions you've had—and I really hope you will share these visions in the circle here tonight—but I'd like to share some of my visions now. I want do to this to make sure that people know you don't have to be a Native American, you don't need to be a medicine man or a shaman, in order to have visions.

"Remember my first visions, Sun Bear? I began to have them back in the early 1970s, in New York City. I didn't know what was happening to me. I would feel the earth shaking and really believe I was in the middle of an earthquake, only to find out no such thing had occurred. I remember once seeing the waters of the East River rise up and run over the city, only to look again and find that wasn't the case. They scared me, those early visions. It wasn't until I met you that I had any idea what was happening to me.

"I had tried to tell people I knew in New York about these experiences, but they had no idea what was happening either, so they looked at me kind of funny. Now I can explain what was happening in any number of ways. I understand those early visions from what I've learned from you, Sun Bear, and I also understand them in terms of several different psychological viewpoints I learned later. But at the time, all I knew was that I was seeing something that wasn't 'really' there, although it certainly seemed like it was to me. I was sure happy when each of those visions ended and I could go back to seeing the world the way other people did. I've been happy over the years to be able to help other people who have come to us with visionary experiences, and no words to put to them.

"Those were my earlier visions, and they were frightening. Others followed after I started to work with you, Sun Bear. I remember going through a period of time when I would hear the songs of various parts of the earth. They would just come into my being and out of my throat. I remember some of the songs I learned that way. I think those were special gifts the Earth Mother gave me in my early times of learning about her. Then I had that whole series of dreams and waking dream experiences where it seemed as though malevolent energies were testing me. It wasn't until I learned to stop fighting the energies I was feeling that those went away. These testings were certainly an important part of my learning process.

"Many times over the years, but I think especially in those early days working with you, Sun Bear, I'd have little visionary experiences when we were inside the sweat lodge. These would be times when it felt almost as if my body would expand so much that I would become part of everything, every molecule of life within that sweat lodge. And sometimes it felt as if I'd expand even more, and become part of everything that was. Those experiences used to scare me, too; they were so unlike anything that had ever occurred to me before.

"Those were some of my beginning visionary experiences. Then there's that large vision I had one night in Nevada, the one I wrote about in detail in *Woman of the Dawn.* That night I saw a burst of blue light, and I began to hear chants in my mind and smell the smell of cedar smudge. I began to dance. And then, and only that one time, I let the presence that was talking to me enter me enough to tell me clearly what it was that I needed to learn.

"I remember that spirit seemed to whisper in my ear, first that I shouldn't worry, he was working only for the good. Then he told me what a difficult human I had been to work with, how my clarity of mind forced the spirit and energy forces to go to extremes. I was so mindful that I resisted all of the energies; I was so caught in my mind that I could not even tell the difference between what felt like good ones and what felt like ones that weren't so good. I was told that I had brought on all the testings I had had, because I had clung to my own mind so tightly. That voice in my ear told me that my mind would not let me trust anyone, not even you, Sun Bear.

"So nothing could break through my barriers with love, since you can't love very well without trusting. I was too grounded on the earth to be able to fall into a trance of ecstatic joy from singing or dancing. That spirit told me there was little choice except to scare me out of my mind enough to open it to the rest of my being. It worked. I finally got frightened enough that I let go, at least for a few minutes every once in a while, of the strong hold that my mind had over my heart and all the rest of me.

"The voice I heard that night told me what my path was to be. Of course, you had been telling me a lot about that yourself, Sun Bear. I was told that the earth is sick with the illness coming from man's mind, the mind working apart from the heart. I was told that humans must heal the diseases humanity has caused on the earth, or else we as a species could end up dying off, just like the dinosaurs. That voice told me the male is the mind, and the female is the heart, and that it was time for the heart to help the mind. That voice encouraged me to find my own strengths, to heal the separation within myself between the male and the female, between the mind and the heart, so I would know how to help with healing the planet.

I was told my help is needed, and that the dance that flowed into my body that night was the dance of life. I was told the dance from that time on would always be within my heart, would give me life and vitality; that each time my heart beat I would remember the dance, and that one day I would share it and help to awaken others.

"That voice kept telling me, 'Remember the dance. All of life is part of the dance.'

"After that night, I had quite a number of other visionary experiences. I've been very blessed in that way. When I went out on a formal vision quest with one of the clan mothers who has helped to teach me, the spirits told me I'd already been given plenty to do, and that I really did not need to look for more. They gave me support and courage to remember the dance, and to teach it. And I've begun to do that more and more, as I've learned that the dance is more than dancing.

"It seems to me that after that dramatic and wonderful night, Spirit didn't need to talk to me in quite as flamboyant a way. Now visions come to me as I need them to guide me: sometimes in my dreams sometimes when I'm awake, sometimes when I'm teaching, sometimes when I'm writing. English is a hard language in which to describe these experiences. Does somebody else in the circle have words to describe how these visionary knowings are different from just regular dreams or intuitions?"

Wabun sets the talking stick down. The thunders are moving away. Everyone sits and thinks and waits. Eventually, Luke Blue Eagle picks up the talking stick. Luke settles his tall, slender body into a chair and holds the stick for a moment to center his thoughts, then he begins.

"The French have another word for these kinds of dreams: *le songe*. This is a dream that is very particular. You remember very clearly the beginning of the dream, and you remember very clearly where the dream ends. It's very contained. Of the dream itself, you remember everything so very clearly that it seems more real than real life, then awakened life. This sticks with you, this kind of dream, it haunts your days; you'll be thinking about it all the time for weeks on end after it's happened to you. This is a straight message from the spirit world. This is a dream that does not belong to the individual in a personal sense.

"Normally, with these kinds of dreams, when the Indian people would have them, they'd go straight to the medicine man and talk to him about it, and he would interpret them. If the people kept this kind of dream to themselves, it could be dangerous for them, because then they would not be accomplishing the nature of the dream, which is a spiritual message. When this straight spiritual message comes to an individual, it doesn't belong to him, it belongs to his community also. *Le songe* also has a community-type responsibility to it, where it has to be talked out—with the proper person, naturally—and he can decide if there's anything that belongs to the community in it. This kind of dream is very special; you really recognize that when it happens.

"There is a correspondence between this kind of dream and a vision. There are also, I feel, different kinds of visions. There are the kinds of images that will spontaneously present themselves to you, pictures that will speak of something that is happening or something that will happen to you in the future. They come without your looking for them, and they're recurrent. Sometimes the same image will come to you for a span of time until you understand.

"There's the other kind that you, Sun Bear, used to call the full-screen Technicolor vision. These come spontaneously, but most of the time they're sought through fasting and prayer, as in the vision quest ceremony. This type of true vision is almost all the time a true out-of-body experience, where the luminous nature of the spirit perceives directly that which the spirit world seeks to show to this person. And this is very similar to *le songe*."

Listening to the cue, Sun Bear waits to make sure that Luke is finished, and then he asks that the stick pass to him. "I think of myself as a dreamer now. Dreaming is one of my strong medicines, and much of my other medicine comes to me through my dreams. It feels good. It's always good medicine to hear from the spirits.

"I think the thing that helps my dreaming medicine most is that I'm always ready for a dream to come. I always make the effort to be prepared for dreams or visions, whether I'm asleep or awake. I keep part of myself open to this type of medicine at any moment. I feel very strongly about these things. I feel that the spirits direct us with dreams to do the work that we have to do. I feel that the understanding of dreaming at this time is something important for all people to learn.

"Everybody needs to listen to their dreams, because dreams are a way of helping us to come into our full power. Dreams have surely helped me in my life. And like you, brother, my dreams started when I was a child. I remember when I was only about three, I used to wake up sometimes, making sounds that my mother told me were like a war cry. They were so loud that it used to scare her. Sometimes my uncle, who was a medicine man, would have to come and work with me in order to get me to stop. I vaguely remember that he used to tell me that it wasn't yet my time. He'd call me a little bear, and tell me that my battle would come later.

"A year or so later, diphtheria was going around, and I got it. I just fell down on the ground one day. My sister got my mother, and she put me in ice water, but I didn't feel it. I was in another place, where everything looked blue. I felt real good in that place. Then I saw these balls coming toward me, and I wanted to play with them. They were colored balls, and I couldn't catch any of them. They rolled past me and lined up. When I finally got to touch one of them, the others began to roll around me, faster and faster, until finally they blended. It was like I was inside a rainbow ball, so beautiful that I did not want to move.

"Outside the ball I saw a brilliant light, brighter even than Father Sun. Through the light, a large bright animal walked toward me. It was a big black bear. And he was surrounded by that rainbow. That bear touched me gently on the hand.

"When it did I woke up, and I saw my mother bending over me, looking worried.

"I remember telling her, 'I can come back now, Mother. I'll stay with you.' It was a powerful vision that I had then, and sometimes I can return to the power place of that vision.

"When I got to be older, I had visions all the time of how my people needed to get back together on the land in communities, like they were in the old days. I went to my own tribe when I was fifteen and tried to talk to them about it, and about ways they could be more economically independent. But nobody listens to a fifteen-year-old. Later, when I was working as economic development specialist for the state of Nevada, I went back at their expense to tell them and a lot of other tribes what I had tried to tell them from my visions back when I was fifteen. It wasn't that way in the old days. Then, people would listen to young men when they came back from a vision quest.

"Here's one that most of you haven't heard, ever. When I was in my twenties, I was working, trying to help some Southwest Indian people run off drug dealers who were messing around with the people on the reservation, down there in Arizona. The drug dealers didn't like the work I was doing, and so they took me out one day and hung me up by my thumbs for a couple of hours. See these white ridges here on my thumb? That's from that day. I don't know, they might have left me there until I died. But some of the other people who had been working with me came looking for me and cut me down. But while I was up there it was kind of like a Sun Dance for me. I did have a vision that it wouldn't only be my own people that I worked with from then on.

"Some of those drug dealer people were Natives who were working against their own brothers and sisters. And I knew then that just because you were an Indian didn't mean that you were a good person working for the good of the earth and the good of the tribal communities. Sometimes I wished I didn't have that vision. It sure has made my life hard, working with non-Natives as well as Native people. There are times when both sides don't like me for what I have to do. But that vision started then, and developed over the years. Eventually, it led to my beginning the Bear Tribe.

"Another vision led to my leaving the original Bear Tribe when things didn't go the way my medicine said they should. That was a hard time. I had believed that the Bear Tribe in California was finally the community I had seen so many times in my visions. When it began to separate, I went out by myself to a hill. I made my prayers, and asked for signs, for directions. I felt as if I needed to have my vision renewed. I didn't know what to do. I prayed to the Spirit, asking for a sign again.

"From the south, a golden eagle came and circled about the hill. It felt to me like I could see into the soul of the eagle, and he could see into mine. I knew the eagle was the messenger, but I couldn't understand what he was telling me, so I prayed even harder. From the southwest, a great cloud materialized and came toward me, even though the rest of the sky was cloudless. That cloud grew and grew, and then it went toward the northeast. As it did a small cloud came off from the big one and began to spin. It spun faster and faster; it seemed as if there was a whirlwind up there, turning it around. Then this cloud separated into two pieces. One of them disappeared. The other one returned to the big cloud.

"I knew that in that cloud was my answer. Part of what I had started would evaporate, but part of my vision would go on to be fulfilled. It might take time, but it would be fulfilled. I knew that some of the people who were with me were not ready to help my vision live. I knew that some would go back to wherever they had come from. Others would grow in a variety of ways, and eventually find some balance. Some of them would split off and never be heard from again, and others would split off for a while and then return. The large cloud, the core of my vision, would blossom. I knew this in my heart.

"After this experience, I went back to Reno, got a little press, and began publishing *Many Smokes* again with the help of good sister Wabun over there. We prepared to try again. Wabun and I traveled around and sold things on the pow-wow circuit and visited with a lot of Indian people. I got my balance back. Then we spent some time in Oregon, but I knew from my medicine that we had to find land that was our own.

"When we started to look for land, I had dreams that showed me a place of enormous power that had fir and pine trees, and cliffs filled with rock caves, and a place you could stand on and look at a river that was not so far away. When we got into the city of Spokane, Washington, I knew the place was close. We rented a resort near a lake and it was beautiful, a nice place to winter. But we didn't want to rent; I knew that the land had to be owned by the Bear Tribe so that it would be there for the people to use for many years to come.

"We looked all around the area, and finally we saw an advertisement in a small paper. As soon as I went to look at that land, I knew it was the right place. I felt it was a power spot, but I didn't know why. It was only later, after we had not only bought the land but also built there, that I learned it was a sacred place for the Spokane Indians, a place they had used for a long time to go and seek vision. There are pictographs at the bottom of the mountain. They tell about the vision quest and also about the caves that are sealed in our mountain, and will stay sealed until the right time.

"It wasn't long after we got Vision Mountain that I had another vision, one that many people think is the most important vision I've had. In that vision I saw a hilltop bare of trees. There was a soft breeze blowing, and the prairie grass was moving gently. I saw a circle of rocks with another circle inside, nearer to the center. Connecting them were other rocks like the spokes of a wheel. As soon as I saw it, I knew that this was the sacred circle, the sacred hoop of my people.

"Inside the center was the buffalo skull. I looked around me, and coming up to this circle were what I at first thought were animals. But then I saw they were people wearing headdresses and the costumes of animals. They came to the circle, and each group entered it sunwise, and made a complete circle before they settled on their place in the Wheel. People came to the North, the winter. Then others came to the East, the spring, the awakening. Then came those representing South, the summer, rapid growth. Then came people to the West, fall, when we harvest what we have planted. All of these people were singing songs of their seasons, of their totems. When they came to their spots, they began to sing songs for the healing of Mother Earth.

"A leader among them said, 'Let the medicine of the sacred circle prevail. Let many people across the land come to the circle and make prayers for the healing of the Earth Mother. Let the circles of the Medicine Wheel come back.'

"In this vision were peoples of all the clans, of all the directions, of all the totems. In their hearts, there was peace. That was the vision I saw.

"From that vision, a lot has certainly grown. I have no idea how many Medicine Wheels there are because of this around the world now. All these Wheels are places where people come to remember the earth, and to heal themselves, and to heal the earth. It makes me feel good. It's good medicine.

"From that vision came the Medicine Wheel Gatherings, and the Medicine Wheel books, and a whole new way for people to work with their relationship to the earth. It's been real good medicine for me, that vision. I think the Medicine Wheel was revealed to me, and then parts through Wabun and others, so that we could help people heal themselves and the earth. The Medicine Wheel is a good tool. It makes people look at the earth again. I feel this about our dream council, too. It's going to remind people of the earth, even in their dreams.

"In my vision, the people who came to the Medicine Wheel came from all clans, all races, all directions. That was important for me to see. That was important for me to tell people.

"I had another vision back in the early eighties. In that one I was on a hilltop again, and everything was dark around me. It felt bleak and desolate, so I prayed. After I prayed, my hand was moved upward. I pointed my finger, and a light seemed to come on. I pointed my finger again, and a second light came on. Together they began to illuminate the void. I turned in a circle and pointed my finger again and again, and more and more lights came on in the darkness. The lights were different sizes, shapes, and colors. These brightly colored, sparkling lights lit up what had looked so hopeless.

"That vision kind of reminded me of the one I had when I was four years old, and I was surrounded by the rainbow light. But in this vision, Spirit told me that these lights represented people who had or would come to me to learn, and then would go into the world again to use their new knowledge. Then, instead of there being only a handful of us on Vision Mountain trying to help heal the whole earth, there would be many people out there who could work together to bring about this healing.

"The lights were of various colors, and that was important for me to see, because it again made me realize that the people who came to learn from me would be of all colors, all races, all nationalities.

"And that's what happened. With the help of that good brother Shawnodese over there, and the sometimes reluctant help of Wabun, we started my apprentice program, which has become our educational program. And there are a lot of lights out there in the world because of the people who have come and studied with us.

"All of these visions, taken together, have a power that pulls me forward every day of my life so that I can accomplish what the Creator wants me to do here on earth. If I am looking for something, if I am not sure how things should go with the Tribe or with my work, then I go out on the earth again, and I pray, like the great medicine people of old, for a vision. Everything I teach has come to me through vision.

"Some of the old-timers used to tell me that a medicine person was one who could see light in the darkness, and that that light often comes in visions. That's surely been the case with me. And you know another good thing? As I've gone around over the years and talked to people about my visions, a lot of them have come back later and told me about their own visions. I think that's how it goes; the more of us who have visions and talk about them, the more vision, the more light there will be on the earth during this time.

"I'm glad that you could all come to be with me, here on Vision Mountain, so that we can talk about our dreams and help to bring healing to the people through our dreams."

Sun Bear puts down the stick just as the loudest clap of thunder of the evening seems to be right overhead. Wabun half expects it to hit the copper bear in the front yard, as it did so many years ago. She even looks at the bear, but the lightning has struck someplace else, and she just sees the beautiful glow as it lights the darkness.

It is getting late. Time to prepare to sleep, and then to dream. Tomorrow the circle will discuss the steps you can follow to prepare to dream so that you, like the people in this room, can help to envision the world.

Chapter 4

PREPARING TO DREAM

A new day has dawned, the third day of the dream circle. A number of participants are now arising with sleep still in their movements and dreams lingering in their eyes. Ellie, a woman from Connecticut, claims that she has never remembered a dream she has had. She wants to hear Shawnodese discuss the way to remember dreams, as he has taught some people she knows. Shawnodese hears Ellie and assures her he will do just that today.

Sun Bear returns from looking at the sky. The air that comes back inside with him smells clean, fresh, invigorating. Wabun takes a moment to go out into the day, marveling at the clouds that seem so clean and light after last night's storm. When she returns Sun Bear, Luke, and Shawnodese, looking ready to talk for hours, sit in the living room waiting for breakfast and the council that will follow. After a leisurely meal, the dream circle comes together. The topic today is Preparing to Dream.

"To make sure I have good dreams,"* Sun Bear says, "I take a moment to think about the day that has passed. Sometimes I put a special dream object near my bed to help me dream: a crystal or stone or special gift or mask. Then I pray for dreams to give me direction or to help me on my path. I hold my dream power object and I pray for a strong dream. I pray that I get the help I need from the Creator and from the spirits so that I know all I can about my life path and what I need to do to go in the right direction on my path. I believe I can bring good dreams to myself if I seek them and pray.

"I also keep a dream net or two in my room. Among my people, the Ojibwas, we make these dream nets usually for young people. They are a net woven on a small willow frame. Commonly they are made out of willow bark or thread of some kind. They have a hole in the middle. We put them above the cradle of a baby when he is sleeping to keep away bad dreams. The bad dreams go out of the hole in the middle of the net. I tell people to keep the nets over a young person's bed as he or she is growing because these nets will also catch good dreams and help the young one learn how to dream.

"There is one other thing I do to help my dreams," Sun Bear says as he dips a quart of water out of one of our spring water jars. "Any of you have an idea what it is?" he asks, taking a big drink from the jar.

"Praying?" ventures Richard, a therapist from Wisconsin.

"Going to bed early?" suggests Tony, a student from NYU.

"One of the ways I have of working with dreams," Sun Bear says, "is to drink a lot of water before going to sleep so I'll have to wake up in the middle of the night to go to the bathroom. Then I'll be able to remember several dreams during the night."

Luke asks for the talking stick and begins. "The first step in working with dreams is learning to remember your dreams. That is the important part. There are a number of things besides water that can help with this. One is purifying the space where you sleep so your dreams will be of a more pleasant nature and be easier to remember. Purifying your space encourages pleasant dreams. It is also good to pray a little before you go to sleep, and then to review your day. If you have a pattern of reviewing your day before you go to sleep, it will also be easier to review your dreams when you wake up. When you wake up in the morning, it is good not to move but first to try to remember your dream, to review it.

*See Appendix, exercise three.

"I also counsel people who have trouble remembering dreams to repeat nine times before they go to sleep that they will remember their dreams. Then I remind them to review their day before they go to sleep.

"Another thing that helps in remembering dreams is beginning to distinguish between the kinds of dreams you can have. I already spoke about *le songe* as one kind of dream experience. I will talk more about this later.

"I find that dreaming comes back to people real, real fast. What doesn't come back is the control over it. That normally develops at a very early stage when young people are close to the dreamtime because they've just come out of the spiritual world. When they receive training at an early age about how to control dreams and how to attribute importance to dreams, they have much more facility in later life to be able to have some mastery or control or remembrance of their dreams. People who come from this Western society have problems remembering their dreams because they have been discounting them all their lives. To change and understand that dreams are a real aspect of ourselves that has true importance in our lives is not all that difficult because on an instinctual level we all know this to be true. With psychology, especially with Jung and Freud, there has been scientific research into this area of human nature that has added some credibility to the dream work."

After Luke has been silent for a time, Wabun asks for the talking stick so she can briefly review how to purify a space for the new visitors who have not spent much time on the mountain.*

"You've all probably had the opportunity to smudge," she says, "and that is one good way to purify yourself and your space. Smudging is a ceremony, used universally and called by a variety of names, designed to allow you to center and clear your energy by 'washing' with the smoke from burning herbs. We often use sage and sweet grass to smudge, but other herbs have been used. What is important is the smoke and your intention.

"Some people use water for cleansing a space, others use salt or sound or prayer. All of these work, and all will purify your sleeping area. It's good to experiment and see which works best for you." Before passing the stick back, she asks Luke whether his people use dream nets or other tools to better prepare themselves for dreaming.

"Yes, Wabun," Luke replies. "We use Herkimer diamonds as a dream stone.** They protect in the dreamtime and they also facilitate a clear remembering of the dreams.

"Some people who have abilities in dream work find working with Herkimer very frustrating, because when they start using it they don't re-

*See Appendix, exercise four.
**See Appendix, exercise five.

member their dreams anymore. In the beginning, Herkimer always sends you to the contrary aspect of what you are. So it is very useful for people who don't remember their dreams at all, because they start remembering them with much clarity. The Herkimer has to be purified with water that has a little salt, a pinch, in it. That's the way the ocean purifies them. First you purify them for a whole week, then every time you use them.

"Usually we counsel people to hold the Herkimer in the hand, to hold onto it. They might lose it during the night, but that's not important. When the Herkimer is held in the hand it has a direct influence on the brain, which hemisphere depends on what hand you're holding it in. Sometimes people will hold it in the right hand to fool the left, logical side of the brain. That way they will let go of thought forms that are not good for their dream remembering.

"Some people will never succeed in working with dreams because of past conditioning. But I've seen people master things in the dream world that I've worked years to master, and they've done it like that. It was very easy for them."

It has been many years since Shawnodese gave his dream lectures in Bear Tribe programs, but the people here have heard of his work through other teachers, as well as through students who worked with the programs in earlier days. Wabun hands him the talking stick, hoping to nudge him into speaking.

"I will begin with a technique I have evolved over many years to help people remember their dreams," Shawnodese says. "I have had tremendous success with this technique, using it with many people who absolutely swore they could never remember their dreams. Much to their surprise and my pleasure, many were able to record remembered dreams on the first night after having used this technique. I have had a few holdouts who did not remember a dream until the second time they applied the technique. On rare occasions there was a person who would take five or six run-throughs before they were able to remember a dream. Among the hundreds of people who have used this technique, the longest anyone has ever gone before remembering a dream was one week."

Shawnodese looks around the circle, then studies the stick in his hand for a few moments before continuing. "A word of caution to the individual who has not been remembering dreams. Before using this or any other technique to bring the events of your dreams into conscious memory, consider this. During the eight years I was giving dream workshops, I noted without exception that there was always a reason why a person was not remembering his or her dreams, and by far the most common reason was the same one that caused the individual to stop remembering his dreams in the first place. To put it bluntly, the dream content involved something the individual did not want to remember. Consequently, the part of the person responsible for remembering dreams got a very clear message to stop the process of remembering. So, as the night progresses and the dreams occur—as they do with every healthy individual—the link that brings the dream into the waking state is not forged because the dreamer does not wish to remember the dream. The dream is forgotten either before or just after awakening.

"The first dream remembered after not remembering dreams is very important. Somewhere within the dream will be whatever it was that the person was trying to forget by shutting off conscious memory of dreams. So if a person is not ready to remember what he has already chosen on one occasion to forget, then he should not use the following technique. If the individual is willing to go forward and face the phantasms of the night using this technique, within a week, maybe less, he will be remembering his dreams.

One of the participants asks for the stick and asks why, if a person was purposely forgetting her dreams, she could not just decide to purposely remember them. She passes the stick back to Shawnodese.

"You could," Shawnodese says, "if you could get in touch with the part of you that has purposely forgotten.

"Let me suggest that the part of you that dreams is much vaster, more aware, more intelligent than the part of you that is awake. Have you heard the line, 'We only use some small percentage of our brain capacity?' Perhaps the part of us that gives forth the dream is the vast unused portion of our brain. I conceive of the part of myself that is responsible for allowing me to remember a dream as something I can talk to directly as if I were talking to another person. I refer to this part of myself as the 'not-conscious' or the unconscious or subconscious part of myself. In order for you to remember your dreams, if you haven't been doing so on a regular basis, you must convince the not-conscious part of yourself that you are serious about your desire to remember dreams. I believe everything we say and do is recorded and processed by this not-conscious part of ourselves. Therefore, my technique for remembering dreams involves a number of steps, all of which are designed to communicate indirectly or directly, with sincerity, to the not-conscious part of myself.*

"The first step to prepare yourself to remember your dreams is either to place a pad of paper and pen or pencil by your bed where you can easily reach it, or to place a tape recorder with a blank tape already in it next to your bed so you can record your dreams as soon as you begin to remember them. You also need to have a light source so you can see to

*See appendix, exercise six.

write or record at any time of the night. By these actions, you are speaking indirectly to the not-conscious part of yourself, saying, 'Hey, you down there, I am ready to start remembering my dreams now. I'm serious. I'm going to record them, and here's my proof.' I like to make sure I'm not sabotaging my attempt to remember my dreams by using the pen to see if it writes, checking the pencil to make sure it has lead, or testing the tape recorder to make sure it records.

"The second step to remember dreams is to prepare yourself for sleep and get into your bed. The position that you choose to lie in is important. It should be comfortable but not 'too' comfortable. You are about to go through a mental exercise in a state of relaxed awareness. To complete the exercise successfully, you need both the 'relaxed state' and the 'awareness.' If you fall asleep too soon, you lose the awareness. If the position is too uncomfortable, you lose the relaxation. For myself, I find lying on my back works well. Others prefer lying on their stomach or their side. The important point is the relaxed awareness.

"If you are already relaxed you can skip this step. But if you find yourself tense, I recommend an exercise of progressive relaxation before you do step four. For example, tense and relax your feet, breathe relaxation into them, then tense and relax your legs, breathe relaxation into them, and so on, working up your body, your hands, your arms, all the way through the muscles of your face. It is especially important for relaxation that the muscles of your feet, your hands, your stomach, and your face, especially your jaw, be relaxed. Once you've achieved a reasonable state of relaxation, move on to step four.

"Step four may be done as a self-directed meditation/visualization. Many people have used it this way successfully. It can also be done as a guided meditation, where a friend or partner reads it to you. Or you might even record the visualization and play it before going to sleep. It works well that way, too.

"Here is the visualization: Imagine there is an old stone well in a meadow. It's a beautiful day, and you are resting beside the well. On the rim of the well are written the words *The well of blank blank's unconscious.* Put your name in the blanks. For example, the rim of my well has 'The well of Shawnodese's unconscious' written on it. Now take a few moments to relax into the scene of the meadow, the well, and the beauty of the day. Next, imagine you have a pen and a pad of paper. Write the following statements: 'I, blank blank (fill in your name), now release whatever I need to release and accept whatever I need to accept to remember my dreams now. You, blank blank, now release whatever you need to release and accept whatever you need to accept to remember your dreams now. He or she, blank blank, now releases whatever he or she needs to release and accepts whatever he or she needs to accept to remember his or her dreams now.' I have found that I am most successful in my efforts to program my unconscious when I address my unconscious in all of the ways it is accustomed to being addressed.

"Because my unconscious is a constant part of me, I am continually addressing it in my own thoughts in the first person, 'I.' It also hears everything that is said to me in the second person, 'you.' And it is aware of much of what is said about me, and therefore I also address the unconscious in the third person, 'he'—or 'she' if you are a woman.

"Next, it is necessary to sign and date the note you've just written. The best way to do this is with the same signature you use on a check. It is also very important to put the correct date on the note, so be sure you know the date before you begin. Next, fold the note up in a small square and drop it into the well of your unconscious. Watch the note as it floats down into the well, getting smaller and smaller until it disappears into the darkness of your unconscious.

"After the note has disappeared imagine you are in bed sleeping. It is a peaceful and restful night. Imagine yourself sleeping, then imagine yourself beginning to experience a dream. Make it a simple dream, perhaps a rainbow after a summer storm. Become acutely aware of the vividness of the colors of the rainbow and of your surroundings. Let the smell of the air after the storm come into your awareness. Hear clearly the sounds of birds singing. Run your hand through the wet grass. Become keenly aware of the texture and feel of the grass. Use each of your senses within the dream as vividly as possible. Then imagine yourself waking up from the dream, feeling excitement and success at having recalled a dream.

"Now imagine yourself recording the dream immediately upon awakening in as much detail as you can. See yourself recalling the shapes, textures, and colors of the rainbow scene. Remember the smell of the air and the feel of the wet grass. Having seen in your mind's eye that you recorded the dream, now allow yourself to feel a sense of pride and exaltation at having accomplished the goal you set out to achieve. Let that feeling flow through you, and then allow yourself to drift off into a natural sleep, the dream-filled sleep of the night.

"I have had people come up to me and tell me that my technique didn't work. When I question them carefully, I usually discover that they left out some part of the technique they didn't feel was important. After going back and using the entire technique as it was given, they would come back and report success. By far the most common difficulty people have with this technique is falling asleep before completing the visualization. If you find this happening to you, if you find your bed is just too comfortable, I recommend that you complete the exercise sitting in a chair. Go through the entire visualization all the way to the part where you are feeling success at having recorded a dream. At this point, get up and go to bed."

Lucy, a counselor from Florida, asks for the stick. "Shawnodese," she says, "I just cannot visualize. I don't know how. How can I use this technique?"

She passes the stick to him. "I pass along to you the advice I received many years ago when I voiced that complaint myself," he tells her. "If you can't visualize, 'imagine' you are visualizing. If you can't imagine you are visualizing, then 'pretend you are imagining you are visualizing.' It worked for me, but if it doesn't work for you then just echo the words of the technique within your head. Even that is enough to allow the technique to succeed.

"I would like to say a little more about the first dream you are likely to have after you have used this meditation. This dream is likely to contain information that on some level of your awareness you do not wish to know. Think back over the meditation. You're saying, 'I release whatever I need to release,' thus you are giving your unconscious permission to bring up to consciousness material that may be unpleasant to face. When you say, 'I accept whatever I need to accept to remember my dreams,' you are telling your unconscious you are ready to accept those aspects of yourself that have been hidden.

"Therefore, the first dream that comes after you've started on the road to remembering your dreams is a very important dream to both record and work with. Unless you do, you will be giving your unconscious a double message. On the one hand, you are doing this elaborate meditation to help remember dreams; on the other hand, you're saying to your unconscious, 'I remember the dream, but it wasn't that important, so I didn't write it down,' or 'It wasn't that important, so although I wrote it down, I didn't really pay any attention to it.' The meditation gives you a direct line to your unconscious self, but everything else you say and do is recorded in that same unconscious throughout the day. Consequently, your unwillingness to face or work with the elements you perceive in this dream may create a louder message than that given in the meditation. If you do the meditation to remember your dreams, expect that the first dream may not be pleasant; but pleasant or not, it is vitally important that you record the dream and work with the dream if you wish to continue the dreaming process."

Shawnodese sets the stick on the floor. Everyone looks as if they want to hear more.

"There are some everyday terms," Shawnodese begins, "commonly used to describe dreaming processes, that are actually very important. I'm referring to phrases like 'drifting off to sleep,' 'falling asleep,' and 'waking up.' These phrases literally describe processes and approaches to sleep and dreaming. The person who is able to 'drift off to sleep' is much more likely to be able to remember dreams than the person who 'falls' asleep.

"For some individuals, part of the problem is the hectic and crowded lifestyle they lead. This lifestyle sees sleep only as a necessary evil. These people often go to bed exhausted, sleep 'dead to the world,' and are jarred awake by an alarm clock before they've had a chance to fully rest. It would take a truly powerful dream to break through this cycle enough to be remembered.

"Two of the most powerful periods for dream work are just as you are falling asleep and just as you are waking up. The 'crash-alarm' method of sleep cheats you out of this prime dream work time. If you are a person concerned with becoming more aware of your dreams, one of the ways to slow the rapid descent into sleep is to plan your day so you can get to bed at least ten minutes earlier than you normally would. Just going to bed a little earlier may by itself give you the experience of drifting into sleep. A technique to facilitate drifting into sleep is to review your day, as Luke suggested, in a nonjudgmental manner, before allowing yourself to enter the dreamtime. A third technique is to lie in bed and imagine yourself 'drifting' off to sleep. Or lie with your eyes closed but mind alert, observing the thoughts that bubble up into your consciousness. Then allow yourself to become an actor within that thought, an active participant. In this manner, cross from wakefulness into sleep.

"Another thing I do on occasion is to close my eyes and watch the shifting patterns of light and color that begin to play within my mind with my eyes closed. As these patterns of color begin to suggest symbols or scenes, I allow myself to move into the symbol or scene, to direct, change, or follow it. In this way I make a gentle entry into dreamland.

"To access the important time and energy of waking for remembering dreams, you might consider getting an alarm clock that has a double alarm system or a 'snooze' alarm, or getting a second alarm clock. Set the first alarm five to ten minutes earlier than the second. Once the first alarm goes off, you begin to awaken but you stay in bed resting peacefully until the second one goes off. During this time, review any dreams you remember, or observe the images that develop in this half-awake state.

"In these twilight states when you are drifting off to sleep or just coming awake—technically referred to as the hypnagogic and hypnopompic states—you can often get answers to questions that are bothering you, interpretations of symbols, or other forms of inspiration.

"If you don't want to use alarm clocks to awaken yourself, you can modify the technique for remembering dreams to help you adjust your sleeping patterns. A word of caution: Do one technique or the other, but not both at the same time. Use the technique to begin remembering dreams, and when you are comfortably remembering at least one dream per sleep period, then use the technique to modify your patterns of sleep. Or first use the technique to modify your patterns of sleep, and once it has been modified for three weeks or more, then use the technique to begin re-membering or enhancing your dreams.

"Here's how to modify the technique so you can awaken and arise at your chosen time without the need for an alarm clock.* Suppose your usual time of awakening is 6:00 A.M. but you have determined that you would like to have ten minutes prior to getting up to just be in bed and experience the postsleep state. Go through the relaxation as it was given, using the visualization to see yourself in the meadow with the well of your unconscious. Then, instead of writing about remembering your dreams, you would write the following: 'I , blank blank (fill in your name), will awaken at 5:50 A.M. tomorrow. You, blank blank, will awaken at 5:50 A.M. tomorrow. She or he, blank blank, will awaken at 5:50 A.M. tomorrow.' Sign the piece of paper as you would a check, date it, drop it into the well of your unconscious, and see it disappear just as you did with the other note. Now, imagine yourself falling asleep. Next, imagine that it is 5:50 in the morning and you awaken peacefully, naturally. You look at your alarm clock and see it is 5:50. You feel happy you were able to awaken early enough to spend some quality time with yourself in bed before the alarm goes off.

"After you have worked with this for a number of weeks, you'll find that your body rhythm has you naturally awakening at the time you desire. At this point you might consider advancing your alarm just one minute. Prac-tice getting up and shutting off the alarm before it goes off. In this way you can avoid the jarring effects of the morning alarm entirely, which I dare to suggest will put you in a much better mood for the entire day. By only setting your alarm one minute past your usual waking time, you won't be late even if you sleep in while your body adjusts to its own rhythm."

The day seems to be cooling, so Shawnodese, seemingly glad of the op-portunity to move instead of talk for a few minutes, gets up to attend to the woodstove. The people in the circle talk quietly until he again takes his seat. Hans, a craftsman from Germany, asks whether Shawnodese has had any experience with dream tools: dream pillows, dream nets, or any-thing of that sort.

"I've seen many dream tools," Shawnodese replies. "Probably the most common one people say works well is the dream pillow. Dream pillows are made for a variety of reasons. One of these is to help you remember your dreams, in which case they should contain one or all of the herbs

*See Appendix, exercise seven.

mugwort, lavender, rose petals, or chamomile flowers. To offer you some kind of protection during your dream state, dream pillows should contain one of more of the herbs mugwort, sage, or cedar. If you are trying to call some specific element into your dreams, include any or all of lavender, mugwort, chamomile, or rose petals. In addition, add something to symbolize the element of creation you wish to contact through your dreams. For example, if you were trying to contact the spirit of the deer, you might include a deer dew claw in the dream pillow.*

"Many people have stones or crystals they take to bed with them, which they say enhance their ability to dream. These objects are either placed under the pillow or held in the hand as you are falling asleep. It is a popular belief that holding a crystal in your hand, as Luke suggests, or having it under your pillow when you go to sleep, amplifies or magnifies your ability to dream.

"A number of people I know have worked to achieve waking awareness in the dream state by wearing a special ring or holding a special stone in their hand while going to sleep. They sleep with the intention of looking for that stone or ring in their dreams. Finding it becomes a trigger for the dreamer to become aware within the dream state that he or she is dreaming.

"I want to share with you something told to me by a Salish Indian woman. Her mother, an elder of the Salish tribe, is someone you might describe as a medicine woman. In her later years, this woman developed a crippling form of arthritis that hindered her traveling as much as she had liked to do in the past. She missed this traveling a great deal. Her daughter, a woman in her late thirties, was also quite fond of traveling and did a good bit of it. The mother asked her daughter to bring back a tiny stone or pebble from any unique place she visited. When the daughter did this, the elder would then sleep with the stone or pebble. She would dream, and within her dream she would see not only the place her daughter had visited, but also all of the things that took place while her daughter was in that far-off place. The medicine woman was able to use that stone as a kind of dreamtime videocassette player. The elder's ability extended to being able to report back to her daughter descriptions of the people she met on her trips and conversations she had with them!"

"I'm sure glad my mother doesn't have that ability," Erika, a medical student from Vienna, says loudly. Many people laughingly agree. "Sun Bear has a similar technique for learning about the power of medicine objects," Shawnodese continues. "Do you want to tell us about it, Sun Bear?"

"You're doing good, brother," Sun Bear replies. "So keep going."

*See Appendix, exercise eight.

Shawnodese continues, "Sun Bear smudges the object and himself, and then sleeps with it. In his dreams he learns about the object, its power, and how he can use that power. He has done quite a bit of traveling in Mexico and Central America. One of his interests is hand-carved masks, but not just any hand-carved mask. He actually seeks out the craftsmen who carve these masks, engages them in conversation about their mask-carving skills, and looks for people who come from families of mask carvers, families where the tradition has been handed down from father to son.

"When Sun Bear locates such masks, he purchases one. After smudging himself and the mask, he places the mask over his face before allowing himself to fall asleep. He describes one such mask obtained in this way by saying that whenever he wears it falling asleep, he experiences a green light surrounding him. Then he dreams about something that is going to happen to him in the future. With another mask that represents a puma, he dreams he is in the tropical jungle, running free as a puma."

"That's how it is, brother," Sun Bear says. "Now let's get these folks moving—maybe to the woodpile so they'll get a better appetite for lunch and we'll get some extra wood for the winter."

DREAMING

It's a sunny, warm, and lazy afternoon. The clouds present this morning have passed, taking the chill with them. After the dream circle, people took a break for some physical exercise—in the form of chopping, carrying, and piling wood—and for a good lunch; everyone wanted to have some time for themselves. Luke decided to take the rest of the day to do his visiting.

Sun Bear went for a walk on the mountain. Wabun and Shawnodese soon followed suit, as did several of the participants. When the circle came together again everyone seemed to be renewed and happy to discuss one of the trickier topics, dreaming itself.

Wabun takes the talking stick and begins. "I feel I understand dreaming historically and culturally. I know how to prepare to dream, and I have opinions on understanding and working with dreams, which we'll be discussing tomorrow. But I can't get a firm handle on just what dreaming is."

"I don't think anyone can," Shawnodese replies. "Scientists say it is a function of the mental processes that occurs when you are sleeping. Some researchers say that dreams seem to have a meaning and serve a purpose for the dreamer, possibly even renewing brain cells. Dreams seem to be a way for people to solve problems that elude them while they are awake.

They help people synthesize information. They allow people to release energy they can't during waking time, even intense anger, sadness, or pain. Consequently, they both release tension and act as a safety valve for instincts that could be dangerous for the dreamer or people around them. Dreams balance the life of the dreamer."

"I agree with that," Wabun says. "I've been doing some research on the subject. I realize some of you have studied this topic extensively, so excuse me if I'm too basic or repetitive. It helps me to understand better sometimes if I can speak the material out loud to someone else.

"I know that physiologically a normal, healthy human enters a cycle of dreams approximately every ninety minutes while they sleep. That means you can have four to seven dream periods in a night. Usually you sleep deeply during your first cycle, going from level one sleep to level four sleep. Level one is when you first let go of the waking world; level four is deep sleep. All of your body functions slow down markedly. After an hour or more, you come back through the levels until you reach level one again. Then you repeat the process but usually don't go as far down into deep sleep. In later cycles there is more activity with Rapid Eye Movement, or REM, when you are in level one. If you observe someone in REM state it almost appears as if they are watching an inner movie. If you wake them at that point, which is usually hard to do, they most often will remember a dream. Sun Bear, remember watching Shasta sleep? That old white dog used to have the most distinct eye and body movements while he slept. Most babies seem to, also. To me that supports the theory that all beings, not just adult humans, dream."

"I do remember how much Shasta moved. We used to joke that he was chasing rabbits in his dream," Shawnodese replies. He then continues, "When you are in a REM state your blood pressure is up, you have higher physiological responses, and an active sexual response. Yet muscle tone decreases, and so it is sometimes more difficult to wake someone in REM sleep than someone in level-four sleep. So REM sleep is also called paradoxical sleep. In early sleep research it was thought that all dreams took place in the REM state, but later research disproved that theory. People can dream in all states, but the non-REM dreams seem to be of a different nature than those in the REM state for most people: less vivid, shadowy, and less intense both emotionally and physically."

"That is all very interesting," Sun Bear interjects, "but none of these researchers seems to know what dreams actually are or do."

"There are several theories on that," Shawnodese replies. "One of them suggests that the brain stem triggers signals which make the brain's sensory channels function in much the same way sensory inputs do during waking time. This implies that the brain tricks the dreamer into thinking he is having real experiences, albeit without external stimuli. Also the production of serotonin and noradrenaline neurotransmitters is reduced during sleep, which means the dreamer is less aware of himself, and less critical. Serotonin is thought to suppress hallucinations, so reducing it increases your hallucinatory ability.

"Another theory speculates that the brain stem activity in REM sleep helps you to remember material you have learned while awake by activating 'higher' areas of the brain. Yet another theory contends we use REM sleep to get rid of unwanted or unneeded information that would otherwise clutter and confuse us. That theory maintains it is better not to remember dreams because they are only composed of mental garbage."

"None of these theories seem to account for dreams actively helping people to solve problems and to have creative inspiration," Wabun says.

"They don't," Shawnodese agrees, "but that isn't surprising. Researchers also disagree as to why we even sleep. Some say it conserves food, since our hunger goes down. Others say it protects us from being eaten by nocturnal hunting animals who can't find us as easily when our metabolism goes down, and thus gives us an evolutionary edge. Some say it gives our brains a chance to rest and renew; others, our bodies a chance to heal. Some, pointing to the reduction of serotonin during REM sleep and the increase in hallucinatory possibilities, even suggest that sleep is designed specifically to let us dream, and to dream as vividly and intensely as we can. 'To sleep, perchance to dream . . .'

"One thing scientists agree on is that most people—not all—get grouchy if they don't sleep for a time, sometimes as little as a night. If you are deprived of sleep long enough, you'll begin to hallucinate, which is sort of dreaming without benefit of the sleep state," he continues.

"I don't know whether this will solve the riddle, but I think it will interest you all. Let me share with you a concept that helps me understand better both dreams in general and how any dream—fragmentary, bizarre, or whole—can shed a great deal of light and understanding for the dreamer. I'm sure you've heard me refer to dreams as holograms."

"Yes," Wabun replies, "but I'm not totally sure I understand what laser light is and how holograms are made."

"Laser light is a beam of very intense light that is generated in such a way as to be 'coherent,' " he replies. "This means that all of the waves of light have the same energy and the same frequency. In the aspect of light that is in a wave form, all the peaks and troughs of the waves are aligned next to each other. This keeps the light in a very tight beam, with little scattering as it travels through space. Depending upon how this laser light is produced or modified, it can be used for a wide variety of functions ranging from communication through delicate surgeries to burning holes in metal.

"An object to be photographed holographically is placed on a very safe, secure, stable foundation. A beam of laser light that is coherent and does not contain enough energy to be destructive is focused on this object. Before the beam actually hits the object, it is split into at least two beams and each of these split beams, through the use of mirrors, are focused on the object from which the hologram is being made. The patterns of light produced by the beams of laser light bouncing off this object make an impression on a special photographic plate. When this plate is developed you have the holographic image. If you look at this plate from certain perspectives in a reasonable light, you are able to see an image of the object that was photographed. Further, if you shine a beam of laser light through any part of this holographic plate, even if the plate has been broken and you have only a small piece of the original hologram, the original object will appear in three dimensions in space at the same distance from this holographic plate as the original object was from the original plate. This holograph will appear to stand freely out in space and it will have the ability to be viewed from several angles as a slightly ephemeral three-dimensional object.

"Now back to dreaming. The still, quiet, safe space where the photography is taking place is our unconscious dream state. Our own life force is the coherent energy that reaches into the dream state and brings forth the dream. The dream state itself is that holographic plate, which when viewed with the right light from several angles will yield an image that is a reflection of whatever was within our unconscious that was the focus our life energy used to produce the original dream.

"Similarly to the hologram, if you focus your awareness in as intense and coherent a manner as possible on the dream, the image of the dreamer will be revealed in multidimensional detail. This is true even if, as with the broken holographic plate, you have only been able to remember a fragment of the dream. The dream fragment is like the fragment of the holographic plate. When you focus the laser on the fragment of the holographic plate, you still get a complete holographic image capable of being viewed in three dimensions. When you take a fragment of a dream and focus intensely on it, you produce an image of the dreamer that is multidimensional and will include an awareness of the forces that helped to create the dream."

After a few minutes' break, everyone returns to the circle.

Misty, a secretary from Canada, asks whether using a brief dream she had the previous night might help everyone to understand the hologram idea better. Shawnodese asks what she remembers.

"I just saw a rose," Misty says. "I know there was more to the dream than that, but all I remember is the rose."

Shawnodese tells her that even this brief dream could reveal a lot about her personally. He asks her whether she wants that to happen in front of the circle.

"Of course," she replies. "I feel everyone here is heart family. Besides, I don't think that short a dream could be very personal."

"You'd be surprised," Shawnodese replies. "This fragment of a dream is our shard of holographic plate," he explains. "We begin the process of focusing our awareness in as intense and coherent a manner as possible on that shard, the rose. Misty," he asks the woman, "what in general does a rose mean in your life?"

Hearing him speak the word aloud leads Misty to think it could be a pun talking about her arising, coming forth, moving up in some manner. Shawnodese then asks Misty to describe the rose she saw in her dream more carefully. She responds that it was a pink rose, a very simple rose. In fact, as she thinks about it, she becomes certain it was a wild rose.

Sun Bear recognizes this as the plant totem of the Strong Sun Moon on the Medicine Wheel, and points this out to Misty. Misty is familiar with the Medicine Wheel, so the circle discusses the possibility she is dealing with the energy of the Strong Sun Moon in some aspect of her life. Since the dream was of a wild rose, which is known for its high vitamin C content, the dream may have had a healing aspect, a German doctor suggests, adding that Misty might want to increase her intake of vitamin C for the next couple of days. Shawnodese discusses the particular shade of pink and how that might be reflecting certain relationship patterns Misty is experiencing.

Shawnodese asks Misty at what point of development was this rose, from bud to wilted bloom, and he applies this knowledge to her pattern of relationships. This helps Misty isolate the specific relationship this aspect of the dream was referring to. Shawnodese asks about the color and texture of the stem and leaves, and whether Misty remembers an entire plant, or just a stem with a rose on it. This, he says, gives him an idea of the rootedness or lack thereof of the relationship being described. Was the stem, which it turned out to be, cleanly cut or roughly broken? Were there thorns on the stem? Were they long and sharp or blunted and dull? How many thorns were there?

As Shawnodese's questions focus Misty more and more back into the dream, she begins to sense a background to the rose, and then remembers the scene from the dream of which the rose was a part. This serves as a trigger to unfold more of the dream. When the circle focuses its attention on the colors of the petals, Misty remembers another dream from the same night in which the same pink had played a prominent part. With this dream of a single image of a rose as the center of the focus of attention, Misty begins to present a very clear picture of herself and the forces at play within her life at the time of the dream.

Misty's physical energy, she reports, has been running a little bit low. She is currently involved in a relationship that is "beginning to bloom." But the other person is not very grounded, and he has a number of personality quirks (thorns) that are bothering Misty. As she remembers the larger dream, she is aware of having pricked her finger on the thorns and feeling that she had to handle the flower (and this person) delicately, so as not to be hurt. Misty sees that on a fairly deep emotional level, she is considering this man's potential as a lifelong partner.

Shawnodese thanks Misty for her willingness to share herself and her dream.

"I used this dream," he says, "to give you an idea of how intense focus on a dream demonstrates many aspects of the dreamer. Just as the laser light focused through any part of the holographic plate will yield the holographic image in three dimensions, so any dream you care to carefully examine will yield many aspects of your own personality."

"That certainly was interesting," Wabun says. "I'm not sure whether I'd want to shine your laser light on some of the dream fragments I've had.

"So we add the hologram theory to the question of what dreams are. Yet I still don't feel as though we have an answer."

"Before we get one," Sun Bear says, "my stomach is going to be way too empty. Let's take our dinner break."

Everyone agrees, and comes together for a blessing of the food. By the time dinner is done the sky is dark. The stars, shining brightly, promise a clear night.

"As I mentioned earlier," Shawnodese says, taking the stick, "I don't think anyone can absolutely say what dreams are. Some things, though, I do feel sure of. There are a number of factors that interfere with dreaming. Illness of any kind can interfere with the dreaming process. Quite a number of drugs are capable of robbing us of our ability to dream. I've particularly noticed that people who are frequent users of marijuana lose the ability to remember and work with their dreams. I know it is true for other drugs as well, including certain prescribed drugs. Also, timing is important. When I'm on a hectic schedule that gives me less than six hours of sleep a night, I hardly ever remember a dream. But when I sleep seven or more hours a night, I almost always remember my dreams. If you regularly sleep with someone, that can create enough of a distraction to make it difficult to remember your dreams. So if you've tried everything else to remember your dreams and nothing seems to work, try sleeping alone for a night.

"I also know, and consider this to be very important: Dreams in no way ever condemn you. They never tell you this is wrong, or this is right. They tell you how you truly and honestly feel about things on a deep level of your being. They never say 'You are doing this wrong,' or 'You are doing that right.' They don't make moral judgments at all. They just tell you how you feel about various aspects of your life and your being. If the feeling in your dreams is generally unpleasant, then perhaps making changes in your life will create happier dreams for you.

"It's often very hard for people to understand the full import of this, but it is a concept that is very important to grasp. If we can understand that dreams are statements of 'isness' and 'beingness,' rather than edicts from on high, it allows us to face more unpleasant dreams and the elements that are unpleasant within dreams with a better sense of balance. Dreams do not condemn; they merely state what is."

Sun Bear takes the stick to say, "On dreams, remember that not all dreams have a deep, powerful significance. Some dreams are just a result of your own paranoia or the work you do. If you're chopping wood everyday—as I hope some of you will—maybe you'll dream of chopping wood at night. But for me, the strong dreams, the medicine dreams, are those that come to me about animals or earth changes. These are very clear to me, and I pray for power in them. These dreams I remember for a long time.

"Your dream time, whatever the scientists say it is or isn't, is very important because it provides a way to reach the spirit world. It is a time when your busy little brain is taken out of its regular circuits, allowing you to explore other avenues of power. Remember that the Australian Aborigines say they have forty thousand years of dream history. They also have a process of very strong healing they do in the dream state. They actually dream the healing. Now that's pretty different from dreams of chopping wood.

"Sometimes my dreams come in sequences, with the dreams of one night continuing the dreams from another. When I work with all these dreams, I have a long sequence of knowledge or information all on one subject. Other times I have short little dreams about many completely different things. With time it becomes easier to determine what is a power dream and what isn't. Speaking of dreams, I'd like to have some now. You folks can continue fine without me tonight." Everyone wishes Sun Bear good dreams. Quite a few of the participants have questions or dream problems they want to discuss with Shawnodese.

When everyone has settled down, Uwe, a visitor from Germany, says, "Shawnodese, your meditation to remember dreams, which I heard from a friend before you even talked about it, worked well for me. I have not remembered a dream since I was a child. From last night I can remember six dreams. I am glad I had a tape machine, or it would have taken me all morning to write them all down."

"That is a lot of dreams," Shawnodese says. "Almost too many. Remember, the normal, healthy human being enters a cycle of dreams approximately every ninety minutes while he sleeps. Which means, as you so vividly show, Uwe, that you could conceivably remember five or six dreams each night. Should you spend the time recording and working with all five or six dreams, your entire life could be spent working on dreams. If you find you continue to have more dreams than you can handle or incorporate, or if the process of remembering your dreams is disturbing your sleep cycle so you are not waking rested in the morning, you might want to curtail the number of dreams you remember in a given night.

"Usually, though not always, when using the guided meditation, you will begin by remembering just one or maybe two dreams the first night. As your record and work with these dreams, the unconscious part of you, being ever more eager to communicate, will help you to remember three or even four dreams in a night. The first few times this happened I thought it was very entertaining, but after a while I realized I was spending too much time focusing on dreams. So after I had been clearly successful at remembering dreams for a while I altered my guided meditation to include a limit on the number of dreams I would remember on any one night. So instead of saying: 'I, Shawnodese, now release whatever it is I need to release and accept whatever I need to accept to remember my dreams now,' I phrased it: 'I, Shawnodese, now release whatever it is I need to release and accept whatever I need to accept to remember one or two of my dreams now.' When you are sure you are continually remembering dreams for a week or so, Uwe, you might want to change your meditation in the same way."

John, a young man from North Carolina, says that he often wakes up feeling a little out of kilter after a night of vivid dreaming.

"I have also had the experience of waking up, usually suddenly, and being disoriented, feeling sort of hazy," Shawnodese replies. "It feels as if I'm even seeing slightly double or fuzzy on into the day. I call this state the 'bad landing.' The two cures I have used are either going back to sleep and waking up again, or sitting quietly in a meditative state and imagining my spirit self stepping out of my body and then stepping back into it in perfect alignment. Either of these techniques end that slightly disoriented state. . . . This isn't a cure for double vision. It's a cure for a bad landing from dreamtime to waking."

"What about bad experiences while sleeping?" Leah, a student at the University of Washington, asks.

"What exactly do you mean?" Shawnodese questions.

"Nightmares," Leah replies. "I rarely get a good night's sleep because I so frequently have nightmares in which. . . ."

"Stop," Shawnodese says, raising his hand, palm out, in front of him. "It's usually better to describe nightmares in a one-on-one situation. Let me answer your question using someone else's nightmares as examples, someone who is not here.

"I have three techniques I use for working with nightmares.* I in no way intend these techniques to be considered a cure for the type of nightmare that accompanies, and is a hallmark of, post–traumatic stress disorder. If you have recurrent nightmares, I encourage you to seek professional help.

"The first technique involves carefully examining the nightmare and all of the elements within it. Try to pay particular attention to the most frightening aspect of the nightmare. Look at that aspect as a symbol. Then go back and very carefully examine the day preceding the nightmare; look for some kind of unpleasant or unhappy situation that might have reflected into the dream world as some frightening symbol.

"For example, John Smith had a series of nightmares where he was being chased by a tiger, a very furious Bengal tiger. After one particularly frightening dream so real that he woke from it screaming, John asked me for help. On first telling, and on several subsequent tellings, John could not quite make an association with the tiger, although he had a vague feeling that it might have something to do with his older brother Bill. With that as a clue, John and I examined his previous day, looking for things that might have reminded him of Bill. Under careful questioning, John remembered he had a telephone conversation with his brother on the day immediately preceding the nightmare. I asked John to tell me about the conversation. At first he described a rather pleasant phone conversation. With some questioning, however, John remembered that he was angry with Bill, because Bill had made some disparaging comments about John's parenting skills. Further question elicited a memory John had of an uncle referring to Bill as 'tiger' when both were younger. I suggested what was now fairly obvious: The tiger chasing John in his dreams was, in fact, his brother Bill, and the trigger for this dream had been the unpleasant aspect of the conversation that John had with Bill. After that time, John reported no further nightmares involving tigers chasing him.

"The second technique I use for dealing with nightmares is to utilize either the period just before you go to sleep at night, the night after a night-

*See Appendix, exercise nine.

mare, or, better yet, the first few minutes upon waking up in the morning after having had a nightmare. Simply take the time to replay the dream and give it a happy ending. So if I had a dream of being chased by someone with murderous intent, I might choose to go back into the dream and dream of that person being apprehended by appropriate authorities, disarmed, and imprisoned. If I don't like that ending, I might try another. Let's say that the person with murderous intent somehow realizes the perceived wrong that engendered his anger in fact never occurred. Therefore, the murderous intent dissolves. I might even dream myself befriending this person.

"A third technique for dealing with nightmare content, especially when the nightmare involves someone chasing you, is to use the Medicine Wheel meditation found on page 296 of this book. Call the frightening element of the nightmare that is chasing you and ask him who he is and what he wants. Going back to my example of John, a Medicine Wheel meditation might involve him smudging, centering, going within his mind's eye to the center of the Medicine Wheel, and calling the tiger to him. Then he would ask the tiger, 'Who are you? The tiger would respond, 'I am your brother Bill.' John would ask, 'What is it that you want? Why are you chasing me?' and Bill might reply, 'I would like you to respect my opinions a little more regarding how you raise your children and not discard them totally before evaluating them.'

"I have used this technique as a guided meditation, taking someone else through the process of confronting a nightmarish aspect of a dream and having this aspect reveal its true nature and true desires. If it works, the nightmare ceases."

Almost before Shawnodese gets the last word out, Richard asks, "What if you are having a dream you find truly interesting, or a nightmare that you want to change, and you've woken up from it? How do you get back to the dream?"

"There's a technique that will allow you to pick up where you left off," Shawnodese replies. "It also works if you wish to continue a dream that you found particularly entertaining. I call it 'enfolding myself back within the dream.'* I literally have the sensation of wrapping the dream around myself as I drift off to sleep. The way I do this is I replay the dream up to the point where I'm awakened and the dream stops. Then I hold that in my mind as I drift off to sleep. Especially with dreams that were interrupted in the night by telephone calls or a baby's cry, I have had very good success with reentering and continuing a dream. Sometimes I go back into the same dream more than once."

*See Appendix, exercise ten.

"Sometimes," Tony says, "I've had nightmares that were so strange I almost felt they weren't mine. I've talked to a good therapist about them, but they still persist. Any ideas?"

"Without hearing exactly what has been happening, I can't give you really relevant information. But I'll tell you about something that worked for a friend of mine, a very sensitive, psychic friend. She began to be plagued by very distressing dreams she felt were originating from a source outside of herself. Together we worked both on the content of these dreams and the elements that were stressful in her life. We were unable to shed light on the origin of the nightmares. She continued to be convinced that they were the result of some kind of psychic attack from outside of her. I was in no position to judge the source of her dreams, but it was clear she no longer felt safe or protected while sleeping and dreaming. This person was familiar with the rite of smudging and had cleansed not only herself but also her bedroom and entire house prior to going to sleep. Still, she could not stop these disturbing dreams.

"I proposed to her the following technique, which I created.* I suggested that she perform her smudging ceremony as she always did before going to bed. Prior to going to sleep, I suggested she place herself in a meditative state. In her meditation I urged her to call out for a spirit of protection to come and stand beside her bed that night. I suggested she summon four spirits, one for each point on the compass. She had a four-poster bed, so I suggested she envision these guardians standing facing away from her at each of the four posts.

"Another form this meditation could take would be for the dreamer to imagine him or herself facing east, and saying within her mind and heart, 'I ask now for a protector to come from the East, a guardian to stand at the east of my bed to guard and protect my dreams this night.' Facing south, in heart and mind she would again call out, 'I ask for a protector to come from the South, a guardian to stand at the south of my bed and protect my dreams and sleep this night.' She would repeat the process to the west and north, then imagine these guardians standing at the four points of the bed. Having called the four guardians, the dreamer comes out of the meditative state and then falls asleep. My psychic friend reported an immediate cessation of the distressing dreams following the use of this dream guardian meditation.

"And with that suggestion there needs to be an immediate cessation of questions so we can all get some sleep and have good dreams to report tomorrow when we set about understanding and working with dreams."

*See Appendix, exercise eleven.

UNDERSTANDING YOUR DREAMS

The morning of the fourth day of the dream council has dawned clear, bright, and sparkling on Vision Mountain. It is obvious that most people dreamed, and dreamed well. There is an air of anticipation, since everyone knows that this is the day the council will start working on understanding and interpreting dreams.

Leonard, a man from Colorado who guides others on vision quests, volunteered to go to the airport to pick up Steven Foster, who has returned from his visit to his family. Leonard has been looking forward to having an hour of private time with Steven. Many people believe that Steven, his wife and partner, Meredith Little, and their School of Lost Borders are greatly responsible for making the wilderness initiation passage available to people from the contemporary society. Steven and Meredith have been working on this process for well over two decades.

From snatches of conversation heard around the breakfast table, it's clear many of the participants are also looking forward to hearing the taped interview with Grandmother Twylah Nitsch that Wabun will play for the group sometime today. While Twylah would have liked to join the dream council, she rarely travels now. Other people are looking forward to hearing the comments from Page Bryant, a well-known author and psychic who has worked with the Bear Tribe for many years and has helped people with dream interpretation for many years beyond that.

Shawnodese indicates that it's time for the circle to come together. Because it's such a beautiful day, people form a circle in front of the longhouse, utilizing some of the tables and chairs that are part of the outdoor dining area.

When everyone is seated, Shawnodese asks Sun Bear if he wants to begin. Sun Bear replies, "You're real good at this, brother. Why don't you begin? I know you have a lot to say to people about interpreting their dreams."

Shawnodese goes and gets the talking stick. When he returns to his seat he begins. "It is impossible for one individual to accurately and completely interpret the dreams of another. While we share a vast amount of similar experiences, and while we all go through similar stages of growth and development, reality for each person is different. Nothing in the universe is equal. There is no way for two people to experience the same thing in exactly the same way. Each person's well of life experiences is different. And because it is different, the connections, associations, and interpretations we place on any event are going to be unique to us.

"Even when a number of people view the same event, they are usually viewing it from different angles, therefore perceiving it in a different light or with their relative abilities to concentrate or focus. Because this is true of every event we experience in our lives, our entire perception of reality from the moment we are born until the moment we die must always be different and unique from anyone else's view. Though we can approach understanding one another because of the many similar experiences we have, there always remains an element of uniqueness and individuality. It is as if each person is wearing an exclusive pair of eyeglasses, each one tinted to a different shade, each one polished to a different angle of refraction."

Hans asks for the talking stick, and when it passes to him, says, "I'm not sure I understand what you're saying, Shawnodese. I think many people have the same experiences and can truly understand one another." He passes the stick back.

"I'm not saying understanding is impossible," Shawnodese replies. "I'm saying that no one sees anything exactly the same way as someone else. For example, if Misty were to stand up now, take off all her clothes and run around the circle before going back to her seat, putting on her clothes, and sitting down, and if I then asked each of you to write down what you had just seen, no two people would give me the exact same description of the events. You would all see the events through your own lenses, which are created by the experiences you've had in life and the ideas, philosophies, and feelings these have given you.

"If you are capable of explaining yourself well, and if another person is capable of listening openly, you can certainly understand what the other person has seen or felt. But even your understanding will have different elements in it. That is part of the human condition.

"Each dream contains within it elements of the past, the present, and the future. Even if what you remember is just a fragment of a dream, it will contain some element from the preceding day, elements of your own past, and, as the dream symbols move into archetypical symbols, elements of the distant cultural past. The dream will also contain a foreshadow of things to come. If we dream it, then it stands to reason that what we dream is likely to come to us in some form barring physical impossibilities. It is quite possible for a dream to seem to focus on only one aspect of life yet contain many other aspects as well.

"I once had a dream where I was talking to Suvy, a lady friend of mine. While I was talking to her, I noticed a gentleman sitting a little ways behind us, reading a paper. In the dream, my attention was drawn to this person momentarily, and I asked Suvy, 'Who is that?' She responded, 'That's Mr. John Doe. He's a graduate of such and such a course of study.' Then I awoke.

"When I woke up from the dream, I knew it was a precognitive dream. I was totally convinced Suvy and I would be talking and she would introduce me to this stranger whose name, through the gift of the dream, I already knew. The dream had been specific about a place, and I even thought I knew when this meeting would occur, though the dream had not been specific about that.

"I knew that on the following Monday night, I would be in the place I dreamed, and that, most likely, Suvy would also be there. Therefore, I assumed this meeting would take place on that Monday.

"As to elements of the present, I had spent part of the day prior to the dream with Suvy. An element of my slightly more distant past was the fact that this Mr. Doe had completed a course of study that I had recently contemplated undertaking myself. The manner in which the conversation was taking place, the indirectness of the manner in which the introduction was being conducted, represented past patterns from my childhood.

"Monday evening rolled around, and I was in the building in my dream. I was there taking a class I normally took on Monday nights, and I was half-keeping an eye out for Suvy, thoroughly expecting to see her so she could get on with this introduction. Much to my disappointment, the class was completed, and she did not show up. I left, at the time chalking the dream up to some kind of wish for a precognitive experience. The dream, however, was vivid and had quite a number of qualities that stuck with me.

"The following Sunday, Suvy and I found ourselves together at a lecture. I immediately asked her where she had been the previous Monday night. She responded she had intended to come to class, but shortly after she left home her car had a flat tire. In the time it took her to deal with this minor upset, she decided there wasn't enough time left to benefit from the class that evening. So she went home.

"I was about to begin explaining to her why I was curious when, out of the corner of my eye, sitting behind me, I saw the very man I had seen in the dream. I was startled, and Suvy noticed my reaction. She recognized the individual and introduced me to John Doe. In the brief conversation that took place, I was able to ascertain that John Doe had in fact been in the same building I had on Monday night. He had been sitting in the foyer, reading a newspaper.

"From this experience, I understood both that dreams can predict the future, and that the future is not fixed. Now you might conclude, as I did, that this experience proves that precognitive things exist. It happened during a period of time when I was working on accessing the precognizant elements of my dream life, so it seemed I had a successful venture from dream to reality. But that was only one aspect of the experience.

"I believe dreams contain not only elements of the past, the present, and the future, but also material that is physical, mental, emotional, and spiritual. Within the term *physical,* I include both the physical health of the body, the day-to-day experiences of life, and whatever it is that a person does, for example a student or a professional. Mental aspects include not only what we think about, but also how we communicate and what we communicate: what we write, say, and do. Emotional aspects include anything that falls within the province of feelings, beginning with the standard feelings of love, hate, fear, sadness, joy, anxiety, and so on, and moving to anything that pertains to how a person relates to people or any element of the entire universe that can be described on a feeling level.

Spiritual aspects cover everything else. Most particularly, I include in spiritual whatever a person's true purpose is in life.

"One critical element of dreaming I find frequently left out of the telling, and often of the interpretation, is how did the dreamer feel immediately preceding, during, and after the dream? This is especially important if the dream caused the dreamer to wake up, or if it was what we refer to as a nightmare.

"Explaining that, I'd like to take you back to the dream I just described and play it again against the backdrop of myself physically, emotionally, mentally, and spiritually. I went to bed a little anxious, involved in my work of trying to tap into the precognitive level of my own dreams. Aside from that, I was generally relaxed, reasonably happy. Within the dream, as I began relating to Suvy, I was feeling comfortable and pleased. Then I was introduced by Suvy to John Doe, and I had a sudden knowing that the person in front of me was totally insipid. I could feel his lack of life in my guts. I was quite surprised. That surprise is what woke me from the dream, meaning I woke in a state of surprise, curiosity, excitement, and, as I have mentioned before, a very clear understanding that the dream was precognitive.

"Relating to my physical life, in the dream I saw myself quite clearly, my entire figure, and there was nothing unusual about me. That is, I appeared in the dream as I saw myself in everyday life, reasonably healthy, things going well. Part of the content of the dream had to do with an educational course of study with which I was involved at the moment, and another I was considering undertaking. Both related somewhat to my potential work in the world and to the work I was doing at that moment as a student.

"On a mental level, the dream was indicative of the kind of conversation I had with Suvy. As already mentioned, the course of study that I had been giving some thought to pursuing over quite a period of time played into the dream as being the course of study Mr. Doe had already completed.

"Emotionally, on an immediate level, the dream very clearly depicted my relationship to Suvy. We were never touching in the dream. In reality, the relationship never blossomed or matured; we never really 'touched' each other. So that aspect of our relationship was played out very clearly within the dream.

"There is the matter of my gut reaction that Mr. Doe was insipid. As you may recall, when I actually met Mr. Doe, I was startled, which was also a precognition from the dream. Within that moment of startle, I again had the same physical gut reaction to Mr. Doe. On the day of the actual meeting, I described the dream and most of its contents, including my feeling of Doe's insipidness, to Suvy.

"As we discussed this, Suvy assured me that although she thought on the surface he appeared somewhat insipid, Mr. Doe was really capable of being quite a lively and entertaining fellow. I was unconvinced, and it was a moot point. I have never again, to the best of my knowledge, reencountered Mr. Doe in my life travels.

"What about the significance of this dream on a spiritual level, on the level that refers to my life purpose, my path? Understand that the precognitive element of the dream kept it near my consciousness over a long period of time. Even today, some twenty-three years later, I didn't need to go back to my dream diary to pull out the important pieces of this dream. I remember it all clearly, as if I had it last night. In that you might say it is a special dream. And it is for me in a spiritual sense. It has served to keep in my consciousness something that is very crucial to me as I follow my own spiritual path: There has to be life in it. There has to be energy. It has to vibrate; it can't be insipid.

"Six months after having the dream, I found myself in a position where I could begin the course of study Mr. Doe had completed. In conjunction with making arrangements to begin that course of study, it was made painfully obvious to me that the people involved in teaching the course were behaving in a less-than-ethical manner. Alarmed by this, I put my plans on hold, and continued on with my regular studies at the University of California. Over the next several months, I was introduced to a number of people who had completed the other course of study. I became firmly convinced these people had not achieved the goals the course of study promised. Further, they had each lost something, some essence, some indescribable but very important part of themselves, through this course. This loss left them insipid. As I drew back even more from the people involved, I began to perceive that they dangled a golden carrot in front of the individual but never actually gave them the carrot. In fact, the more I saw the more I believed the carrot was probably wood with fake gold paint on it.

"What at first seemed like a simple precognitive dream was telling me something my unconscious self had clearly processed but my conscious self was not yet ready to accept: that course of study was not for me. There was some very important energy missing. It was insipid. As I retell the dream and the events that followed, I can see other points in the past twenty years when part of the equation that goes into choosing my life path has always been that it have a vibrancy, a life within it. And that the people I associate with and learn from have that vibrancy also.

"I feel as if I've presented so much material that I'd like to recap. In most dreams you will find elements of your present, the immediate past, the far past, and the future. In addition, the dream presents you with a view of yourself physically, mentally, emotionally, and spiritually.

"What I'd like us all to do now, with the agreement of the other teachers, is to break up into groups of four. When you're in your groups I'd like each of you to take some time to write down a short dream that you've had during the course of our dream circle, and also to write down how you see that dream reflecting your present, your past—both near and far—and your future. I'd also like you to write down how that dream reflects where you are physically, mentally, emotionally, and spiritually. Then I'd like those of you who feel comfortable doing so to share both your dream and your analysis of it with the other members of your group.* If it feels comfortable, I would then like you to allow the other people in your group to add anything they see that you might have left out."

All of the teachers seem happy to let the people begin to work with their dreams in this way, and so the group breaks up into smaller groups. About an hour and a half later, after people have had the opportunity to work with their dreams and take a short break, the group comes together again. This time, because the sun is rising higher in the sky, the circle meets in the living room of the longhouse. Shawnodese again takes the stick and begins.

"When interpreting a dream and the depth of its significance, it's very important to take into account how removed you are from the dream content.** The further removed you, the dreaming person, are from you, the dream content, the deeper and more repressed the dream content is.

"Let me explain this a little more clearly. There are three perspectives common in dreams. The first is that you are a person taking part in whatever scenario that dream is presenting. The material in this kind of dream represents something very close to your consciousness. The more dissimilar the dream you is from the real you, the more removed from your waking consciousness the content of the dream is. When I find myself in a dream as Shawnodese, and I look and act my age, the content of the dream is most likely focusing on something very present in my current life. If I experience myself as much older or much younger than I am now, or if I experience myself as a woman rather than a man, or as an animal, plant, or elemental, then the dream is going to be aspects of myself that are more removed from my conscious life.

"For example, if I'm within a dream and I am myself as I am now, and I'm buying clothing, this dream is dealing with myself as I am now, or as I soon hope to be. And it is dealing with what I am doing to clothe myself. It is a very 'now' dream. But if within the same dream, I suddenly see myself twenty years younger, I know the elements being brought to my

*See Appendix, exercise twelve.
**See Appendix, exercise thirteen.

attention revolve around things that have been going on in my life for at least twenty years or that originated within the time period of the age I see myself in the dream. So the first series of ways we remove ourselves from conscious to unconscious is our perception of ourselves in the dream. The more changed and transformed we are, the further removed the content of the dream is from our conscious waking life.

"The second dream perspective I refer to as the point of awareness. In this kind of dream we're not aware of ourselves as a participant, nor are we aware of ourselves as a nonparticipant. We seem to be some kind of point of awareness within the dream, observing, almost directly experiencing, but not quite. When we're at this level of awareness, the dream is dealing with something we are not quite so willing to look at in our conscious life.

"A third dream perspective is where we are aware of ourselves as existing separate from the dream. We seem to be watching the dream as one would watch a play or a movie. Instead of taking place around us, as with the point of awareness, the dream is taking place somewhere in front of us or behind us. We distance the dream from us as we distance the content from our conscious awareness.

"Then there is the phenomenon of people who actually dream they are dreaming. They have a dream, and they dream themselves waking up into the second dream, and then, from that dream, they eventually wake up to their normal waking consciousness. The material in the dream just before they woke up is much more accessible to them. The symbols in the dream within the dream represent thoughts, feelings, actions, parts of being that are much more difficult for them to access on a daily basis.

"Moving in the other direction, when you have a dream where you question whether you were asleep, the content of that dream is something that is very, very close to the conscious surface of your mind. So your state of participation in a dream gives you an idea how far removed from your conscious mind the material is that created the symbolism of that particular dream."

Shawnodese stops and passes the stick around the circle. Several people tell of dreams they had that corroborate what Shawnodese has just been saying. When the stick comes to Thelma, a retired homemaker, here with her husband, Jimmy, she says, "I want to be sure that I have this right, now. If I'm having a dream that I'm seeing home movies of myself as a baby, that means that I'm seeing something about my own childhood that I really don't want to see very clearly. Is that correct?"

Shawnodese nods.

"But I had a dream like that recently," Thelma continues, "and in it the movies of me as a baby were very clear. I'm not sure what that means."

Shawnodese says, "I would take that to mean that whatever was happening to you in the movies is something you are almost ready to bring fully into your conscious mind, but you still want to keep the material one step removed. Does that make any sense to you?"

"Yes," Thelma replies, "in the movies I seem to be crying, and the people around me were laughing at me for crying. But I wasn't aware, or couldn't see, what had been happening to me that made me cry."

"When you're ready to see that," Shawnodese replies, "then you may be ready to dream yourself as the baby, and not be watching it as a movie. That would be a big step toward making the dream content more accessible to your conscious mind."

The stick continues to make its way from hand to hand around the circle. When it comes to Luke, he holds it for a moment and prepares to speak.

"Those are all very helpful ideas, Shawnodese. Thank you. I would like to add some ideas that I have come up with through working with people. I've identified different types of dreams, or qualities of dreams.* The first level is just dreams that are digestive dreams, or dreams that are doing things on a physical level, or processing things on a physical level. These are dreams where the images are of absolutely no importance, they don't have any particular meaning.

"There's another kind of dream where you're mentally processing things that happened in the day, or in the previous days. Those dreams also don't have much importance. They're not of a level where you should sit down and work with them. It's just daily stuff that hasn't been done that needs to get done. You know, we live lives where there's too much information. We have to process a lot of it in the night time. So that type of dream also is not worth sitting down to work with. But you can practice remembering them if you want.

"Then there's the third level, the dream that's talking about the person's psychology. It's a spiritual type of dream that speaks symbolically to the dreamer of the way he is, what's happening in his life, how he's reacting, and how he is in a general way. This kind of dream makes it easier to evolve and perfect your being through understanding what the dream is telling you. This type of dream never offers solutions, all it does is show you in a symbolic way how you're living your life.

"When you start looking at these kinds of dreams, it gives you very deep insight into who you are, and how you can work to better your understanding of how you should enter into a relationship with yourself and the world around you.

*See Appendix, exercise fourteen.

"There's also another level right there. It's what I call the fun dream. There are a lot of dreams where I have fun, and there are many times I'll be flying in these dreams, indicative of an out-of-body experience. It's like experimenting and having a pleasant time, but it's on a level that's very spiritual; it's one of the higher levels of dreams.

"Then we come to the final level, which I have already spoken of—*le songe*. This is a dream that is very particular, clear, and contained. You remember everything in it so very clearly that it seems more real than real life, than awakened life. And this sticks with you, this kind of dream, because it is a straight message from the spirit world, meant to be shared with your people."

Luke finishes and passes the stick again. When it comes to Marilee, a business consultant from New Jersey, she questions, "I'm not sure I understand the difference between levels of dreaming."

Wabun motions for the stick, and when it comes to her she says, "Understanding the different sorts of dreams you can have is probably one of the most difficult things for someone who is just beginning to work with their dreams to learn. Basically, you are going to be the only person who can tell whether a dream you're having is a dream that is psychological, a dream that is a fun dream, a dream that is a digestive dream, a dream that is a visionary dream. Probably, in the beginning, you'll make a lot of mistakes in interpretation. And we will discuss a bit later different methods of interpretation you can use that will help you. I think the most important thing when you're beginning is to write down or record your dreams and to also record what kind of dream you feel it is. After you've done this for a while, and seen the mistakes you've made in earlier classifications, you'll be much better prepared to know what kind of dream it is that you're having.

"Most people err in the beginning in the direction of thinking that every dream is a major transcendent dream, when in fact very few dreams truly fall into that category. Maybe that's good, however, because when people think the dream is very important they will take a lot more care in writing it down and working with it. And on one level of being, every dream you have is very important."

Wabun passes the stick to Shawnodese.

"It's common to be confused about your dreams, not only when you first start working with them, but even after you've been working with them for quite a while. That's why it's sometimes good to have a dream circle or council get-together so that you get input from other people about the meanings and the types of dreams that you've been having. It's also important to remember that while this input can be helpful, interpreting your dream is ultimately your responsibility. The world of dreams is a world of symbols. Each dreamer's symbols contain elements unique to that dreamer. But there are patterns of symbols that play out within most dreamers. It is to these patterns that I refer when I begin to try to understand a dream.

"One such pattern I see is that all dreams that occur within one night of dreaming, and often all dreams that occur within three nights of dreaming, all revolve around the same theme. If I am having difficulty understanding a specific dream, and I have a second dream on that night, as I come clear about the meaning of the second dream, often that which eluded me in the first dream becomes clear.

"We have also found this to be a common pattern when people go out to fast and pray for their direction in life. Sometimes all the dreams they have during their time in what Steven calls the threshold—even though the dreams might seem wildly different in content—are in fact about the same theme.

"Another pattern is that dreams speak in symbols, except in the rare instance of a truly precognitive dream. As I have demonstrated by my own experience when I talked to you earlier, even a truly precognitive dream contains within it symbols that reverberate far beyond the events foreseen. So, for example, if you dream of the literal death of someone, the dream is not necessarily about that person dying. The dream is about letting go, or transformation, or ending, or whatever else you associate with the symbol 'death.' "

Wabun asks for the stick. "Quite a bit of the material Page shared with me in our taped interview is about dreams of dying," she says. "This seems like a good time to bring that material forth." Wabun sets up the tape recorder, presses the play button, and Page's recorded voice begins to speak.

"I always remind people studying with me," Page says, "that the dream is a message from the self to the self; it's you talking to you. It really has little or nothing to do with anyone else. Dreams are real intimate and personal messages. That's how I view dreams, as messages. They're telling me something about me. So, because I feel that way about them, and I also have a way of using my psychic ability to interpret dreams for others, I definitely stress the importance of dreams, and the importance of keeping a dream record.

"People tell me that they dream about people in their families or friends who are deceased. They're talking to that person or getting messages from that person. Another common one is people dreaming of themselves or loved ones dying. It frightens them because they think it means they're going to die. Another one is being chased, in dreams. Another is trying to make a phone call or get a message to someone, and continually failing. Those are some real common ones. But the ones that have to do with death, those are the ones that more people ask me about than any others."

The dream circle then hears Wabun's voice asking Page, "What do you usually tell people about such dreams?"

"I tell them," Page replies, "it can mean one of two things as far as I'm concerned. It can be spirit communication; literally, the deceased person has a message, or there is a communicative relationship going on. In that case I tell the person to take it literally. But most of the time, I would say that the deceased person someone is dreaming about represents an aspect of the dreamer. So therefore, if I, for example, having lost my mother recently, if I dream of my mother, as opposed to it being a spirit communication from her, I am probably dreaming of some part of her that is in me, or I'm responding to some fault or feeling or whatever she had. Or I'm dealing with something left undone in the relationship that had to do with me, not with her. I keep trying to make people go back and remember that the dream has to do with you. Even if what you dream is about a place, it has to do with you; it's relative in some way to you."

Wabun stops the tape and passes the talking stick back to Shawnodese. He takes it and says, "I would certainly agree with everything Page has said. To reemphasize some of her points, and the point I was making about the symbolic language of dreams, I'd like to give you an illustration of a couple of dreams I've had.

"In 1972, when I had a dream of a man I knew falling back into a black chair, turning black and dying, my understanding of my own death symbology allowed me to see that this was not a precognitive dream predicting the death of that person. Rather, it was a dream talking about an emotional dream relationship between myself and that person and the endings that were taking place within that relationship. The dream showed me the drain that relationship had been having on me, and that it would soon cease.

"Eight years later, I had a three-day series of dreams. I only learned they were dreams at the end of the third day. I was spending some time in a trailer at an outdoor educational center. Every morning, a gentleman would walk through the various encampments, cabins, and trailers ringing a bell to let us know it was time to gather for the beginning of the day's activities. I would hear this bell in the far distance, and it would become louder and louder until it was right outside my window. Then I would hear it fade off into the distance and I would be fully awake. I assumed the bell was the real thing. The second day the dream was identical to the first. The third day was identical but had one element added. This time, as the bell was being rung, I heard a voice saying to me, 'Ask not for whom the bell tolls, it tolls for thee.'

"Now that got my attention! That morning I went immediately to the person who was the bell ringer and asked him where he began ringing the bell. He said, 'Truth be told, I start every morning outside your window.'

"At that point I realized all three mornings I had been dreaming of this bell ringing, not hearing the actual bell ringing. With the addition of the voice in the third dream, I had a sudden and complete awareness that my father, who had been in ill health for a very long time, was at that moment dying. I completed the commitment I had for teaching in that wilderness program that morning. By the time I was able to get to a phone and check in, the message was already waiting for me that my father had, in fact, passed away.

"The dream I had years earlier of a person dying was symbolic of change in a relationship. But this highly symbolized dream of a bell tolling was, in fact, a clear and vivid premonition of the imminent death of someone close to me."

Sun Bear asks for the talking stick. "My mother had a powerful thing with dreams," he said. "At least twice that I remember, she dreamed about relatives dying. Within three days those relatives had died. She became frightened of dreams because of this, and didn't want to be a dreamer anymore. That can happen to people, too; they get so afraid when their dreams actually come true that they decide not to dream anymore, or not to remember dreams. That's what this good brother Shawnodese's been talking about when he tells you that what you dream when you first start dreaming again will tell you what it is that you didn't want to remember for whatever period of time in your dreams." Sun Bear passes the stick back to Shawnodese, saying, "Keep up the good work, brother."

"Death isn't the only subject that figures prominently in our dream symbology. Sexual expression is clearly food for the dream world. I have often found people embarrassed to discuss certain elements of their dreams with me. Yet driven to understand those elements, they will tell me what they consider to be bizarre sexual escapades within dreams. When we look at those escapades as a symbolic language of acceptance and rejection, of giving and taking, we see that they are often not the undercurrents of feared sexual preferences or perversions. They are symbols, highly charged symbols, of other types of relationships within the life of the dreamer.

"What I'll tell you next really happened, but I have changed the names for obvious reasons. A man named Harold had a dream of shooting Maude with a ray gun, and seeing Maude evaporate in a burst of light. Harold was in fact dreaming of his desire to have sexual union with Maude, and his unconscious belief was that he was armed with a weapon that would give an energy jolt or an orgasm to Maude, that would literally blow her away—that is, enliven and enlighten her entire body.

"At the time of the dream, Harold was a very frustrated young man and Maude was a beautiful, angelic young woman. Harold was convinced that Maude was his 'soulmate.' Maude was convinced Harold was a pest. Maude eventually dumped Harold. Harold found happiness in the arms of another. Knowing that, let's look at Harold's dream, and instead of looking at Maude as the woman he knew, let's look at Maude as the part of Harold that is truly a beautiful person. Once Harold was able to focus his energy, to shoot his ray gun, at that part of himself that truly was beautiful, Harold experienced a profound sensation of enlightenment. So, after Maude dumped him, Harold had to refocus his energies on himself, on his own growth and development. In the process, he began to discover in himself many of the qualities he had projected onto Maude. In his own way, Harold became enlivened. Harold's happiness came not from bedding Maude, but rather from losing her.

"Another way that dreams speak to us, a very common way, is through the pun. For example, you might have a dream involving a bear. You might be inclined to believe you are having a medicine dream involving a totem animal, the bear. As you play with the dream and work with the dream, the portrayal of yourself as having the bear for a totem never quite rings true. It doesn't even seem like a possibility to you. But if you turn things around and spell bear 'bare,' you suddenly see that the dream is describing a part of you that is naked and exposed to the world. The 'Ah ha!' sensation of the truth of that interpretation floods through you, showing that this dream had a trick interpretation; it was in fact a pun that you needed to understand in order to see what the dream had to tell you."

Shawnodese holds the stick up to indicate he is done, and to see if anyone else wants to take it. Wabun asks to have it passed to her, and when it is she comments that it has certainly been a full and long morning, and that perhaps before the circle continues its discussion of dreams, it would be a good idea to break and have lunch and a little chance to incorporate some of the information that has been given this morning. People nod their heads in agreement.

When lunch is completed, people take some time to walk or talk before coming back to the longhouse and sitting once again in the dream circle.

Once everyone is settled, Wabun takes the stick. "I think this would be a good time to share Twylah's words with you," she says. People indicate that they would very much like to hear what Twylah had to say, so Wabun gets the tape set up, and when she is seated again, pushes the play button.

"When we dream at night," Twylah's voice says, "we are being counseled by all our teachers. That's why dreams are so prolific at times. The dreams that you remember, you should record. If you don't remember your dreams, then you're just releasing energy. That's what dreams do. When there's pent-up emotions and all that kind of stuff, they release the unnecessary emotional stuff that otherwise would affect our health. When you record them, then you've got a handle on some of your ideas. Then you can use them during the day. We use our dreams during the day, only we're not aware of it.

"We're always receiving impressions, and these impressions are a spin-off of our dreams. And we're always thinking; no matter what we're doing, we're thinking. These impressions are flying through our minds at all times. Sometimes we pay attention to them, sometimes we don't. The impressions organize our lives for each day. We set up what we are going to be doing, and then we plan how to do it. Most of us have all of these directions we give ourselves in the morning, and these come from our dreams. How we process them depends upon how much we listen to our inner knowing."

On the tape, people hear Wabun asking Twylah, "Which do you feel comes first, Twylah, the impressions or the dreams?"

"The dreams are first. The dreams are definitely first, because they come in with us. We're born with all these dreams, and when we come into this earth walk, we have a mission in life. It's based on our gifts. Our dreams are constantly tapping into our gifts so we can process what is necessary throughout the day. Each day we shift, filter, and screen. That's how we discipline ourselves.

"But this society is the kind of society that wants to control everyone's thought process. That's why they insist that children be sent to school. And they tell the kids how they must learn, and what they must do. And they keep pounding it into their heads, day after day after day. When they get home, the parents are doing the same thing. So then the child doesn't have the opportunity to follow his own dream. He's fitting into a mold that someone else is building for him."

Wabun's voice asks Twylah, "How would you teach a parent to allow their children to begin to follow their own dreams?"

"Listen to what the kids have to say," Twylah says. "Most parents don't listen. The parents want everyone to listen to them, but they don't even listen to themselves, nor do they listen to anyone else. In the past, in the Wolf Clan way, we used to teach children to become more sensitive to their environment by asking them, 'What did you see that was beautiful today? Or, 'What did you hear that made an impression on you?' We asked, 'Am I happy in what I'm doing? What am I doing to add to the confusion?

What am I doing to bring about peace and contentment? And how will I be remembered after I'm gone?' We ask these questions all the time, not only of children but also of adults.

"When I used to travel more and teach, I would encourage children to remember their dreams. I'd have the kids lay on the floor on their backs, with their arms right next to their sides, and all their heads in the middle. There'd be a circle, and I would ask them just to close their eyes and listen to their thoughts. Then I would ask them to watch the pictures as their thoughts materialized in their minds. I had them do that for five minutes, and then I had them sit around and tell what they saw. I made it kind of a game.

"I would also ask them at different times whether they remembered a dream they had that was important. And then they would tell me some of the horrible dreams they had. And those dreams are fears; they're fed through fears.

"If you want to help children or adults who are having nightmares, in the first place the person shouldn't eat before they go to bed. If they eat, their body is not ready to sleep because it's working, taking care of the food they had eaten.

"I also teach each person to take a few minutes, maybe five minutes a day, to sit and just daydream. If you get used to daydreaming that way, then you won't be afraid at night. A nightmare is a body revolting against something that has been done through the day. Sometimes parents will have whipped the children for something they have done. Maybe the child was wrong, or maybe the parent didn't have a real reason for the punishment. That creates a nightmare. Nightmares are fears. The biggest fear is not being accepted, the fear of abandonment.

"To work with that fear, people have to look at their own gifts, and to love who they are. It's good to find a place where you can sit alone and be grateful for everything that you have. It's good to constantly be grateful for your gifts. It's also good to remember that every vision and dream has a reason behind it, and that all these reasons are based on a person's gifts."

Wabun stops the tape for a moment and says to the group, "What Twylah is going to explain next in the interview is her method for interpreting dreams, so I think this is a good place to take a break. After the break, we'll come back together in the groups of four that we used earlier. What I'd like you to do in your small group is to bring out any of the questions you have from any of the material we've covered this morning. The teachers will circulate among the groups, and you'll have an opportunity to ask those questions and perhaps get some of the answers you're seeking."

INTERPRETING YOUR DREAMS

By the time people have completed their small-group discussions about understanding dreams, it is late afternoon. Nonetheless, the dream circle decides to meet for several hours before dinner; they are all excited to hear the conclusion of Grandmother Twylah's teachings, and they know there is a lot more material to cover before they go to bed to dream tonight.

When people are settled, Wabun asks if everyone is ready to hear Grandmother Twylah's information on interpreting dreams. When she sees affirmative nods from most of the people, she turns on the tape recorder.

"As I said before, Wabun, everything is based on a person's gifts. When I start to work with people on dreaming, the first thing I do is find out their birth month. The month they're born represents their faith. The month directly opposite is how they express their faith. Let's take you, for an example. Your birth month is . . . ?"

"April," Wabun answers.

"Being an April person you're a worker." Twylah continues. "You're also a seer, and you're into prophecy and philosophy. That's your birth gift. Opposite April is October, which is creative, so you could well be doing anything creative. Being a writer is a good thing for you to do. Your birth month and the month opposite establish your truth line. I tell people to put their birth month in the south of their personal wheel, and the opposite month in the north. Then the months that fall in the east and west establish the earth path.

"Knowing how to live, that's what the earth path is. No matter what your birth month you are always sitting in the south, perceiving your wisdom, which is directly across from you, to the north. To your right is your east, and to the left is your west. East is your inspiration, and the west is your future. Also, east is behavior, and the west is the will. Together, they give you the will to live the truth. We call this our Wisdom Wheel, because that's what it is. In it is the Medicine Wheel, but sometimes the term *medicine* confuses people.

"Being born in April means your earth path is January and July. That means you like to learn through love, or you love to learn. Again, that's your earth path.

"In order to dream, you focus on your south and look toward the north, which is your wisdom. Wisdom for a dreamer is the counselor."

Wabun asks Twylah to explain the gifts of the other birth months.

Twylah replies, "January is learning, February is honor, March is knowing, April is seeing, May is hearing, June is speaking, July is loving, August is serving, September is living, October is working, November is sharing, and December is thanking. These are the basic twelve gifts a person can come into the world with. You come in with the gift, and you also have the gift that's opposite to help you use your birth gift.

"I think the most important things I'd like people to remember are that every vision and dream has a reason behind it, and everything is based on a person's gifts. So it's very important to know what your gifts are."

Wabun turns the machine off. She passes the talking stick around, and people express their gratitude for Twylah's input to the dream circle.

When the talking stick returns to Wabun, she says to Steven Foster, "Steven, I know from the conversations we've had that you have a system of understanding dreams using four shields, and this is part of the ecopsychology you're currently writing about. I'd love to hear more about it."

Steven takes the talking stick and first expresses his appreciation at being back on the mountain in this dream circle. Then he begins to talk about
the four shields and ecopsychology. "I'll try to keep it simple. The four
shields are the four seasons of human life. The temperate zones of the
world have four seasons. So do the human beings who live there. The four
seasons of human life can be lived in a lifetime, and they can be lived in
a day or an hour. We move through the seasons of our life again and again
and again. Over and over again we spiral through the four seasons. This
is the dream of Mother DNA. The spring is bound to lead to fall. The summer of life is bound to lead to winter. The fall of life is bound to lead to
spring. And the winter of life is bound to lead to summer. Now I'll trans-
late this more clearly in terms of human experience. Spring is that which
is newly born, that which comes from death, that which is illumined. Summer is the child, the children, the way of the child. Fall is the fall from innocence into adolescence, the inward constriction of summer, the reaping
of the rewards of childhood, the preparation for winter. Winter is the adult,
the man or woman who bears responsibility for the survival of the people through the dying of winter. These are the dimensions of the human
dream of life and death, and they form the basis of a psychology based
on human nature. They also compose a system of balancing, as the four
seasons balance, the human self.

"So in addition to what people have already learned about remembering dreams, the four shields concept offers them a way of interpreting the
dreams. In one shield we have everything associated with childhood. In
another shield we have everything associated with adulthood. In another
shield we have everything associated with the psychological, the inward
life. In another shield we have everything associated with the expression
or out-working of a dream, or what might be called vision, or imagination, or illumination. It's an all-inclusive system; we can put almost anything into the four shields. What we get, then, is an idea of which shields
in a person are strong and which ones need work. We train people in
mostly self-help activities that will help them strengthen their ability to
experience all four shield systems.

"A person can take their dream, and then use the four-shield system as
a way of understanding it, as a way of seeing what the dream is teaching
them.

"For example, if the dream strongly suggests the fall shield, or persona,
then it is best to examine the contents of that shield. The adolescent is inward, psychological, self-conscious, in a labyrinth of shadows, and intro-
spectively engendering an inward mirror of the opposite sex, anima or
animus. But in every shield its opposite is implied. Hence, the opposite

of fall is the expansion and birth of spring. Also implied are the workings of the other two shields, summer and winter. A dream can reveal shield imbalances."

Steven pauses for a moment and Erika, the medical student from Germany, asks for the stick and then asks Steven whether he could be more specific about what he puts into each of the four shields in his system. She returns the stick and Steven, after a minute, begins to speak.

"South, or summer, is the child. In that shield we find the emotions, the instincts, the erotic nature. The child is irrational. The child of summer is the innocent body that has to survive in a world of violence and destruction. You can see it in the play of children. 'Let's play war.' 'Let's be cruel to the new kid on the block,' 'Bang, bang, you're dead,' that kind of thing. You see the same thing in animals, fox cubs and lion kittens, pouncing on each other in mock battle. Young animals play at survival. This is the shield that we associate with war, with revenge, with death-dealing toys. In the summer shield, we see blood, we see abundant life and abundant death. It's summer; everything is at its fullest; everything competes for space. Survival of the fittest.

"The summer shield is the interplay of sensuality and desire. The child needs. The child seeks to possess the object that gratifies the need—to eat, drink, multiply. It's the ego and all those primal urges and reactive emotions. The ego's need to possess. So when we see much of this in a dream, then we tend to posit that dream in the south shield.

"In order for summer to become winter, it always has to undergo the fall. The fall shield, quite literally, is the shield of initiation. It is innocence becoming experience, having to go through the dark, being tested, becoming self-sufficient. It's the ordeal, and much of it is inward, as in adolescence. Adolescence, although it seems relatively short in terms of a life span, is a very significant time. That's why the ancients spent so much time initiating their children at the onset of adolescence. For the children must become adults. A child has to become reasonable, has to learn self-control, self-discipline, work, responsibility, and awareness of what is good for the people. And the only way they can learn that is to go through the dark part of themselves. They have to fall, they have to leave the garden of Eden.

"In the fall, or west shield, we find the source of dreams and the wounds that form 'personal medicine.' We find the feelings, as opposed to reactive emotion, addictive behavior, and self-consciousness. The inner monsters lie here, in feelings like guilt, remorse, and loss. In the dark shield we also find the anima, the inner woman, and the animus, the inner man. In adolescence, we learn to see ourselves through the eyes of the opposite sex, particularly the opposite-sex parent.

"But the fall shield must give way to the winter, or north shield. The adolescent must be initiated into adulthood. If the species is to survive the winter, it must look to those who are mature—the initiated men and women who fashion and use the tools, strategies, and ethics that benefit the people at large, especially in times of hardship and want. Marriage, parenthood, occupation, law and order, duty, responsibility, and all the rights and privileges of adulthood are found here. The adult makes, heals, serves, facilitates, arbitrates, teaches, leads, and assumes the role of elder. The adult shield is the mind of winter, the rigidity of the frozen seed, the life of contemplation, discipline, and thought.

"The winter shield is responsible for rites of passage, science, technology, logic, mathematics, medical science, philosophy, theology, and all the other 'ologies,' and is quite the opposite of the child, or summer shield, which is irrational and governed by emotion, instinct, and bodily hunger. Winter is the life of the mind. That which knows: 'No pain, no gain.' Dying also occurs under the sway of the winter shield. Winter must die so that spring can come. So the adult must be initiated into the powers of elderhood, the greatest of which is the knowledge that the self must die.

"The spring or east shield lies at the end of the passage of winter. With the spring comes expansion, opening, a surging of potential, transformation, and illumination. Here we find the miracle, the divinity, the gods and goddesses, the Spirit. Dark fall has entered the passage of winter and has been transformed into spring light. Old forms have been shattered so that the wholeness of new growth can spring forth. The newly born comes into the light, trailing clouds of glory. Vision starts here.

"The stages of a wilderness rite of passage correspond to the four shields. Severance is the setting forth from childhood—summer. Threshold is the sacred time/space of initiation—fall. Incorporation is integration with maturity, a new life stage—winter. From the first three stages comes the fourth, new life, new growth, expansion, illumination—spring. Which brings us back to summer and the continual need for the child to be reinitiated into the mysteries of adulthood and its resulting expansion.

"You can see the same kind of initiatory movement within a dream. The child, the ego, the 'I'—summer—confronts a passage, a dark forest, a monster, a task—fall. The impediment must be assimilated, for that is where the 'medicine' lies. This medicine then becomes the credentials of the mature adult—winter—who, when the life change has been effected and the work has been done, is the recipient of new life or illumination—spring."

Lucy, one of the therapists attending the workshops, asks if she can have the stick for a moment. When it passes to her, she says, "Steven, I think I'd like to understand this a little better by having an example. I'd like to give you a recurrent dream that one of my clients has, and see how you would fit that into the four shields."

Steven nods affirmatively, and Lucy continues. "In this dream, the client is standing by the ocean, watching the waves come in higher and higher. She always has the sense that a big wave is coming. Sometimes she'll be trying to run away from it, and sometimes she'll know there's no running away. How would you work with that dream using the four shields."

She passes the stick back to Steven. "The dream is one of initiation," he replies. "There's an engulfing, a clouding of the way; it gets dark, it gets shadowy, it gets overwhelming. The child is standing at the edge of the ocean, contemplating the threat of being engulfed by the great tides of life. She knows that in the engulfing there will be a sea change into something rich and strange, a new birth. The dreamer is sometimes ambivalent about the need to again encounter the dark tides of life for the sake of the people. This is a kind of shamanistic dream. The shaman goes down into the darkness to find a cure. So this dreamer must endure the darkness so that she can become adult, so that she can become illumined, so that the people can prosper.

"In our way of teaching fasting and initiation, we say that what you encounter when you go into the wilderness, to the smallest, littlest thing, is part of your dream, and very important. Taking that into consideration, you run into a lot of natural entities, potent symbols, from the four elements and their various manifestations to things like silence, tracks, shadows, nakedness, the sun and the moon, the rhythms of day and night, the conflicts between psyche and spirit. The quester's place of power, all the various animals, plants, ceremonial objects, all are important, including the processes of urination and defecation. For a lot of people, these symbols form the very basic core of their experience during the threshold time. We will often use those particular symbols as ways of looking at their lives, and at the way in which they deal with such entities within their lives.

"Nothing is too small. And a lot of times people overlook the obvious."

When Steven is finished, people get up and take a fifteen-minute break, stretching, going to the rest rooms, taking a brief walk, talking. After the break, Shawnodese takes the talking stick and begins.

"Steven, I particularly enjoyed what you said about nothing being too small, and everything being capable of being considered a part of the vision or a part of the dream. I believe that anything we experience in the course of our waking day, including our daydreams, can be addressed and interpreted as if it were a dream. For example, many years ago I was associated with a group of people who met together for the purpose of spiritual study and meditation. One member of that group, whom I will call Regina, remarked she had just had her third windshield cracked, within as many months. She was becoming very frustrated with the annoyance and the expense and was wondering if there was any 'significance' to this series of cracked windshields.

"I suggested we view these unfortunate events as if they were a repeating nightmare in an attempt to understand if there was a symbolism in the shattering of the windshields. Regina and the group agreed to do this. We proceeded to have Regina describe each event leading up to the cracking of the windshield as if it were a dream. I asked Regina and the other people present to suggest possible interpretations. Working with the events as if they were dreams, Regina revealed she was experiencing a growing unhappiness with the way she was going through life at this time.

"It became apparent that the stone striking the windshield and breaking it carried at least two meanings for Regina. On the one hand, she was very certain that her worldview, as represented by the windshield, was distorted—the distortion symbolized by the rock striking and cracking the windshield. The rock symbolized an outside force or influence capable both of distorting her view of the world and, at the same time, of forcing her to obtain another, possibly clearer worldview—that is, to purchase a new windshield. Regina was then able to use her understanding of the serial cracking of windshields as the impetus for some substantive changes in her life. When I last checked back with her there had not been another broken windshield.

"I felt that this was a very interesting way of looking both at dreams and at waking life, and of seeing that the difference between the two might not always be as large as people imagine.

"At this time, I'd like to go into a number of techniques I've developed for helping you to interpret your dreams. The first I call a dream council.* This is a group in which a family, or a group of individuals living together, or a group of individuals who get together regularly for personal growth, meet to discuss their dreams.

"The individuals involved would begin by smudging themselves as a ritual of cleansing away negativity, drawing positive energy, and focusing attention. After each individual in the circle has smudged, the talking stick is passed through the smoke of the burning herbs. It is given to the person upon whose dream the council is going to focus. That person, while holding the talking stick, tells the circle his or her dream. Having done that, the person passes the talking stick to the person to the immediate left. Each person in turn is allowed to question the dreamer on the finer points of the dream—colors, qualities, feelings, nuances—that may have been missed in the first telling. The talking stick can pass around the circle of the dream council up to three times, or until no one else has any

*See Appendix, exercise fifteen.

more questions about the actual content of the dream. The dreamer then tells the council what he or she feels the dream means. In their turn, each member of the council, as they hold the talking stick, tells the dreamer what he or she feels the dream means. When the stick has gone completely around the circle, the dreamer may elect to repeat what the dream means if his or her feeling has changed at all after the input of the other people.

"It is very important to understand that each person's interpretation of the dream is true and correct, but not necessarily for the dreamer. It is true for the person who heard the dream. Each person interprets the dream from their own frame of reference, even when they are using information they have about the dreamer. Therefore, the interpretation they give to the dream is actually what is true for them, not necessarily what is true for the dreamer. Further, the dreamer hears what he or she allows through his or her own filters. By sharing the dream in the dream council, the dream becomes a dream of that council. By meeting in dream council, every person participating in effect gets to have more dreams."

It's dark when everyone returns to the longhouse living room after a break for dinner.

Shawnodese takes up the stick and continues where he left off. "I would encourage you to take the time when you get home to try the dream council if you have a group with whom to do it. If you don't, it might be a good excuse to get together with some new people.

"The next technique I'm going to share with you I call 'owning your dream.'* Though I've never had the pleasure of working with them, I am told this technique is similar to one employed by Joyce and John Weir in their organizational development workshops. The dreamer first writes out the dream in as much detail as possible. As an example, I will use a dream I had twenty-one years ago. In this dream, I am an observer. I'm not aware of my own body. Looking downward, I see a yellow rose. It's a very large rose, filling my entire field of vision. It is fully open. In the dream I know it is somehow associated with an artist friend of mine, a woman I'll call Karma. Karma was a famous artist who had a terminal illness at the time I had this dream.

"After writing down the dream, the next step is best done with two or more people who can help keep the dreamer on track, and not avoid understanding parts of the dream. Owning is also more powerful when it is done out loud. Owning the dream always begins with the statement: 'I am dreaming, and the dreaming part of me is a . . . (fill in the blank).' Every

*See Appendix, exercise sixteen.

aspect of the dream is brought into the present tense, first person, and described as a part of the dreamer.

"With my rose dream, I would say, 'I am dreaming, and the dreaming part of me is an observer part of me. It is a part of me that is not aware of my own body. This observing, unaware part of me sees a downward direction part of me. In that downward direction part of me there is a yellow part of me, a rose part of me, a yellow rose part of me. This yellow rose part of me is a very large part of me. It fills the entire part of me, the field part of me, the vision part of me, the entire field of vision part of me. It is fully a part of me, it is an open part of me, it is a fully open part of me. It is an artistic part of me, a friend part of me, an artistic friend part of me. It is the Karma part of me. And I am awake.'

"I used 'And I am awake' to indicate the end of that round of working with the dream. Owning your dream always begins with 'I am dreaming' and ends with 'I am awake.' Now it is quite possible that just speaking the dream the way I have demonstrated will trigger enough insight that the meaning and intent of the dream will become clear to the person speaking.

"However, if that is not the case, or if there are particular parts of the dream that are confusing or difficult to understand, or if you want to get at other levels of interpretation of the dream, then the dreamer and, if applicable, the dreamer's helpers take some time to make a list of words they each associate with the words used to describe the dream. Then they proceed with the second round. For example, take the words *yellow rose*. 'I am dreaming, and the dreaming part of me is a yellow part of me, which is a cowardly part of me, which is a hopeful part of me, which is a fearful part of me, which is denying part of me, which a spiritually powerful part of me.' I'd go from there, describing all the things I would associate with the color yellow.

"Then I would take the word *rose*. 'The rose part of me is the flower part of me, is the open part of me. It's a having gotten part of me, it's a potentially thorny part of me, it's a growing part of me.'

"As I went through and processed each part of the dream this way, I became aware that the dream on one level is speaking about my own denial of death; my hope the person who is sick would survive her illness; my sense of the beauty and completeness of the artwork Karma had created; my intuition her work was complete, that she would do no more artwork. There was more to this dream, but this is what I feel comfortable sharing with you now."

Luke Blue Eagle asks for the talking stick. When it has passed to him, he says, "I also want to make sure people know about the trick of taking every element in your dream and writing down very fast all the first things that come to mind. That's very valuable, because it can give access to a person's private symbolism. The important thing is to just let it flow out. Sometimes the analogies will be very surprising, because we all have very different symbolisms, because of what we've lived, because of our experience in life. This is one way of having access to that: just put down the elements of the dream, then write down very fast, without thinking, the analogies. Whatever comes off the top of your head when you're thinking about it." He passes the talking stick back to Shawnodese, who thanks him for this suggestion, and then continues.

"Another very powerful way to understand the meaning of a dream," Shawnodese says, "is to act the dream out. A very clear description of how this process works can be found in the book *Black Elk Speaks* by John Neihardt. The book describes how the entire tribe got together and reenacted the dream of the young Black Elk. I've never personally reenacted an entire dream. But I have gotten very deep understanding of parts of a dream by acting those parts with one or two individuals.

"Yet another way of understanding dreams is to reinterpret the symbolic language with yet another symbolic language. This can be done by the individual, taking the dream and using it to create something else: a painting, a song, a poem, a piece of music, a sculpture.

"As you begin to study your own dreams and their interpretations, you will very quickly learn to recognize that gentle sense of 'Ah-ha!' that flows through you when you have hit upon a correct interpretation. There will be no doubt in your mind what this dream means. You'll know with a deep sense of knowing, one you can feel in your own body.

"I know that you'd all like to try some of these techniques that I'm suggesting, and you will have time to do that yet this evening. But there are a few others that I want to present to you first. And Lucy, I have not forgotten about the dream you presented. What I'd like to present now is an exercise for working with your dreams that is based loosely on Evelyn 'Mahadjuni' Eaton's work with the Medicine Wheel.* If you have constructed a Medicine Wheel, be it tiny or large, go to that Medicine Wheel and sit at whatever place feels right to you. If you are unfamiliar with working with the Medicine Wheel, the best place to start is the position that corresponds to your birth. As I'm sure you remember, if you were born in the spring, you sit in the East; in the summer, the South; in the autumn, the West; in the winter, the North.

"If you don't have a Medicine Wheel or if it is impractical to sit at a Medicine Wheel, sit anyplace that is calm and conducive to meditation. Once you're sitting comfortably, begin focusing with the smudge ceremony. Perhaps chant or drum for a few minutes to get yourself centered and fo-

*See Appendix, exercise seventeen.

cused. It is possible to do this entire meditation drumming or listening to a drumming tape. Some people have found that to be a very powerful method. Once you've smudged and centered yourself, close your eyes and imagine the Medicine Wheel in front of you.

"In your mind's eye, get up and walk to the center of the Medicine Wheel. As you stand in the center of the wheel begin by saying something like: 'Creator, I come with honor and respect for those who have gone before me, with honor and respect for those who walk beside me in this earth walk, and with honor and respect for those who have yet to come, the great grandchildren of my children's grandchildren.I come seeking truth and understanding about the dream I have had. I ask only that which is of the light and love and truth and life. All else, all negativity be banned from this circle. This is my dream.

"At this point you would tell your entire dream within this inner circle. You would end by inviting your own internal dream council to come and share with you. You might do this in the following manner: 'I now invite the members of my sacred dream council to come and sit with me in the circle of the ancient Medicine Wheel. I call my child, male and female, from the East; I call my adolescent, male and female, from the South; I call my adult, male and female, from the West; I call my elder, male and female, from the North.' Imagine these eight figures stepping into the Medicine Wheel and sitting down with you in a circle. Address each one, one at a time. Begin with the child that is of the same sex, and say something like: 'I ask from you the gift of understanding of this dream. Tell me what it means to you.' Be peaceful, quiet, and listen to the response from that still, small voice within you. As each member of your Medicine Wheel circle finishes speaking, thank them for the gifts they have shared with you. You may use the words: 'Thank you for the wisdom you have shared with me. I ask that I use this wisdom in a good and wise way.'

"When the last of these eight teachers have spoken to you and you have thanked them, thank them as a group again before you leave the circle. Words that you use could be: 'I give thanks to you, my dream circle, thanks to you and thanks to all of my relations. It is good.' Then, if you haven't done so already, imagine these teachers leaving you. Imagine yourself getting back up from the center of the Medicine Wheel and returning to where you were sitting. At that point gently become aware of your surroundings. Stretch, open your eyes, feel the earth beneath you and the sky above you. Again, give thanks for the wisdom that has been shared with you.

"Now I want to give you one other technique I use when I come across a symbol in dreams that really does not make sense to me, no matter how I look at it, work with it, or talk about it. I use this technique to bring light to that symbol. I was taught this form of meditation by a woman in the

San Francisco Bay Area named Betty Bethards. She referred to it as con-centration-meditation.* It has two phases, the concentration phase and the meditation phase. The concentration phase can be from one to ten minutes long, and the meditation phase can be equal to or up to four times longer than the concentration phase. So, for example, five minutes of con-centration allows you five to twenty minutes of meditation.

"To begin, you sit in a comfortable chair. Your body attitude should be somewhat closed. I recommend you sit with your ankles gently crossed, hands either folded together or lying on your thighs, palms down. In this position you begin to concentrate on any one thing.

"You can use any single sense for that focus of concentration. For ex-ample, you can use the sense of sight, where you focus on a burning can-dle or a picture that has specific spiritual significance to you. There are quite a number of forms of meditation where the essence of the medita-tion is to visualize a specific picture. You can focus on a sound, either a mantra, which is a word or words repeated over and over again inside your head silently, or a chant, or a word. I've found just using the word *love* produces a very pleasant, focused, concentrated state. Or you can use a Tibetan bowl, or bells or cymbals. You would strike the instrument once, and then listen and focus all of your attention and concentration on that sound as it slowly fades into silence. You may have to strike the in-strument several times during the period of your concentration to renew the sound you are focused on. Eventually, you'll be able to strike the in-strument once, and the sound will carry throughout the concentration phase. Incense or smudge can be a focus for your sense of smell.

"There are a number of 'mystical schools' that teach techniques of fold-ing the tongue back within the mouth, tasting, and using that taste as a focus of meditation. Or you can concentrate on the flow of your breath or the flow of energy as you inhale and exhale. It really doesn't matter what you concentrate on, as long as you concentrate.

"Now this concentration may sound easy, but just give it a try. Your mind can produce all kinds of garbage in order to interfere with your process of concentration. The appropriate way to handle this is to realize that your focus has wandered and, gently, without recrimination, bring your focus back to whatever it was you were concentrating on. No matter how many times you find your mind has wandered, gently bring it back. It is impor-tant not to change what you've decided to concentrate on in the middle of the process. Keep with it through one concentration period, and prefer-ably through five more concentration periods, before you select another point of focus.

*See Appendix, exercise eighteen.

"I recommend five minutes for your first run through this, and I recommend you have a watch or a clock easily within your field of view, so you can open your eyes and see what time it is. There is nothing more disturbing in a concentration than to have some kind of alarm go off. At the end of your concentration phase, you want to uncross your feet and turn your palms face upward to the sky. At that moment, you ask within your inner being, 'What is the meaning of this symbol?' Then you meditate or observe, and this is just as difficult as focusing.

You'll find yourself wandering off into daydream and patterns of thought, and not observing. When you find yourself doing this, gently remove yourself from it and observe that daydream or pattern of thought. Pull yourself back into the position of observer, someone who watches the thoughts that go by, and gradually you will begin to develop a sense of knowing. It may take more than one or two attempts at this technique, but I guarantee that if you use the technique of concentration for five minutes, ask the question 'What does this particular symbol mean?,' and then allow yourself to be open for an answer to that question for the next five minutes, without hanging onto daydreams or thoughts, eventually an answer will come to you.

"It is very important you don't ask about another symbol before you have the answer to the first one. Now, the answer may not come to you within the observation phase. It may come later during the day, it may come within another dream. It may come out of the mouth of a friend, or it may come from a book you open intentionally or by accident. I've worked with many people using this technique, and I know other people who have used it. I've heard many stories of books falling off shelves and opening to chapters or sections that gave an answer to the question asked.

"The most bizarre experience I ever had with this technique involved a question I had asked in the observer state on a Tuesday. Saturday had rolled around, and I wasn't really thinking about the question anymore. I had spent the day with friends scuba diving. Two of us were driving back from the diving site, both fairly physically exhausted. My companion, who was driving, was talking about his thesis on theoretical physics, a subject I did not find overwhelmingly interesting. All of a sudden, quite out of nowhere, this gentleman gave me a detailed answer to the question I had asked in my meditation four days earlier. He then proceeded with his discussion of theoretical physics, totally unaware he had answered the question I had asked.

"Gradually, as you get better at using this technique, the answers about a symbol may come more and more quickly, until you get to the point where you merely have to think of asking the question. 'What does this symbol mean?,' and the answer will come clearly into your mind, without the need for the concentration and meditation. Again, this technique has to do with convincing your unconscious that you are serious in your quest for understanding. I actually knew one person, Abby, who was so clear in her intention and focus in not only remembering but also understanding her dreams that at the conclusion of each dream she had she would see within her mind a written interpretation of the symbols within her dream. We should all be so lucky.

"Now Lucy, concerning the dream your client had, I think Steven has given you a wonderful interpretation of it. What I've given you are several other methods that you can use for interpreting the dream for you and for her. I think we've had plenty of talking for today, and so I'd like to suggest that we again go into our smaller circles and spend whatever time people in the circle feel comfortable spending with actually using one or another of these methods of dream interpretation that have been presented here today. I'm happy to stay around. Are you, Steven?"

At Steven's affirmative nod, Shawnodese says, "Steven will stay here also, and perhaps some of the other teachers who can help you with utilizing these methods of dream interpretation. Are there are any questions about what we're doing before we begin?"

John asks whether each group has to use each method of dream interpretation, and Shawnodese replies that it is entirely up to each group how they want to use the material that has been presented.

Someone else, looking at her watch, notes that it is now nine o'clock, and asks how late they should stay up interpreting dreams.

Sun Bear answers this time, saying, "That also is entirely up to you. But for me, I'm going to just be available for a couple of minutes, and then I'm going to go get some new dreams to work on myself. I intend to be up early tomorrow morning, and if any of you have questions for me you can present them then. Thank you all, good brothers and sisters, for all the information you've given to people here. Good night now."

With the stars shining brightly in the sky, some small circles go out to experience the crisp, cool autumn air, while others gather in the living room at various distances from the woodstove. An owl hoots in the darkness, as if to give her approval to all the work with dreams that has gone on here this evening.

WORKING WITH YOUR DREAMS

The fifth and final day of the dream council dawned clear, but shortly after sunrise clouds began to come in from the west. Most of the people in the circle look very excited from the work they did the previous evening on interpreting their dreams. A few people look upset. Prior to breakfast, most of the teachers are present, making themselves available to any participants who need to talk about problems that might have come up in working with their own dreams.

After people have had the opportunity to enjoy breakfast and to talk more about their own dreams of last night as well as previous nights, the circle meets in front of the longhouse, enjoying the intermittent sunshine and the sight of the wonderful pine trees that surround the longhouse.

Luke Blue Eagle takes the stick this morning and begins to talk about working with his dreams. "After you have started remembering your dreams, and you have differentiated between the types of dreams you have, you can go to the next stages. There's the stage where you try to awaken in the dream—that is, to try and be conscious you are dreaming the dream while you are dreaming. The following step is to act consciously in the dreamtime. Moving on to another step, you learn to consciously go places in your dream. Usually in the beginning of dream work we choose power spots because we can easily be drawn to them. Then you can go to a stage where you can do healing consciously in the dreamtime.

"Something personal that I have worked out, in wanting to perfect my dream work, is that I started calling upon a spirit to help me in the dreamtime. At some point the spirit did manifest to me, and it was a shape-shifter. I call him my dream wizard. The first time he was a dragon, and then he was a dog—and the way I knew he was a shape-shifter was through indications given by the dragon aspect of him. Then he would be there, the same presence, only he would have different forms.

"Then I made what I call a dream altar, where I have a fetish representing this dream wizard, with Herkimer diamonds sitting on a mugwort pillow. They say mugwort helps you remember your dreams. It holds the dreams. So when I have specific things or dream work I want to do, I'll use this dream altar, and I'll try to get in touch with my dream wizard to help me with my dream work. To me and to many people, dreaming is a very important part of life, and a very powerful way of looking at who we are, because it puts everybody on the same level. Everybody can be respected for their participation in the spiritual creation of life through the dreamtime.

"This is why the dreams of certain people are always listened to, like the women in the Moon Lodge. These women were considered to be in a spiritual time, so when they had dreams, people listened to them. What saved Chief Joseph at one point was when one of the women from the Moon Lodge came and told him she had the dream of many, many horses coming that had steel shoes. He knew that was the white people's horses, so he left where he was. Some hours later the army got to where Chief Joseph's people had been camped, but the Nez Percé had moved on. This is just one example of how dreams were very important to the lives of Native people."

When it is obvious Luke is done speaking, Wabun asks for the talking stick. "I think this is a perfect time for me to play for you part of the interview I did with Brooke Medicine Eagle. A very important part of her medicine is the Moon Lodge and teaching women today about this aspect of life. She talked about this in the interview I conducted with her for our dream council, and I'd like to share that with you along with some of the comments she made about dreams and visions in general. If you'd like to take a stretch break for a few minutes, I'll set up the tape so it's ready to go when you get back."

After the tape is set up and people return to their seats, Wabun turns on the recorder and Brooke's voice comes forth. "If you really work with your dreams—remembering them, writing them down—it's a very powerful way to start being able to bring the information of spirit back into your daily life. I think many of us have had dreams and visions that could be important to us, but we didn't know how to remember them and bring them through that very strange veil which you encounter when you come into the waking state from a dream. We've all had the experience of having this vivid, wonderful dream, and then it kind of goes *vrowwww.* . . . Pretty soon you wake up and you can't remember one thing about it.

"Continuing to work with our dreams begins to help us bring dreams and information back from the side of spirit and illumination, and then helps stimulate nonsleeping dreams or visions. The better we get at bringing things back from that non–time-space, nonphysical side, the more easily we can get to this place in many forms. Then it becomes a powerful guidance in our lives.

"I have a very rich visionary life. It seems as if I live my whole life based upon that. These visions roll out in front of me all the time, and that's what I'm following as I live my life. The visions often come in pictures and images, details of a larger vision. It's like small vision after vision helps me understand and work out my larger vision in the world. I did a series of four vision quests that were very formal, and then it seemed as if the ball was rolling and I didn't need to go out and sit anywhere special for them, they just seemed to come very much at will.

"Concerning dreams, I have had something very interesting happen as I travel around and teach: Many people who have heard me speak have images afterward of what they assume is White Buffalo Woman, a mystical Native woman associated with the White Buffalo, who came to the Lakota people long ago. What fascinates me most is that some of them come to me to relate that *before* they heard me talk about White Buffalo Woman, they had no way to identify the woman in white buckskin who was coming to them in dream!

"White Buffalo Woman is a teacher who brought the sacred pipe to the Lakota people, which is a teaching about unity and wholeness and holiness, about sacred ecology. I think she's coming back to people today because the message she brought so long ago is vitally needed in our world at this time. Here is a message of the feminine, nurturing renewal of the world. It's a message of global harmony and working with All Our Relations. It's absolutely vital in the crisis we're in, where we haven't paid attention to wholeness and to All Our Relations, and have come to exist in such disharmony.

"I have another symbol that's really present with me, and that's a black jaguar, which represents to me the feminine, the deep, unconscious realms of the dark and the richness of nighttime."

On the tape, Wabun questions Brooke about her work with women and moon time, and how this relates to dreaming. "The moon time, if it's done well, is a full-blown vision quest," Brooke says. "If you take four days and really spend that time in quiet and work on opening your vision, that's the same amount of time and, in a sense, energy, that's put into another kind of vision quest. So, the moon time can be very powerful, and can really bring that same kind of *big* vision, or numinous vision, that comes when you go out on the mountain. It's just a different, more feminine form of it."

Wabun talks to Brooke about the work she has done with women and moon time and notes that many women report they are more able to dream vividly and powerfully when they're on their moon.

Brooke replies, "Yes, that's what I'm taught is the precise function of that time for women. In the moon time there is an openness to the realm of dream and vision, and that's why it's important to take advantage of this time. A woman has a much easier access than she would normally to her dreams, and may be able to go deeper than anyone else in the human form, if she knows how to take advantage of that time of openness. I advise women to take time off and quiet themselves as much as possible. I tell a woman that, when she can, she should literally make it a vision quest every month! That's the way it was traditionally done. In this day and time it's not very easy to take four days a month for yourself, but I believe that anything we can do to quiet ourselves is good.

"The first day of the moon time is an especially powerful time. If we women could just take that, or the second day, and spend it quietly, and not be doing *anything* outwardly—which means to eat lightly or just drink juices, to help get ourselves into a quiet space without demands on us—then we can really open up that visionary side. When women do this, they find it's a very powerful time to tune in and get centered and connected with themselves and the deeper mysteries.

"Also, if a woman's eyes are keyed strongly enough by being in the moonlight, it will help her to come into a natural cycle where her bleeding takes place on the dark of the moon. That's the most powerful time for visioning, when that combination of dark of the moon and the moon time takes place.

"It's very important to work with your dreams and interact with them," Brooke continues, "to talk to the characters in them, to talk to the objects and the beings, in such a way that you come to understand what each symbol or event means, in this moment, in this time of your life. The symbol could be different than it has been before. It's very powerful to know from your own inner self what meanings are there, because then you can begin to enrich and deepen your experience of the dream. It's not important to have one exact meaning, because your consciousness loves to teach you in an individual and moment-to-moment manner. It's just like the difference between seeing a car pass you on a busy city street, or seeing a car pass you when you're starving in the desert! It's the same *object,* but it has very different meanings and implications according to the situation. The same is true of your dream.

"Much of the guidance we receive from the Great Mystery, and from our deepest selves, can come from dreams if we invite this and commit ourselves to working with our dreams. And I also believe that Mother Earth is really in dire need of this kind of guidance, which comes directly from Spirit, at this time in evolution."

When the interview with Brooke is done playing, Wabun turns off the recorder and asks whether the women in the dream council would be willing to talk about some of the dreams or visionary experiences they have had during their own moon time. It turns out that this indeed is a powerful time for many of the women present, and the qualities of their dreams at that time are very different from the qualities of dreams during other times of the month.

Wabun encourages the women who have not observed the difference between moon time dreams and other dreams to begin to do so, and to always note that in the journals or dream diaries they are keeping. She tells the men present that it would be interesting for them to note when the women to whom they are relating are on their moon time, and whether this has some effect on the dreams the men have.

"There is a very real shift in the energy of a woman who is on her moon time," Wabun says, "and sometimes her energy is so expanded, so vast, that it will have a very real effect on the people around her. I've even read of studies where children would always know when mom was on her moon time, because there was such a difference. Sometimes this would also affect the dreams of the children. As with many things having to do with women and their reproductive cycle, there hasn't been nearly enough research done in this area. I encourage you all to become experimenters and to begin to perceive the differences that the varying cycles make in a woman, and in those to whom she relates. Don't expect these to be negative differences by listening to all that old 'on the rag' business we've grown up with. It's very possible that the energetic difference in a woman as she goes through the parts of her cycle is very positive, and can help both her and you, not only with your work in the dreamtime but with your life in general."

Since several hours have passed since breakfast, Wabun suggests that people take time to restock on tea, water, or coffee; to stretch their legs; and to talk with one another about any reactions they have to the material presented thus far.

After the break, Shawnodese takes the talking stick and begins. "Sun Bear, I hope you're going to talk this morning about how you can appear in other people's dreams. I just want to mention here, folks, that I've had many reports that Sun Bear regularly appears in other people's dreams, even in the dreams of people who have never met or even heard of him. In the eight years I traveled with Sun Bear, it became almost a given that, as we moved into some new place, someone would come up and excitedly tell Sun Bear about a dream in which they had seen his face or had heard him beckoning to them to come and learn from him. They would report that only later had they seen his picture in a book and written for more information. Now, I know Sun Bear, and I know he doesn't go out each night and say, 'Well, tonight I'm going to go out and tickle the unconscious of these six people to get them to come to my next workshop.' It is something that is a part of his energy that draws people to him.

"So, brother, are you going to tell us more about just what that is?"

Sun Bear nods, and Shawnodese passes the talking stick to him. After examining it, Sun Bear says, "Sometimes I do go to people in their dreams if I need to communicate with them. If I have trouble communicating with somebody, or I can't communicate with them in the normal ways, I'll pray for a dream that night in which I can reach them. Maybe I don't know where to reach them. Sometimes I have a very powerful dream, and I bring them into the dream and talk to them and share things with them. Then, maybe a couple of days or a week later, I get a call from the person, and he is telling me about having this powerful dream and my being in it with him. This is something that makes me feel really, really good about my dreaming power.

"One time a friend called and told me about her dream from the night before in which we met at a farm and spoke of important things having to do with her growth. When she was done I said, 'I know this farm well, I was there, too.' I do this by projecting myself out in the night. However,

I do not encourage new dreamers to try this without help from a dream teacher or a dream guide.

"I'll tell you a couple of other stories that people have told me. There was one man I used to meet at arts and crafts shows, and he would buy our magazine, which was then called *Many Smokes* but is now called *Wildfire*. He told me he never read the magazines; he'd just buy them and put them under the counter. Eventually, he had a couple of years' supply.

"At about this time he started having problems with his health, and felt he needed to get away from the pollution and stress of the city. But he had no idea how to live in the country, so he did nothing and his condition grew worse. Finally, he told me, I came to him in a dream. For four nights, I stood near the stack of magazines and I just kept shaking my finger at him.

"It was quite a while before I saw him. When I did, he came up to me and said he had to tell me what had happened in his life. He told me about his health being bad. He told me how, though he knew he should leave the city, he didn't feel he had the knowledge he needed. Then he told me about his dream. Apparently, the dream shook him up so much he sat down and read all the back issues of *Many Smokes*. Well, *Many Smokes* had a lot of good information about living outside the cities, and he said reading the magazine gave him the confidence he needed. When he did move away, he regained his health. He also remained a faithful reader of the magazine. So on both sides, good things can come out of dream travels.

"Now, I have the power also when I go to sleep to project my image out to people in dreams. Sometime back, there was a lady who had continuing migraine headaches. I came to her in a dream and put my hands on her head and healed her. Now she's studying with me as a student.

"I had a similar dream myself one time. My eye was bothering me for about a week. It was all swollen and sore and I didn't know what to do about it. Then I had a dream in which Rolling Thunder, another medicine man, came to me. He spit on his fingers, and he ran his fingers over my eye, and the next day my eye was fine. It was healed.

"I had another man who had a dream in which I came to him and told him to study with me. He had never heard of me. The next day he went over to Berkeley to the bookstore and he walked into the store and my book *The Path of Power* fell off the shelf in front of him. Since that time he's been studying with me.

"I did a workshop sometime back in Florida and three people had come there because they had had dreams about me, and five people had come because they had been to a psychic and a spirit had told them to come and study with me. Many, many times people have come up to me at different workshops and programs who have had powerful dreams in which I've come to them and helped them and healed them.

"Sometimes when I'm having a dream and I seem to be having trouble in it, or somebody's getting the best of me, I wake up, and then I'll pray over that dream and go back into it and try to make it turn out better.

"If you have dreams that are fragmented or you can't remember your dreams, I would encourage you to have a dream object and to pray with that dream object before you go to sleep. Focus yourself and pray for good, strong dreams that will give you more centering. I always have a lot of dreams at night, and I'm able to increase my dreams. As I've told you, before I go to bed I drink lots of water or tea. Then when I go to sleep I'll sleep for a couple of hours and have to get up and go to the bathroom. Then, when I go back to bed, I have a different dream. This way sometimes I'm able to have four or five dreams in a night on different topics.

"Traveling in a dream state can become a common occurrence. When I want to do this, I prepare myself by praying and focusing before I go to sleep. My two most frequent forms of dream travel are as an eagle or as part of Brother Wind. The sky is the pathway for my journey. It's a very powerful experience to see all of the living Earth Mother below, or to feel and be a part of the wind.

"Being the wind can be a wild and exciting feeling, like an unending flow of powerful emotion. Or it can be as gentle as a caress between loved ones. The wind has been my powerful ally in many situations. Because I travel with the wind in my dreams, a part of me is the wind and, at times, the wind will come when I call in a sacred way through prayer. This occurrence has been helpful for turning the heads of some participants at events who have been slow to grasp the power and reality of the medicine path. After a little windstorm, they are usually convinced that other realities exist. Sometimes, then, they even begin to believe that the dreamtime exists, and they can in fact work in it. And that's good. That's good medicine."

When Sun Bear puts the stick down, several of the people in the circle ask to have it to recount dream experiences they have had with him. These corroborate the stories he and Shawnodese have just finished telling. When others are done speaking, Shawnodese asks that the talking stick pass to him.

"I want to talk about some specific methods of working with your dreams.* I'd like to begin by saying it is possible for two people who share

*See Appendix, exercise nineteen.

their lives together to have dreams that contain the same symbol as the main element. I have heard of couples who often dream dreams that are remarkably similar. My wife and I have upon occasion had dreams that contained the same element, and it seemed to be, if not exactly the same dream, parts of an identical dream.

"I know of groups of people who have done ceremonies together and prayed for their group to receive a dream that would be a dream for the whole group. I have worked with such groups and can verify it was possible for a number of people to have a dream that had shared elements. One way to accomplish this is for the group of people to sit and pray together. Another is for each person to make a dream pillow or pouch that they pass around the circle, with each person holding each item for a moment and then passing it on until the pillow or pouch returns to its original owner. Everyone would then sleep with a pillow or pouch under their pillow or beside their bed.

"I also know of groups of people who have gone to sleep in the same room, forming a wide circle with their heads toward the center so they sleep as if each were a petal of some large daisy. I've experienced this situation yielding a number of people within the group who have dream elements very much in common.

"Dreaming together can be very interesting if everyone agrees that it is something they want to do, but I need to tell you a story now about what can happen if you try to dream with someone without their permission and cooperation.

"My wife and I were staying at the house of one of Sun Bear's apprentices for a few days, one Azakir by name, who begged me to teach him how to enter another person's dream. Being young, arrogant, and ego-flattered that Azakir would ask me. I took the time to teach him how to enter another person's dream, cautioning him at each step in the process that this was not something to be done lightly, and definitely not to be done without the permission of the person whose dream Azakir wished to enter.

"He assured me my conditions would be met before he would attempt such a journey. But I had an intuition that Azakir would use this knowledge incorrectly. Yet out of my own ego I proceeded to complete the instruction. I had an uneasiness that night, a restlessness. My wife sensed it also. We lay in bed without sleeping for quite some time, mulling over the day. We both heard the front door of the house open and close, and we heard footsteps walk through the house, from the front toward the back. We were concerned, and we got up to see what was happening.

"The house was dark in the front, but there was a light on in Azakir's bedroom. We knocked at the door and a voice croaked for us to come in.

We found Azakir in great physical distress. His eyes were large and puffy, his lips were swollen up like sausages, and he was having some difficulty breathing. We were out in the country, an hour from the nearest medical attention. It was evident that Azakir needed medical help immediately. Fortunately for all of us, my wife had with her some Benadryl, which we gave to Azakir. This and a healing pipe ceremony fairly rapidly began to relieve what was evidently the symptoms of a severe allergic reaction that was becoming anaphylactic shock.

"By coincidence, Azakir had gone through all the steps to prepare himself to enter someone else's dreams that night. Under the misguided delusion he was in love with her, he had attempted to enter the dream space of a person I will refer to as a medicine woman. This particular person had been recognized within her own culture as having a special gift and ability to work with dreams and the dreamtime. Because this gift had been recognized when she was still a young child, ceremonies had been done to protect her while she dreamed. The way she describes it is that they placed guardians around her to protect her from those who would intrude so that the powers of her dreams would remain clear and pure. I knew this medicine woman. My wife and I went to speak with her the next day, to ask her if anything strange had occurred within her dream state the previous night. She said she had a vague memory of some energy that approached her guardians, but they struck out at it as one would swat a fly. She had given it no further thought. I have not taught anyone else how to enter someone else's dream space, except through the meditation I am going to share with you.*

"The first and most important thing to remember about this meditation is that it can only be done with the conscious permission of the other person or people involved. Now, given that you understand this, the following is a device for two people who wish to dream together, to share the same dream or at least elements of the same dream. I recommend you discuss with each other your desire to dream together, and you become very clear on the reason why you wish to dream together. The clearer you can be on your reason, the more likely you are to have a pleasant and successful experience.

"Once you both are clear that you wish to dream together and why, the next step is for each of you to make a dream pillow. Be very focused in your mind when you are making this dream pillow. All this is done with the thought that you are giving this pillow to the other person as a gift so you might share dreams together.

"Go to a Medicine Wheel, or some other place where the two of you

*See Appendix, exercise twenty.

can sit together quietly in meditation. An important part of this meditation is that you hold hands while you are doing it. You begin by sitting at the agreed-upon position by your Medicine Wheel, or in some other safe space. Prepare by smudging yourselves and your dream pillows. Sit side by side at a point on the Wheel that feels mutually comfortable. Center yourselves either in silent meditation or by chanting or drumming. When you feel centered, reach out with the hand closest to the other person. Join hands, palm to palm. You can continue doing this as a guided meditation, with one of you being the guide or with each of you doing the visualization in your own heart and mind.

"In your heart and mind's eye, with your hands joined together, get up and walk to the center of the Medicine Wheel circle. Once there, ask the life force, the creative energies, to bring each of you into harmony with the other, so that you might walk together in the dreamtime. Imagine that the forces of the center of the circle play through you, making adjustments in the frequency of your vibrations so that, from head to toe, there becomes a harmony between the two of you.

"When you feel harmony has been achieved, return to the place where your bodies are sitting in meditation. Gently squeeze the hand of your partner, release it, and stretch. Become aware of your surroundings. If you were going to do this silently, you might cue each other with gentle hand pressures. A first pressure would indicate you are ready to go into the center of the circle. The second pressure would indicate you are ready to leave and are waiting until you feel your partner's response.

"When you are back in normal time, give each other the dream pillows you have made, and agree upon a day and time the shared dream is to take place. On the night of the shared dream, prepare as you always would for remembering your dreams. Be sure to have the paper and pencil, or tape recorder with tape in it, by your bed ready to go so that should you wake up in the middle of the night remembering the dream, you can record it. Place the dream pillow under your own pillow, beside your head, or underneath your head, and allow yourself to drift off to sleep. Make a point of recording all the dreams you remember from that night. Get together with your dream companion the next day, if possible, and compare dreams.

"It may take several attempts before you succeed in having a shared dream. I recommend you continue with the guided meditation on a daily basis until you have success with the shared dream. After your first success, I recommend you continue with the shared meditation until the pattern of dreaming together is firmly established. Once it is established, all you need to do to dream with the other person on any given night is to take out the dream pillow and sleep with it.

"Based upon the example of my own youth, I don't believe people heed cautions. But I do have to give one in regard to this process of dreaming together. I do not recommend this technique for people who do not wish to become deeply involved emotionally with each other. In my mid-twenties, I used this technique with a person who was a good friend, with the express intention on both parts of merely being able to experience the phenomenon together. Though we succeeded with little difficulty at perfecting the technique, the pain of emotional entanglement that ensued destroyed our friendship and left scars that I can still feel today.

"This calls to mind pictographs Sun Bear often speaks to me and others about. These described the development people go through when reaching for higher and higher realms of spiritual power. They also give the warnings and show the consequences of reaching beyond your ability or readiness. One such pictograph showed a man with half of his head bald, and the other half full of hair. This is a symbol of great imbalance, indicating that the seeker had lost his mind in his search for knowledge and power. Therefore, my advice to you in dreaming and in all areas where you seek to grow beyond your current self, is to allow the growth to occur naturally, one step at a time. Then you will have few difficulties. Reach too far and too fast, as I have in the past, and as Azakir did, and be prepared to face the consequences."

The clouds are coming in closer together, promising, if not a visit from the thunder beings, at least a visit from the rains. It is time to break for lunch, and to give people a chance to digest all of the information they have received this morning. When the circle meets again this afternoon, it will be to discuss how the teachers have put all this information to work in their own lives, and how the participants can also make their dreamtime a larger part of their waking hours.

LIVING A DREAM LIFE

The thunder beings are heading toward the mountain. There is no sound of thunder or flash of lightning as yet, but from the dark gray thunderheads that are gathering, people know it is only a matter of time. Everyone seems glad they spent part of the morning talking outside, since it is clear the afternoon session will take place in the living room of the longhouse.

"How appropriate," Tony says. "We began our dream council in the longhouse living room with the thunder beings all around us, and now it looks as though we're going to end that way."

Wabun smiles at Shawnodese. They both know how often the thunder beings are around when Sun Bear is speaking. What surprises both Wabun and Shawnodese is not the fact they would be present for the last session, but rather that they had not been there every night during the dream council.

Wabun takes the talking stick. "I certainly feel full from all I have learned during this dream circle," she says. "However, there are still a few points some of the teachers told me they wanted to stress, and this afternoon will be their chance to do so. I think throughout this afternoon's information, you should keep in mind something Steven Foster spoke about yesterday. And that is, what really counts is not the dreams you have as much as your willingness and ability to make them a real and present part of your life. One of the big differences between Earth societies and the mainstream Western culture today is that to Earth peoples, dreams and visions are the guiding forces of life. They did not just have a dream, write it down, interpret it, and then wait for another. If they had a dream they knew would serve their people, they felt obligated to fulfill the mission they had been given by the dream. I hope you have already started to think of ways of doing this in your own life, and that what we share with you this afternoon will help give you even more impetus and support in doing so."

Wabun says she has some information from Page Bryant with which she would like to begin. Wabun turns on the tape recorder. Page's voice comes out, saying, "Ancient indigenous peoples have long held beliefs regarding the special power at sacred sites. While their legends and descriptions of the power that various places have over human life and consciousness differs, their underlying premise remains the same. Sacred sites are the homes of the gods, locations where the natural, raw earth energy is at its most intense.

"Yet it's another of the powers attributed to sacred places that I think provides the best help to humans, or at least the most practical help, and that is the fact that holy places are where one can go to communicate with the spirits. These spirits include the Creator, angelic and elemental presences, the spirit forces of nature, and even the human ancestral spirits whose existence, advice, and guidance play an integral role in a person's psychic health and spiritual growth and well-being.

"Among quite a number of Earth cultures, Native American included, it's a rather common practice to sleep in a sacred site. This might precede a vision quest, be part of a vision quest, of an initiation ceremony, or of some other special and sacred rite. The purpose of sleeping at a sacred site, of course, is for the person to seek a dream that would connect them with the Great Spirit or other higher powers; a dream that might offer some special guidance and direction, or contain a useful message.

"The ancient Celts had a practice of sleeping at or near sacred sites, other places of intense Earth power, or on the lines of energy—ley lines—that connected them. When people from Earth cultures obtained a dream by sleeping at a sacred site, I think we can safely assume that such a dream was considered to be a revelation of some sort, and would be interpreted accordingly."

When Wabun turns off the recorder, Shawnodese asks for the talking stick. "I think it's important for us to realize that, besides sleeping at sacred sites, we can sometimes create the situation for a special dream to happen. That's basically what happens when people sleep at a sacred site. Another way to do this is a 'mini-walkabout.'* To do this, you would set aside some time when you can go out to the country, ideally into the wilderness, but since that is not available everywhere at least into a park that has some chance of a few birds and wild animals. Ideally, this would be on a day that you are fasting, at least from solid foods. You would go to an area you had scouted out ahead of time, and knew you felt comfortable and safe in.

"You could begin by cleansing yourself if you had access to a sauna or a sweat lodge. If that is not the case, you could smudge yourself as we have described and demonstrated several times during this council.

"You arrive, cleansed, at the area you have chosen on the day you are fasting. Then you begin to walk. You open yourself up consciously by observing every aspect of nature. You note the physical surroundings, the plants and animals, changes within the sky, the wind, the temperature, everything.

"The first time you take a mini-walkabout, it should only last for one or possibly two hours. At the completion of the time you have scheduled, take your journal and write down everything you saw, everything that happened, as if it were a dream. This is very much like what Steven talked about doing with people who come back from a wilderness quest. After you write things down, you work with it. You work with all the symbols that come to you as if they were a dream, coming from your subconscious, speaking to you.

"If you approach this with sincerity, I believe you'll find it a truly remarkable experience, potentially life-changing. And if you've been having difficulty remembering dreams, this might help you recognize and work through whatever blockages you've not been able to release from the unconscious. As I've worked with people who have gone to seek their direction in the wilderness, I have uniformly observed that the events that take place in nature are at least as important to the person as the visionary experiences they have. I've also observed that these events need to

*See Appendix, exercise twenty-one.

be interpreted just as if they were visionary dreams.

"Interpreting them this way clearly reveals the person and the path that the person walks in life. If you truly work with your dreams, and understand your dream language and how it speaks to you, then take this method and apply it in the walkabout tradition, you will see beyond the shadow of a doubt the deep truth that everything you experience is a reflection of your self. At the same time, you will have the opportunity to experience the equally profound truth that tells you that you are an important and connected part of the whole web of life."

Misty asks for the talking stick and questions Shawnodese, "Have you ever had the feeling when you go into the woods that you've been there before? This has happened to me a couple of times, and I never know what to make of it."

Shawnodese takes the stick and replies, "I believe that a lot, if not all, of what we experience as déjà vu—the eerie sensation of having been in a place before, or having seen the same thing or done the same thing—may in fact be related to precognitive dreams. I know for myself, especially when the déjà vu has extended over a period of time, I've been able to go back to my dream journals and actually find the dream that predicted the event that would occur. Rightly or wrongly, I've used that as an indication I am still on the path that is right for me. In some cases, the déjà vu would relate to a dream I had as much as five years earlier. This is a really good reason to keep dream journals. If I had not, I would not have been able to know for certain that it was in fact a dream that contributed to the déjà vu experience."

Marilyn asks Shawnodese whether he has any advice as to how someone could differentiate between a shamanic dream and a normal dream.

"It is very important for the dreamer to understand," Shawnodese says, "that it is not the dream symbol per se, but rather the energy and quality of the dream symbol that differentiates between a shamanic or medicine dream and a normal dream. It was common for Earth peoples to have dreams filled with the elements of nature, because the elements of nature were so much a part of their everyday lives.

"Those of you who have read of Lame Deer or Black Elk, or other famous Native American men of power, have heard, perhaps with some longing, of power dreams with eagles soaring or herds of buffalo or horses thundering across the plain.

"It is not the eagles or horses or buffaloes that made those dreams power dreams. In each of these scenes, the animals were part of the life history of the person who dreamed it. It was the energy of the dream, and the knowingness of the person upon awakening of the special quality the dream possessed, that made it a medicine or shamanic dream. Because most of us in Western society are so far removed from nature, when one of the elements of nature comes into our dream state, it is more than likely to have a deeper significance than if it was something we saw everyday. However, given the right dream, an everyday object can also have a powerful significance, or be a powerful part of a shamanic dream.

"I'd like to emphasize here something that I said near the beginning. Unless you are a psychologically well-balanced person, your emotional garbage will continually color your dreaming process, and make it almost impossible to sort out wish fulfillment from the true shamanic dream. If you know yourself, it becomes easy to sort out the extraordinary, the spirit gift aspect of a dream, from the merely bizarre psychological aspects of a dream. Remember, it is possible for a dream to contain powerful elements of both a psychological and spiritual nature. It is only through knowledge of yourself that you know how to sort out the elements and act upon them.

"Sun Bear often says, 'If your philosophy doesn't grow corn, I don't want to hear about it.' A shamanic dream is nothing but a dream, unless you act upon the shamanic power that it gives you. If your emotional or physical act is in disarray, you will be unable to respond appropriately to a vision dream.

"The dream that Sun Bear had of the return of the Medicine Wheel, on first telling, was just a dream. A hill, two circles of stone, some animals coming up the hill, seeing that the animals were people, that they were singing and dancing, and that a voice was saying, 'Now has come the time for the return of the Medicine Wheels, now has come the time for the healing of the Earth Mother.'

"It was a dream; a beautiful dream, but a dream. If Sun Bear had lived with his head in the clouds, and his two feet off the floor, or if he had lived continually replaying the conflicts of his childhood, his dream of the return of the Medicine Wheels could have amounted to nothing. Because Sun Bear walks his life upon the Earth Mother in balance, he was able both to recognize the power of the dream and to use the power of the dream to move him forward. With that dream, and the help of the people working with him, he was able to create a powerful teaching that has spread around the world and affected the lives of hundreds of thousands of people. If you wish to walk your life in power, first walk your life in balance."

Sun Bear asks for the stick. "And the good brother and sister here were also very responsible for that dream of the Medicine Wheel becoming a reality," he says. "If sister Wabun had not had the gift for writing that she does, I don't know if that vision would have spread anywhere near as far around the world as it has. If brother Shawnodese had not offered his gift of organizing people and programs, I'm not sure I would have had the number of students and apprentices I do today. It was a wonderful gift Creator gave me in that vision, and it is a wonderful gift Creator gave me in supplying me with such good people to help me carry that vision forth."

Looking just a little bit embarrassed by his praise, Wabun asks for the talking stick and suggests that, on that happy note, everyone take about a half hour break to stretch themselves and relax.

After the break, Wabun takes the talking stick again. "What I'd like to mention now," she begins, "is the concept of transcendent dreaming. This is a term I've come to use to describe the sorts of dreams we seem to have had problems describing during the dream circle. Transcendent, according to the dictionary, means a number of things that make it an appropriate term. It means 'to be beyond the material universe,' which is usually said of a god, and 'that which is altogether beyond the bounds of human cognition and thought.' I like both of those definitions for the kind of dream that just is very special. It's the kind of dream that stays with you throughout your day or throughout your life. It's the kind of dream that can guide you, heal you, give you understanding, revelation, and foreshadowing of your own future. I think it's the kind of dream the Huichols are talking about that makes you feel as though you are a god. It's the kind of dream that everybody always thinks they want to have, and then wonders what they've gotten themselves into when they actually do have them. Prophetic dreams, shamanic dreams, medicine dreams, would all come under the category of transcendent dreams. I understand that Sun Bear, a little bit later, will be sharing some of his transcendent dreams with us. And when I spoke with Page Bryant, she also had a transcendent dream that I thought you'd like to hear. I'd like to pass the talking stick to Page now, via the tape recorder, and give an example of transcendent dreaming."

Wabun turns on the tape recorder, and again Page's strong voice comes through: "In early 1989, I made a pilgrimage to the volcano on the big island of Hawaii, to make 'contact' with the goddess Pele. I had, for some time, felt drawn to make this connection so that I would have a better understanding of both the goddess energy and the constructive and destructive forces within myself. I had long considered Pele's power to be a clear manifestation of the pure creative power. The home of Pele lies in stark and sterile evidence to the destruction brought about by episodes of volcanic eruption that have sent hot lava pouring onto the landscape. However, amid the devastation there exists small twigs of new plant life whose seeds began to germinate some thirty minutes after the lava had cooled. There are also acres of new black pebble beaches, pebbles that the relentless ocean waves have not yet pulverized into sand.

"During the night, after my initial visit to Kilauea, I experienced the genesis of what I have come to call my Pele dreams. In the first dream, I saw a long mountain ridge that seemed to stretch for miles, over which poured a torrent of hot lava!

"The next day, I came across a centerfold in a photo book I had purchased in the visitor's center. There, in the photo, was what I had seen in my dream. It was an actual image of a recent eruption that had, in its destruction, created over two hundred acres of new land.

"Since that time, I have had many Pele dreams. They always contain images of hot, flowing lava. Sometimes the dream images show me a spectacular display of nature's force. Sometimes the lava endangers someone I know, and I set out to save them. These dreams always leave me with the paradoxical feeling of knowing that I need to pause for caution in my life, while at the same time I need to be bold, strong, and more aggressive in my nature. One thing that stands out most is when these dreams come, whether they leave me feeling uneasy or empowered, I am always left with an inner knowing that the images have touched and stirred archetypal forces from within the deep recesses of my soul."

When Page has finished describing her Pele dreams, Sun Bear indicates he is now ready to speak. The talking stick passes around the circle to him. "I regard myself as a dreamer," Sun Bear says. "I have had many dreams that have helped me and my people in a variety of ways. Sometimes my dreams would bring me money or food I needed for survival. When I lived in Reno, Nevada, I had dreams about the numbers on a Keno board, and even which casino to go to. I'd go in and mark the numbers that I'd dreamed. Six times I won money: four times $1,100, one time $535, and one time $112, all with the number I had dreamed about. Any other time I could go down to the same casinos and mark Keno tickets all day long and never win anything. But whenever I would have a strong dream telling me what numbers to play, I would go there and I would be very successful.

"I also remember a time when I was hungry for meat. I'm not a vegetarian, so I prayed to the Creator to give me some meat. I went into the supermarket and I looked at the meat they had at the meat counter. It looked as if they had just painted it over fresh for the next day with some red paint, and it didn't even smell good. So I left, and on the way home I was praying to the Creator. I said, 'Creator, I want meat, real meat, deer meat.'

"That night I had a dream. In the dream I saw two deer lying dead on a familiar highway north of Reno. The next day, I jumped in my car and drove north on the highway, and sure enough, right across the California line was a deer lying dead, freshly killed. So I put it in the trunk of my car and I drove down the road again. After another two and a half miles, there was another dead deer lying alongside the road. I pulled over in my car to load it into the trunk. Just as I was doing it, a California highway patrolman came around the bend—he hadn't been in my dream. He said to me, 'What are you doing here?' I said that this deer is just going to lie here and rot in the sun. I told him, 'I want to take it home, cut up and use the meat, and make something out of the hide.'

"He said, 'Well, California Fish and Game might not like it, but I'm not California Fish and Game. Take it.' I said to myself, 'Thank you, Great Spirit. This is good medicine.'

"Besides dreams that help me with survival, I often have dreams that are prophetic. Back in 1978, I had a dream in which I saw a map of Iran and the word *Iran* vanished off the map. I was told by Spirit that Iran would eventually be destroyed by earthquakes and by its neighbors. Following that, Iran had a devastating war with Iraq that caused great destruction. Since then, it has also had a couple of major earthquakes.

"Back in 1983, I had a dream in which I saw Russia struck by major earthquakes. That has also happened now. There have been three major earthquakes in Russia, and I see three more before the year 2000.

"I've had dreams that have showed me the cities of the United States shaken down by major earthquakes. The power lines were lying in the street. People were trying to flee from the cities. So many different things similar to this have been given to me in dreams.

"I had another dream one time where I saw these great space ships moving over the land. They were able to fire laser beams and strike and ignite areas. The ships were equipped with all kinds of weapons of warfare. They were also being used for powerful space exploration. Later on I realized they were the space shuttles *Challenger* and *Columbia* I was seeing.

"Sometimes I have dreams in which I see airplanes that are crashing. Occasionally, I even see the name of the airline on it. I'm afraid to tell people about this, because they might panic.

"On December 1, 1988, I had a dream that I shared with Jaya, my wife. In that dream I saw two airplanes catch on fire in the sky and burn, explode. Within three weeks, this had happened to one over England and another one over Scotland. The one over Scotland was the one that got so much publicity because it was destroyed by a terrorist bomb. These are some things I have seen. I believe that the spirits try to reach us in different ways to teach us.

"Sometimes my prophetic dreams are very personal. I had a dream in which I was getting ready to do a workshop in Rochester, New York. In this dream, four rattlesnakes came to me. The next day at my workshop, one of my apprentices came to me and brought me four silver rattlesnakes as a gift, which I now wear on my power necklace around my neck. That was the fulfillment of the dream.

"One time I had a dream that one of the people with the Bear Tribe went to town and got a speeding ticket. Unfortunately, I forgot to tell her about the dream. Sure enough, she went to town, and sure enough, she got the speeding ticket.

"I think prophetic dreaming may run in families. My mother had a dream back in 1932 when we were living in Idaho. The dream was very vivid. She saw a big two-story white house, and it seemed that someone was stealing a child from this house. There was a ladder against the house. The people in the dream were speaking German. My mother became so frightened over the dream that she went to see if my brother and I were safe. And we were all right, of course. But the next day, my dad went to town and he came back with a newspaper and said to mother, 'Here's your dream.' The newspaper told about the Lindbergh baby kidnapping.

"There is another kind of dream I have. In part, it is prophetic, but it is more. It is Spirit telling me things I need to know. Some people call these shamanic dreams or medicine dreams. Wabun just told you that she calls them transcendent dreams, so here are a couple that I've had.

"One is a dream I had when I was in Germany. In it, I found a wolf skull in the forest. It had hair and rotting flesh on it. I was cleaning the hair and flesh off with my fingers. I asked the Spirit what this was. The Spirit said that this wolf skull represents the ancient spirit of Germany, and that the hair and rotting flesh represent the political things that some people are still trying to do. But, Spirit said, eventually, the German people will return to their original spirit.

"The next year when I went to Berlin, a woman came to me. She told me she had a dream in which she was holding a wolf skull, and the spirit told her this wolf skull represented the ancient spirit of Germany. I found out later this was true, that many German people regarded the wolf as their protector or guardian animal. That's why the name Wolf is so common in Germany.

"When I was in England, I had a dream in which there was a beautiful white horse—a white stallion—running free over the land. I told the English people about it, and they said that this was the ancient spirit of England I was seeing. Later on they took me north of London to a place called Ridgeway. There they showed me a white horse carved into the side of a hill. I found out later there were six of these around England. At one time there had been a white horse society that regarded white horses as sacred.

"When I was in Australia, the Australian Aborigines asked me to dream for them. I had a dream in which I saw a big sand dune by the ocean. Behind it was lower land. In the dream, I saw the water rising and the land sinking. I shared this with the Aboriginal people. They said, 'We know exactly where that place is. Many of our old-timers have had similar dreams that this would happen in the future.'

"I had another dream when I was in London one time in which a woman brought me into a room and showed me a collection of books. She told me that these were forty of two hundred and forty books that contained the knowledge of the nations. She said, 'These belong to the lion and to the dragon. There are books for the wolf and for the eagle and others.' She mentioned others, and she mentioned different ones that I knew were the ancient spirit keepers of nations. She said in the dream that the seventh and eleventh earls were magicians. This was the end of the dream.

"The next day I was doing a lecture and I told the people at the lecture about the dream, and there was a man sitting in the back of the room. He looked very impressed by what I was saying. During the lunch hour he came up to me and said, 'You have very powerful dreams, and you have a lot of wisdom.' He said that the seventh and eleventh earls were magicians. He told me they were his uncles. He also told me he was part of one of the royal families.

"Another time my protector bear, the great grizzly bear, came to me in a dream. There was a cage under a tree and it was held to the tree by a chain. The cage was made out of tree saplings. I was on one side of it, and the grizzly bear was on the other. There were five people in the cage. The bear and I were shaking the cage back and forth between us. And in the dream I said, 'That's what I'm doing with my bear medicine power. I am shaking the cage of these people to wake them up.'

"I had another dream that a new teacher was coming to me. In this dream, a bear came and told me how he was going to teach me to work with the dream world. He said that eventually I would be able to go into the long sleep like the bears—in other words, hibernate for periods of time. He said that I could do this and that I could come back when I wanted to and work again with people. He said in this way I would prolong the life of my vision. I felt very good about this dream, very strong about it."

Not surprisingly, the thunder beings are right over the longhouse at this point. The clouds have darkened the sky long before sunset. The grayness is lit intermittently by the glow of the lightning. As Sun Bear finishes speaking about this bear that had told him he could go into the long sleep, and then work again with people, a loud crash of thunder sounds overhead, as though in agreement.

Everyone sits in silence for a few minutes, seeming to feel, without verbalizing it, that no one can "tie on another story" to what Sun Bear has just said, or to the sounds of the thunder beings.

Part Two

A Dream Language
of the Earth

INTRODUCTION

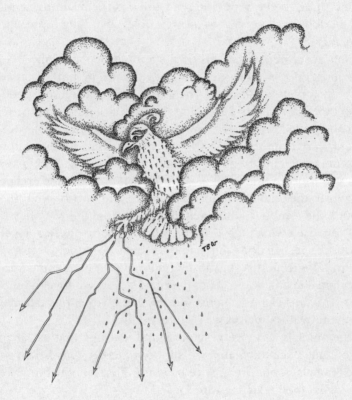

On the evening of the fifth day of the dream council, more people still remain on Vision Mountain than had originally intended to. The thunder beings have come with force. The Spokane airport is closed because of the winds and clouds, and a number of people decided that it would be more pleasant to spend their time waiting here than at a hotel in Spokane. There is plenty of food, so the cooks are agreeable to having extra mouths to feed at dinner. People wander around the house, talking in small groups, relaxing, unwinding.

After dinner, Wabun, Shawnodese, and Luke sit down in the living room and begin talking about the concept of dream dictionaries.

"Although the idea of a dream dictionary originally didn't appeal to me at all," Wabun begins, "it really seems that people need to have some sort of guide to the natural symbols, many of them coming from the Medicine Wheel, that have started coming into their dream world over the past several years. So many people have asked me for this that I feel it would be a service to have one. Yet I don't want people to feel that symbols mean the same thing to every person who dreams them. In my opinion that would be doing a disservice to the symbols, what they represent, and to the dreamers."

"I think every person has his own symbolism," says Luke. "For example, for most people eagles are a very spiritual sign, but for other people it can be completely different. The eagle can be a sign of greed and all kinds of things that are of a ferocious nature. It depends on the life of the person and on the dream. For sure, there are some universal symbols that Jung said were from the collective unconscious, and these will manifest in the same way in transcendent-type dreams, in *le songe*. Otherwise, every person has his own relationship with the symbols and the archetypes.

"However, the animals do teach humans, and part of what they teach is through the symbolism that mainly comes from the way they live their lives. They teach what their responsibility is on the physical level by carrying out the instructions that came to them from the Creator. Humans can learn a lot from that, because you'll never see an animal go against those original instructions. That's the big difference between humans and animals. Humans can go against the original instructions that have been put in them by the Creator.

"So the animals can give very profound teaching that can help us humans to come back to what we're supposed to do. This is why when we see the animals in our dreams we have to reflect on what their responsibility is, what their teachings are for us."

"That's one of the things I'd like to emphasize in this dream language I am writing," Wabun says. "It's something we emphasized throughout the Medicine Wheel books that have already been written. I feel it's very important that people look not only at the animals and their lessons but also at the plants and the minerals associated with the Medicine Wheel. I don't just mean they should look at them in the book either. One of the most profound ways people can learn from the Medicine Wheel teachings is to use them as a reason to go out in nature and observe these beings in their own world. I always tell people when I talk about the Medicine Wheel that if they'd just observe, really observe, one animal or plant or stone in nature, it will make a profound change in the way they perceive their entire life. I believe that's true.

"I also think that a lot of the symbolism of people who live closer to the earth—Earth people—has entered the collective consciousness of people worldwide. That makes sense to me. No matter what race we are, we all come from people who lived closer to the earth at some point in history. I think a lot of people go toward the Native American symbolism because the Native Americans lived closer to the earth until later in history than people in most other parts of the world."

"I think the dream dictionary will benefit people if you do it very carefully," says Shawnodese. "You have to emphasize that absolutely no one but the dreamer can interpret his or her dreams. Consequently, it might seem somewhat bizarre to present a dream glossary as part of a book on dreaming. But for a number of reasons, I believe a dream language section can be a very valid and useful tool in understanding the symbolism of dreams.

"The first reason is that we share a common language, so we have agreed upon the meanings of many words. Our dream experience calls forth the language that we share, and the meanings of those words.

"The second reason, which is more difficult to prove, is that there is what we're referring to as the collective consciousness, symbols that seem to be common to mankind and that stretch across both time and culture. This is easily seen in symbols that pertain to parenthood and childhood.

"No matter who we are, we have all had the experience of floating within our mothers' wombs. So the symbol of water, even to a desert dweller, on the very deepest level of being, connects us with our source. Carl Jung described other images that are shared within the collective unconscious. Because it appears there is a collective unconscious, I think it's important to study the symbols contributed by the Earth traditions as well.

"Also, if you believe that thought directs energy to create things, then consider the amount of thought that thousands of years of Native cultures focused on symbols. Understand that on one level those symbols are created and have existence.

"A third reason is, if you accept my premise that the unconscious is desperately trying to communicate with us at all times, then you'd understand that by reading the dream dictionary, you'd be programming into your consciousness a vast set of symbols with ready-made interpretations. Thereby, you give your subconscious a language with which to communicate with you. I recall quite clearly, when I first began to study my dreaming process seriously, that I would read this or that book on dreaming, and I would then begin to dream with the symbols presented within the context of that book. A benefit was that it made it easier for me to understand my dreams.

"So, for example, when I studied astrology, my dream patterns and symbols revolved around symbols consistent with astrology. After reading *Man and His Symbols* by Carl Jung, I remember having the most delightful dreams of epic proportions using the symbolism of ancient cultures.

"So when you have this dream language completed, Wabun, I think we should tell people to read through the entire section before they attempt to use it to interpret their dreams. That way they will give their dreams a lot of help in speaking to them. That's not to say that reading the section after they've had a dream won't help in interpreting it. It may be the exact trigger they need to become aware of the meaning of the symbol. But they have an even better chance if they've read through the dictionary first, because then they will have given their subconscious a new language with which to speak. And the more symbol languages you can give your subconscious, the better, because that part of you expresses and communicates through symbols, rather than through words. When it does use words, it also uses the words as symbols."

"What I've done first in this glossary," Wabun says, "is to take all of the symbols associated with the Medicine Wheel and define them. To that I've added all the symbols—minerals, plants, animals—that people have asked me about over the years. These are beings from the other kingdoms that have been very important to the people asking. I have often wished we could have many times the number of positions on the Medicine Wheel so that we could honor so many more of our brothers and sisters in the mineral, plant, and animal kingdoms. In my dream language, I've done just that.

"The way I've started this section of the book is to give not only key words about the symbol, but also to describe the being as a part of nature. Then I've given people what I believe to be the most common dream meanings, and I've also given them trickster meanings—puns, plays on words, plays on thoughts and feelings. I've also formulated a transcendent meaning for each symbol. The transcendent meaning is the gift, the revelation, or the deep understanding that dreaming of this particular being can bring to a person.

"It seemed to me that, with these different meanings, a lot of images would be triggered in the dreamer, and if what I wrote wasn't right for them, perhaps reading it would allow them to find the correct meaning for the dream they had."

"I've been dreaming about the osprey a lot," Richard says. "Any mention of that in this glossary that you've been working on?"

"There sure is," says Wabun. "Osprey is one of my favorite birds."

"Flies keep coming into my dreams lately," says Pete. Do you have any meaning for those?"

"Uh-huh," says Wabun.

"One of my vision questers recently came across a lot of mushrooms when they were out in the wilderness," says Leonard. "Do you have anything about those?"

"I sure do," says Wabun.

"I have an idea," says Shawnodese. "If you have some of this on paper already, why don't you bring it down and people can start to look up what they're interested in. That way we'll get a chance to see how this dream language works for the dream circle here."

A DREAM LANGUAGE
OF THE EARTH

The best way to use the "Dream Language of the Earth" is to read through the entire glossary before you begin to work with your dreams. By doing this, you will begin to incorporate even more of the dream language into your own dreamtime. Then, when you go back to this section as you dream, you will have gained the ability to understand more specifically what each of these symbols means in your own dream life.

Abalone

KEY WORDS: DEEP; HIDDEN; BEAUTIFUL; CLOSED.
DESCRIPTION: Abalone is a single-shelled mollusk generally found off the west coast of the United States. It has an iridescent inner shell that was used by many Native people for tools, decoration, and ceremony. The

mollusks had to be successfully scraped off rocks to be used for food.

COMMON MEANING: your deeper emotional nature, hidden from the rest of your feelings.

TRICKSTER MEANING: a lot of baloney.

TRANSCENDENT MEANING: a very obscure and tenacious part of your nature that can have great value if uncovered.

Acorn

KEY WORDS: BEGINNING STRENGTH; HOPE.

DESCRIPTION: Acorns, the seeds of the oak tree, are extremely nutritious when prepared correctly. Acorns from some oaks can be eaten raw, others need to be leached by putting them in running water for several hours, or by several boilings in water. Sun Bear used to advocate putting them in a mesh sack in the tank of your toilet and letting the flushing do the leaching.

COMMON MEANING: the seeds of your own strength; your endurance; a new beginning in your life.

TRICKSTER MEANING: a corn; corny; a joke.

TRANSCENDENT MEANING: endurance; a gift of strength.

SEE ALSO: *Oak Tree*

Adolescence

KEY WORDS: INTENSITY; SEXUALITY; NEW BEGINNINGS; FRUSTRATION; FULFILLMENT.

DESCRIPTION: Adolescence was a time when, in earth-oriented cultures, a child was allowed to seek vision and come back as an adult. It was a time of increased freedom, sexual exploration, and occupational experimentation. Today, adolescence is often a time of frustration because the natural exploration and experimentation is blocked.

COMMON MEANING: increasing sexuality, sensuality, intensity, exploration, or frustration.

TRICKSTER MEANING: a lot less sense; or less cents.

TRANSCENDENT MEANING: understanding the roots of your own sexual nature or lifeway choices. Having an opportunity to correct bad decisions from the past.

Adult: see Maturity

Agate

KEY WORDS: COLORFUL; THIRST-QUENCHING; PROTECTING.

DESCRIPTION: Agate is a chalcedony, with either bands or irregular patches of color, found throughout the world. Historically, agate was believed to ease the thirst, so it was carried by ancient travelers. It was also said to

be a charm that would keep storms, lightning, and poison spiders away.
COMMON MEANING: a colorful aspect of yourself that protects and nurtures you emotionally.
TRICKSTER MEANING: a gate.
TRANSCENDENT MEANING: the picture you see in the agate is a dream key.

Air (element of) see *Butterfly*

Alabaster
KEY WORDS: SOFT; HARD; MALLEABLE; FOUNDATION STONE; PARADOX; GIVEAWAY; WABOOSE.
DESCRIPTION: Alabaster, the mineral associated with Waboose, Spirit Keeper of the North, can be found in both a soft and hard variety and in colors from colorless to brown. Soft alabaster has been carved by many Earth peoples, and hard alabaster has been used for construction.
COMMON MEANING: in keeping with the paradoxical nature of Waboose, alabaster can mean you are either at a time of great malleability or of great rigidity. Note the texture and use of the stone for more clarity.
TRICKSTER MEANING: "all, a bastard," or "a bastard."
TRANSCENDENT MEANING: help with discovering the softness that is the key to your true strength. Help to guard against becoming too inflexible.

Algae
KEY WORDS: VARIETY; WATER-LOVING; NUTRITIOUS; POTENT; CLEANSING; FROG CLAN.
DESCRIPTION: Algae, the plants associated with the Water or Frog Clan position in the Center Circle of the Medicine Wheel, is found throughout all of the earth's waters. Algae is a group of plants, one-celled to many-celled, that contain chlorophyll but have no true root, stem, or leaf. Earth peoples around the world used algae as both foodstuff and condiment. Algae is known to be nutritious and high in vitamins and minerals. It is purported to give energy, help disinfect the body, and protect and help rid the body of toxic after-effects from radiation.
COMMON MEANING: floating in the deep waters of the life energy; willing to work with your deep emotions that can lead to true spirituality. Such a dream can have spiritual, sensual, or teaching connotations.
TRICKSTER MEANING: Al (name); "Al, gee" or "gee, Al"; "gee!" in surprise or consternation.
TRANSCENDENT MEANING: help with flowing through whatever dream experience you are having; sustenance in the dream, or a dream that can sustain you.

• • •

Alligator

KEY WORDS: ANCIENT; POWERFUL; AGGRESSIVE; SURVIVOR; BASIC; PRIMITIVE.

DESCRIPTION: The alligator, like the sturgeon, is an animal that has existed in its present form for untold numbers of years. Alligators, who have few enemies (man being one of them), will eat any flesh—living or dead—they can swallow. With their sharp teeth they can tear most things into pieces small enough to eat. Alligators can exceed fifteen feet in length; such an alligator would be capable of eating a cow.

COMMON MEANING: your most basic survival needs and nature: where you live, how you work, what you work at, what you eat, the state of your health; the most primitive aspects of your emotional nature; where you have "tough skin."

TRICKSTER MEANING: Al (name); Al who cuts; what you cut or what cuts you; what is eating you; what you eat.

TRANSCENDENT MEANING: increasing vulnerability; hidden aggression and/or power; root desire for survival; ancient wisdom.

Amber

KEY WORDS: PREHISTORIC; STRENGTHENING; LONGEVITY; ENDURANCE; HEALING; SOLIDITY; STRENGTH.

DESCRIPTION: Amber, associated with strength, the third Spirit Path stone of the West, is a fossilized resin that comes from pine trees dating back to prehistoric times. Dragonflies or other insects are sometimes found completely preserved inside this stone, which can range from clear to yellow to brown. Amber is said to be one of the oldest stones used for ornamentation. In German, amber is called *bernstein,* which means "bear stone." There is a soft amber resin, nonfossilized, which has been used as a fragrance and is currently used in modern aromatherapy.

COMMON MEANING: the most primal part of life, and of your own being; the original source of a situation.

TRICKSTER MEANING: person's name.

TRANSCENDENT MEANING: a gift of endurance; ancient wisdom; healing.

American Ivy

KEY WORDS: PERSISTENCE; TENACITY; CLINGING.

DESCRIPTION: American ivy is one of the most familiar plants found throughout the country—in cities, suburbs, and forests. Ivy can ascend as much as a hundred feet in the air by supporting itself on trees, walls, or anything available. It has green or white flowers, which are not frequently visible. Ivy is purported to have had medicinal uses as a tonic, astringent, and expectorant.

COMMON MEANING: your own tenacity and persistence; where and how you cling, and to whom.

TRICKSTER MEANING: I.V., or intravenous feeding or medicating; unnatural nurturing; healing.

TRANSCENDENT MEANING: persistence or endurance in dream or dreaming process.

Amethyst

KEY WORDS: VALUE; ROYALTY; GOOD JUDGMENT; PROTECTION; ATTUNEMENT; BALANCE; HARVEST MOON.

DESCRIPTION: Amethyst, the mineral totem for people born during the Harvest Moon (August 23–September 22), is a crystalline form of quartz that ranges in color from lilac to purple and is found in areas all across the world. Amethyst has been a popular gemstone throughout time and is found in many historic pieces of jewelry. Amethyst was considered to symbolize good judgment, justice, and courage; to protect its wearer from black magic, lightning, hailstorms, and intoxication; to bring about spiritual attunement, balance between the energies of the physical and spiritual levels.

COMMON MEANING: a valuable and possibly ancient part of your being with good judgment and courage; a warning to protect yourself.

TRICKSTER MEANING: anarchist; am a this; am a twist.

TRANSCENDENT MEANING: a gift of ancient wisdom and/or protection.

Animals

KEY WORDS: BASIC NATURE; INSTINCTUAL NATURE; HELP; NURTURANCE; THIRD KINGDOM OF CREATION.

DESCRIPTION: Animals are considered to be the third order of creation, which is divided into four parts: those who swim, those who crawl, those who fly, and those who walk. Animal beings are more dependent than the plants because they need the help of the plants as well as the elementals for their lives to continue; they are more independent than man, who needs their help for life to continue.

COMMON MEANING: ancient knowledge; instinctive energy; your basic nature; help needed or given.

TRICKSTER MEANING: an animal, a lower order of creation; a boorish, insensitive human.

TRANSCENDENT MEANING: a gift of help, knowledge, food, song, qualities.

SEE ALSO: individual animal listings for more specific information.

Ant

KEY WORDS: STRONG; ENDURING; PERSISTENT; DEPENDABLE; BUILDER; AGGRES-

SIVE; COMMUNITY-MINDED; CONFORMING; STRENGTH.

DESCRIPTION: The ant, the animal associated with strength, the third Spirit Path position of the West, although small, has the capacity to carry four times its weight. Ant colonies with their limited and defined social structure provide survival for the species, but little if any respect for the individuals.

COMMON MEANING: ways to use your strength for the benefit of all your relations; conformity; endurance.

TRICKSTER MEANING: aunt.

TRANSCENDENT MEANING: understanding of the collective consciousness that allows for survival of the whole as it relates to individual strength; ability to bring your knowledge of the dreamtime into everyday life.

Antelope

KEY WORDS: GRACE; SPEED; BEAUTY; CHANGE; PROTECTION.

DESCRIPTION: The antelope, also called the pronghorn or the goat deer, is a horned member of the deer family. There were an estimated 30 to 40 million in North America before Europeans came and began hunting them. Through conservation, the antelope population has come from near extinction to numbering close to half a million. Most of the remaining herds are found in the far west. Antelopes are among the quickest animals in the world, able to run at speeds close to seventy miles an hour.

COMMON MEANING: grace; speed; change.

TRICKSTER MEANING: aunt; elope.

TRANSCENDENT MEANING: help to move quickly either in the direction of something or away from something; impetus and protector.

Armadillo

KEY WORDS: ARMOR ABOVE; VULNERABILITY BELOW; PROTECTION.

DESCRIPTION: The armadillo, a mammal with heavy bony plates armoring its upper body, has a soft underbelly, like the porcupine. It likes to burrow, preferably close to creek banks, run swiftly, and swim for short distances.

COMMON MEANING: your armor; that which you put between your essence and the world.

TRICKSTER MEANING: arm a dill, oh!; arm a dildo; arm a dodo (idiot).

TRANSCENDENT MEANING: help in seeing the mask you present to the world; recognition of your true nature.

Arnica

KEY WORDS: PAIN RELIEVING; HEALING; GOOD IN EMERGENCY; SKIN AID.

DESCRIPTION: Arnica, a variety of thistle that grows in the northern mountain states of the United States and in Canada, is a perennial with yellow flowers. The plant has been used both internally and externally. Internally, it is purported to help with shock and pain, although too large a dose can be poisonous; externally, as a salve, it is said to help sprains, wounds, bruises, and skin conditions.

COMMON MEANING : a view of your old pains, bruises, and wounds; aid to the skin, either literal or figurative.

TRICKSTER MEANING : are; Nick (name); a?.

TRANSCENDENT MEANING : a gift of healing; emergency help.

Arrow

KEY WORDS : TOOLS; TALENTS; GIFTS; THOUGHTS; HELPERS.

DESCRIPTION : The arrow, one of the four additional symbols associated with the Medicine Wheel when used as a stone or card set, appears in the eastern quadrant and symbolizes the tools that you have for thinking and doing. The arrow represents the power of thought, communication. The arrow also represents the tool that enabled the hunter to have success.

COMMON MEANING : your talents; your gifts; your ability to seek and find what you need; your work; your living; goals.

TRICKSTER MEANING : a row; an argument.

TRANSCENDENT MEANING : a direct message pointing you to the path that you should take, or the tool you need.

Autumn

KEY WORDS : HARVEST; SERVICE; HEALING; TEACHING.

DESCRIPTION : Autumn, the time of harvest, is when all of earth's children reap the benefit of the intense internal and external growth they have undergone in the time preceding. This is the time of maturity, service.

COMMON MEANING : harvesting; reaching a goal; achieving maturity.

TRICKSTER MEANING : awe or wonder; "tum," a slang word for stomach or name for a stomach medication.

TRANSCENDENT MEANING : an indication of the gifts you will have as you reach your maturity, or of the ultimate goal of a project.

SEE ALSO : *West* and *Mudjekeewis.*

Azurite

KEY WORDS : HEALING; PSYCHIC; RECEPTIVITY; REBIRTH; BUTTERFLY CLAN.

DESCRIPTION : Azurite, the mineral totem for the Butterfly Clan (Air Clan) position in the center circle of the Medicine Wheel, is a copper carbonate that is usually blue but can range to black. Azurite has been used to strengthen intuitive abilities.

COMMON MEANING : working with your intuition; inspiration; creativity.

TRICKSTER MEANING: as you write; as you right.
TRANSCENDENT MEANING: a time of intense psychic opening and inspiration.

Baby, see *Infancy*

Badger

KEY WORDS: ATTACK; VICIOUS; ANGER; COMPACT; STOCKY; AGGRESSIVE; PROTECTOR OF THE ROOTS.

DESCRIPTION: The badger, a small, compact animal, has the ability to attack powerfully, aggressively, and viciously. Consequently, larger animals avoid badger as judiciously as they avoid skunk. Both exude a musk that is quite offensive. Badgers don't see well but have a highly developed sense of smell. Generally, they do not attack people except in self-defense.

COMMON MEANING: the aggressive, protective aspects of your being; the vicious part of your nature; anger; rage.

TRICKSTER MEANING: to "badger" is to annoy in the extreme.

TRANSCENDENT MEANING: a strong protector and ally, or an opponent capable of viciousness.

Barracuda

KEY WORDS: FEROCIOUS; LARGE; PREDATOR OF THE WATERS.

DESCRIPTION: Barracuda is a large fish found in the Mediterranean and West Indian seas. It is similar to a pike, large and elongated, attaining lengths of ten feet. It is a ferocious predator.

COMMON MEANING: the fierce or predatory aspect of your emotional nature; demanding feelings; feelings demanding to be expressed.

TRICKSTER MEANING: slang for a tricky, ferocious, aggressive person; often used in referring to a lawyer.

TRANSCENDENT MEANING: fierce determination for emotional understanding; aggressive emotional practices, detrimental to spiritual growth.

Basket

KEY WORDS: HARVEST; USEFUL; TOOL; FEMININE; BOUNTY.

DESCRIPTION: Baskets, originally made as tools to hold food or water, have come to represent the bounty of the harvest. Since baskets were most often woven and used by women they also represent the feminine.

COMMON MEANING: harvest from a project; feminine aspect of a person or project.

TRICKSTER MEANING: "make a basket," as in sports, meaning to achieve a goal; winning. "Basket case," someone who is extremely vulnerable or someone verging on insanity.

TRANSCENDENT MEANING: a gift given; a goal achieved; understanding of your feminine being.

Bat
KEY WORDS: ADAPTABLE; OMNIVOROUS; QUICK; SHADOW; NIGHT.
DESCRIPTION: The bat, a warm-blooded mammal, resembles a mouse with large wings. It hangs from its long, narrow tail to sleep, and generally flies at night. Bats are the most numerous mammal excepting rodents, and the only mammal that truly flies. Bats play an important part in human imagination, eliciting fear in some, wonder in others.
COMMON MEANING: messenger; guide; shadow side of self; fear; wonder.
TRICKSTER MEANING: bat, to hit; baseball bat; crazy.
TRANSCENDENT MEANING: a messenger of magic, either good or bad; shape-changer; gift of wonder, understanding of fears.

Beans
KEY WORDS: NURTURING; FOOD; SEED.
DESCRIPTION: Beans are the seeds of a variety of plants. They have long been used by animals and humans as an important source of nourishment.
COMMON MEANING: what you eat; what eats you; nourishment; nurturing; seed; new beginning.
TRICKSTER MEANING: bean as used in "bean pole," someone small and thin; someone who eats beans; slang for Hispanic people.
TRANSCENDENT MEANING: a gift of a seed, of a new idea, of a new way to nourish yourself.
SEE ALSO: *Corn* and *Squash*

Bear
WOLF CLAN TEACHING: the West; strength; love (especially black bear).
SEE ALSO: *Brown Bear* or *Grizzly Bear*.

Bearberry
KEY WORDS: EVERGREEN; PRAYER; EARTH CONNECTION; FEMININE.
DESCRIPTION: Bearberry, an evergreen shrub that grows low to the ground, has white flowers that become red berries, and leathery-looking leaves. It is called upland cranberry or uva-ursi, and was one of the major smoking herbs used in the pipe ceremony by Native people in areas where it grew. It is purported to treat various forms of blood sugar disorders and is a potent diuretic. The berries have nutritional value but very little taste and a mealy texture.
COMMON MEANING: being close to the earth; providing an avenue for

prayers; getting rid of excess water or emotions.

TRICKSTER MEANING: bare berry; berries that look tasty but are gastronomically disappointing.

TRANSCENDENT MEANING: a revelation of the part of you willing to sacrifice in order to make potent prayers to the Creator.

Beaver

KEY WORDS: STABILITY; STUBBORNNESS; DAMMED-UP EMOTIONS; LEARNING TO COMMUNICATE; APPRECIATING HARD WORK; BUILDER; RESOURCEFULNESS; SUSTENANCE; FROGS RETURN MOON.

DESCRIPTION: The beaver, the animal totem for people born during the Frogs Return Moon (April 20–May 20), is the only animal outside of man that can drastically change its environment in order to provide for its own peace, security, and contentment. The beaver is the largest rodent in this country, and is a land mammal that spends a lot of time in water. Beavers were trapped for both their pelts and their musk gland, which secretes castoreum, regarded as a cure-all.

COMMON MEANING: bringing your life into more balance; reengineering your life; seeing the dams you've built; building necessary dams; learning about communications ability; learning about emotions; needing to express more feelings; needing to increase acceptance of life; struggling against rootedness and stubbornness.

TRICKSTER MEANING: a slang term for the female genitals; also a slang word for a woman.

TRANSCENDENT MEANING: a gift coming from hard work; a revelation about communication; seeing a truth about your emotional nature.

WOLF CLAN TEACHING: honor; clan animal for February.

Bee

KEY WORDS: COMPLEX; SOCIAL; HONEY-PRODUCING; STING; GENTLE; PROTECTIVE; SERVING.

DESCRIPTION: The bee, an insect that produces honey by ingesting pollen from flowers, has long been a source of wonder to humans. Bees, which help to pollinate flowers, have a complex social structure, with a queen, workers, and nurse bees. Most bees are not aggressive, only stinging if they feel attacked. When a bee stings, it dies because part of its stomach comes off with the stinger.

COMMON MEANING: ways to serve the earth and her other children; protective aspects of being; healthful; useful; digesting aspect of being; nonaggression; willing to sacrifice for the good of the whole.

TRICKSTER MEANING: the letter b, or "to be."

TRANSCENDENT MEANING: a messenger who will bring your attention to an aspect of the dream that would otherwise be unnoticed; help with understanding your true feelings about community; revelation about a part of you that died in self-protection.

Beetle

KEY WORDS: HARD-SHELLED; COMMON; HUNGRY.

DESCRIPTION: Beetles scientifically belong to the order *Coleoptera,* a family that has more than three thousand species having in common biting mouth parts and sheathlike front wings that appear to be hard. Many beetles eat crops that humans also enjoy and so are often considered pests.

COMMON MEANING: a hard-shelled or tough part of you that you consider to be both common and annoying; persistence; neediness.

TRICKSTER MEANING: a wooden club; putting on a glossy finish; a stupid person; jutting or overhanging.

TRANSCENDENT MEANING: knowledge of your defenses and your protection.

Bigfoot

KEY WORDS: INTERDIMENSIONAL; EXTRATERRESTRIAL; BIGGER THAN LIFE; PROTECTOR OF EARTH.

DESCRIPTION: Bigfoot, an interdimensional being, is known to Native peoples in various parts of the world, particularly those who dwell in mountain areas. Bigfoot—called Sasquatch in the United States and the Abominable Snowman, or Yeti, in Tibet—is a huge creature who is purported to appear and disappear at will. Some Earth people believe Bigfoot lives in underground caves; others believe Bigfoot is connected with extraterrestrials; still others believe Bigfoot is a spirit that can sometimes manifest in form.

COMMON MEANING: parts of your nature that seem to appear and disappear at will; parts of your being you might consider alien; parts of you that are larger than life; parts of you that feel as though they come from another world.

TRICKSTER MEANING: literally big feet, or big foot.

TRANSCENDENT MEANING: often a literal messenger from other realms; a gift of wisdom that is either ancient or from a different realm of creation.

Bighorn sheep

KEY WORDS: HEIGHTS; SOCIAL; MAJESTIC; STRONG; SURE-FOOTED; MATRIARCHAL; PERSISTENT.

DESCRIPTION: Bighorn sheep, mainly found in the Rocky Mountains, are very muscular and active. The rams have large brown curving horns. Bighorns live in herds led by an old ewe.

COMMON MEANING : a part of you that seeks the heights, is social, or community-oriented; feminine-focused; matriarchal.

TRICKSTER MEANING : big horn; very horny; sheeplike or thoughtlessly conforming.

TRANSCENDENT MEANING : a gift of knowledge from matriarchal times; understanding of relationships; a guide to the heights of your own being.

Birch

KEY WORDS : COMMUNICATION; CLEANSING; CONTAINING; BARK; CLEARING THE AIR; EARTH RENEWAL MOON.

DESCRIPTION : The birch tree, the plant totem for people born under the Earth Renewal Moon (December 22–January 19), was used by Earth people for communicating. The bark provided their actual writing scrolls. Birch is also purported to have a variety of medicinal values, particularly being helpful to the digestive tract. Salicylic acid, a predecessor to aspirin, can be extracted from its inner bark. Birch switches were used by Native people to thrash the skin; some people have used birch rods as an instrument of punishment.

COMMON MEANING : power of communication, either through speech or writing; understanding of digestive disturbances, whether figurative or literal; cleansing, either internally or in relationship with other people.

TRICKSTER MEANING : birch beer, a sweet and unique beverage; to thrash or hit.

TRANSCENDENT MEANING : understanding of ancient traditions; a gift of ancient wisdom.

Black

KEY WORDS : SHADOW; FEMININE; INTUITION; VOID; MATURITY; MYSTERY; LOOKING WITHIN; REBIRTH; LOSS; DESTRUCTION; WEST; MUDJEKEEWIS; LONG SNOWS MOON.

DESCRIPTION : Black, along with blue, is a color associated with the West and with Mudjekeewis, Spirit Keeper of the West; also with the Long Snows Moon (Elk). Black, which is really the presence of all colors, is often looked upon in this society as being the void. It is the color of the night, the color of the darkness, the color that you go into when you step into the shadow part of your nature. In older times, black was considered to be a very feminine color, to be the color of the void from which all things can come, rather than the void into which all things are inexorably pulled.

COMMON MEANING : a deep intuitive part of your being; apparent nothingness containing all things; the void; the night; your relationship with darkness within and without; your shadow, an unknown or unrecognized aspect of being.

TRICKSTER MEANING : a person of African descent.

TRANSCENDENT MEANING: the void from which all things come, which allows entry into all realms of creation; a gift of feminine power.

Black Bear
WOLF CLAN TEACHING: the West; strength; love.
SEE ALSO: *Brown Bear.*

Blackbirds
KEY WORDS: THE SHADOW; THE FEMININE; THE VOID; MAGIC.
DESCRIPTION: Blackbirds are a group of birds that have sharp, pointed bills and flat profiles. Most look both black and iridescent. Some have other colors on the wings or head, most commonly red or yellow. These birds are frequently seen near the water.
COMMON MEANING: shadow part of your nature; examination of your feminine being.
TRICKSTER MEANING: black, as in of African descent; bird, giving someone a gesture of contempt; bird, slang for female.
TRANSCENDENT MEANING: entering the void; receiving a gift of magic that can be used for good or bad.

Black Spruce
KEY WORDS: TALL; STRONG; AROMATIC; ANTISEPTIC; CLEANSING; NURTURING; LONG SNOWS MOON.
DESCRIPTION: Black spruce, the plant totem for the Long Snows Moon (November 22–December 21), grows in many regions of the United States to heights of more than forty feet. The wood is soft, strong, and free from knots; the tips of the tree contain vitamin C; the gum was used medicinally as an antiseptic, purported to loosen mucus, to clean cuts and wounds.
COMMON MEANING: a deeply rooted part of your nature; your connection with the earth; your desire to reach skyward; relationship with the forest, either literal or figurative.
TRICKSTER MEANING: a black person; spruce, to fix up, beautify.
TRANSCENDENT MEANING: understanding of the forest; a gift from the forest.

Black Widow Spider
KEY WORDS: DEVOURING; FEMININE POWER; THE SHADOW.
DESCRIPTION: The black widow, a poisonous spider, particularly the female, is a black spider with a red hourglasslike shape on its stomach. After mating, the female of the species devours her mate.
COMMON MEANING: fear of feminine; a devouring aspect of your nature; an unexamined part of you.

TRICKSTER MEANING: black, someone with black skin; widow, we dough; spider, spied her.

TRANSCENDENT MEANING: a gift of the shadow feminine; a revelation of either what you would like to devour or what is devouring you.

Blanket

KEY WORDS: ORNAMENTATION; PROTECTION; WARMTH; PRACTICALITY; GIFT.

DESCRIPTION: Blankets, woven for household ornamentation, for clothing, and for warmth, were also often used for ceremonies. There were special blankets for special ceremonies. Blankets were also a frequent medicine gift given to a shaman either as an honoring gift when requesting a healing or as a gift of thanksgiving when a healing had been completed.

COMMON MEANING: that which covers you, protects you, warms you; also an area where you can consider ridding yourself of some protection keeping you from direct contact with the world.

TRICKSTER MEANING: to cover; blank it.

TRANSCENDENT MEANING: a gift that you are being given; a gift that you should give to a teacher or someone who has given you important lessons.

Blue

KEY WORDS: SPIRITUALITY; SATISFACTION; RELAXATION; TRANSCENDENCE; ATTUNEMENT; FATHER SUN; WEST; FROGS RETURN MOON; ILLUMINATION; INTROSPECTION.

DESCRIPTION: Blue is the color associated with quite a number of positions on the Medicine Wheel. Father Sun is associated with sky blue; the West is associated with blue and black; the Frogs Return Moon, the Beaver people, are associated with true blue; the quality of illumination is associated with fluorescent blue; the quality of introspection is associated with royal blue.

Like green, blue is one of the most predominant colors shown in pictures of the earth that are taken from space. Blue is the color of the waters of the earth, and also of the sky that we see above the earth on clear days. Blue is the color that reminds us to look skyward. Some people feel that blue is the color of the most fundamental energy that exists upon the planet. Other people feel that the color blue is the color most closely associated with real spirituality, with your true connection to the Creator.

COMMON MEANING: spirituality; connection with the sky; connection with waters; true purpose; deep emotions.

TRICKSTER MEANING: depressed; "blue."

TRANSCENDENT MEANING: understanding of what is most sacred to you; the deepest part of your own spirituality.

• • •

Blue Camas

KEY WORDS : STAPLE FOOD; SWEET; BALANCE; DANGER.

DESCRIPTION : Blue camas, the plant totem for those born during the Frogs Return Moon (April 20–May 20), is a wild member of the lily family, similar to wild hyacinth. Blue camas was a staple food for Earth people in the West. It is important to distinguish between blue camas and the death camas, which has yellow or greenish-white flowers. Blue camas was often used to sweeten other foods and to provide spice to an otherwise monotonous diet. The bulb of blue camas appears starchy, although it does not contain starch. It contains inulin, a complex sugar that helps to balance the blood sugar level. Too much blue camas can act as a purgative and emetic. It is important to note the color of the flowers in dreams about camas. Dreaming of death camas can mean that you have something of danger in your environment or your life.

COMMON MEANING : discovering your ability to sustain yourself and others; sweetening your disposition or attitude; bringing about a balance within yourself.

TRICKSTER MEANING : "blue, came us." Death camas (white or yellow flowers) indicates a possible danger in your environment or your life.

TRANSCENDENT MEANING : a gift of balance.

Blue Jay

KEY WORDS : NOISY; LOUD; CHANGEABLE; MIMIC.

DESCRIPTION : The blue jay, a crested blue bird that is larger than a robin, has white spots in the wings and tail, is gray underneath, and appears to be wearing a black necklace of feathers. Blue jays can mimic the call of red-tailed hawks and utter many other notes. They are very noticeable for the loudness of their cries and their apparent delight in making them frequently. The blue jay begins life as a black bird, and turns blue as he grows older.

COMMON MEANING : change; changeability; loud; noisy; annoying parts of your nature.

TRICKSTER MEANING : blew; Jay (man's name).

TRANSCENDENT MEANING : understanding of your ability to communicate, or of an annoying part of your being.

Bobcat

KEY WORDS : DECEPTIVELY APPEALING; WILD; DANGEROUS.

DESCRIPTION : The bobcat, tawny with black spotting and a short tail, is the most common wildcat in America. The bobcat is an expert climber who makes a variety of calls and has the capacity to sound like a domestic cat.

COMMON MEANING: a part of your nature that appears cute and appealing but is in fact wild and potentially dangerous.
TRICKSTER MEANING: Bob (name) cat.
TRANSCENDENT MEANING: a deep understanding of the parts of your nature not conforming to the culture around you.
SEE ALSO: *Lynx*.

Bobwhite

KEY WORDS: SELF-IDENTITY; SPIRIT NAME.
DESCRIPTION: Bobwhite is a small bird with ruddy feathers and a short, dark tail; males have a white throat. The bobwhite's voice is a whistle that sounds like *bobwhite* or *poor bobwhite*. Consequently, it is a bird who has named himself.
COMMON MEANING: calling your own name; naming yourself; self-identity.
TRICKSTER MEANING: Bob (name); white, color associated with people of northern European descent; white, Bob; poor Bob; poor white.
TRANSCENDENT MEANING: a deep understanding of your identity; a gift of a new spirit name.

Bonfire:

KEY WORDS: ELEMENTALS OF FIRE; MAGIC; TRANSFORMATION; RADIANCE; HEAT; LIGHT; CLEANSING; PURIFICATION.
DESCRIPTION: A bonfire is usually a large fire purposely lit to provide warmth and heat. In several Earth religions, bonfires also play an important role in ceremony and in magic.
COMMON MEANING: transformation; release; radiance.
TRICKSTER MEANING: bond; fired.
TRANSCENDENT MEANING: a ceremony; magic; an initiation; the elemental power of fire.
SEE ALSO: *Fire* and *Thunderbird Clan*.

Borage

KEY WORDS: HEART; HEALING; INTERNAL AND EXTERNAL; FLAVORING; STABILIZES; TRUST.
DESCRIPTION: Borage, the plant associated with trust and the first Spirit Path stone of the South, has been used medicinally and as a culinary herb. The flower of borage can resemble a purple starburst. Borage reportedly tastes like cucumber. It was purported to increase milk in nursing mothers and to bring balance to a person's moods.
COMMON MEANING: trust in the healing process; trust in the power of growth; nurturing.

TRICKSTER MEANING: Bo (name); B.O., an abbreviation for body odor; rage; Bo's rage.
TRANSCENDENT MEANING: a gift of balance or of nurturing.

Brown

KEY WORDS: PERMANENT; STRUCTURED; CONNECTED; GROWTH; DEPENDABLE; GROUNDED; EARTH AWARENESS; ENVIRONMENTAL CONSCIOUSNESS; TURTLE CLAN; DUCKS FLY MOON.

DESCRIPTION: Brown is the color associated with the Earth Clan or Turtle Clan position in the Center Circle of the Medicine Wheel, and also with the Ducks Fly Moon (Raven).

Brown is the color of the earth, home to both our domesticated and wild plants. Brown is the color of connection, growth, stability. It is a color that encourages spirit to enter structure and form, a color that raises environmental consciousness and awareness of the earth.

COMMON MEANING: connection with the earth; earth energy; structure; stability.

TRICKSTER MEANING: Brown is the color used to refer to the race of people of Mediterranean, Hispanic, East Asiatic, or Middle Eastern descent.

TRANSCENDENT MEANING: a gift from the Earth.

Brown Bear

KEY WORDS: COMMUNICATIVE; OMNIVOROUS; CURIOUS; DELIBERATE; ADAPTABLE; CLEVER; STRONG; DEFENDING; DISCRIMINATING; HARVEST MOON.

DESCRIPTION: The brown bear, the animal totem for people born during the Harvest Moon (August 23–September 22), is identical to the black bear. They are careful, quiet creatures with a good vocabulary of sounds, a healthy appetite, a lot of curiosity. Their only enemies are humans and forest fires. They are curious, slow, cheerful, good-natured, and deliberate. They incompletely hibernate throughout the winter. In the latter part of hibernation, females have their cubs, and nurse them while still hibernating. Bears can do many things humans do, like stand on two legs and walk, climb a tree, remove honey from beehives, and spear fish.

The bear was very special to Earth peoples. In many legends of the animal world, the bear was the head of the council of the animals because of his fairness, strength, and courage. The bear was attributed with having healing abilities, leadership abilities, and the ability to defend.

COMMON MEANING: leadership and healing ability; power to defend; defensiveness; discrimination; balance.

TRICKSTER MEANING: brown has a racial connotation; black has a racial connotation; bare or naked; overbearing or forebearing.

TRANSCENDENT MEANING: a time of power; a revelation of your true capacity.
WOLF CLAN TEACHING: learning; clan animal for January.
SEE ALSO: *Bear* and *Grizzly Bear*

Buffalo

KEY WORDS: ALMOST EXTINCT; DOMESTIC; LARGE; POWERFUL; INSPIRATIONAL; REMINDER OF MAN'S EXCESS; LONG LIFE; POWER; ABUNDANCE; MEDICINE.
DESCRIPTION: The buffalo, once 50 million strong, were almost hunted to extinction by Europeans. Native people had used the buffalo in a very sparing and respectful way, to provide them with meat, clothing, homes, and tools. Many Europeans killed the buffalo for sport and left the carcasses to rot. Most buffalo today are domestic.
COMMON MEANING: powerful, primal wild aspect of being; roaming free; contact with the earth.
TRICKSTER MEANING: buff, either to shine or to be naked.
TRANSCENDENT MEANING: understanding of the giveaway, and ways in which you can serve the earth.
WOLF CLAN TEACHING: the North, or wisdom.
MEDICINE EAGLE'S TEACHING: giveaway; nurturing.
SEE ALSO: *White Buffalo, North,* and *Waboose.*

Butterfly

KEY WORDS: TRANSFORMING; MOTION; NEWNESS; ACTIVE; MANIPULATIVE; SERVING; GRACEFUL; EMERGING; HEALERS; INTELLIGENT; CREATIVE; EXOTIC; VISIONARY; BRIDGING; AIR; AIR CLAN; MENTAL.
DESCRIPTION: The Butterfly Clan is the clan associated with the element of air. In the Medicine Wheel, people of the Rest and Cleansing Moon (Otter), the Cornplanting Moon (Deer), and the Ducks Fly Moon (Raven) are all members of the Butterfly Clan. Air can bring changes, either gradually or rapidly. People associated with this element have the power of transformation. They tend to be people who are always in motion, with a lot of life energy coming through them. They are active, not afraid to change. They enjoy finding ways to serve their people. They are intelligent, creative, and quick to see the weak points of any plan. This is the clan associated with the mental aspects of your being.
Butterflies are masters of transformation. They all begin life as caterpillars, feed on plants until they can form a cocoon, and then, after a period of apparent dormancy, transform into the butterfly, which feeds on flowers, helping to pollinate them and thus bringing the gift of beauty to the rest of creation. Butterflies are often one of the first creatures to leave a damaged or dying ecosystem. There are some parts of Europe in which

the only butterflies you see are those in special butterfly houses, which are really zoos for these winged ones.

COMMON MEANING: transformation; rapid change; communication.

TRICKSTER MEANING: butter; fly, an insect; fly, a zipper in pants; flies.

TRANSCENDENT MEANING: a gift of transformation or understanding of change.

Butterfly Weed

KEY WORDS: GRACEFUL; POWERFUL; DEEPLY HEALING; CATALYTIC; TRANSFORMING; AIR OR BUTTERFLY CLAN.

DESCRIPTION: Butterfly weed, the plant associated with the Air or Butterfly Clan position in the Center Circle of the Medicine Wheel, is known botanically as *Asclepias tuberosa*. Butterfly weed resembles the dandelion with a large seed pod. It is also known as milkweed or pleurisy weed. Healers believed the plant could help bring milk to nursing mothers, and could help cleanse the lungs. Too-large doses can cause problems with the digestion.

COMMON MEANING: rapid change; healing; releasing blockages; indication of caution in reaching beyond your grasp.

TRICKSTER MEANING: we'd; we'd better fly; see *Butterfly*.

TRANSCENDENT MEANING: the ability to breathe fully; deep release of blocked energy.

Cactus

KEY WORDS: PRICKLY; ARID; FEAR OF VULNERABILITY; EMOTIONLESS; DESERT; TENACIOUS.

DESCRIPTION: Cactus, a variety of desert-dwelling plants that need very little water to survive, generally have moderately to very prickly thorns. Some bear fruit that is edible or medicinal. They provide a source of water in the desert if you know how to tap them.

COMMON MEANING: hidden emotions; protection for vulnerability; fear of hurt; thorny part of your nature; emotional repression; connection with waters of the earth.

TRICKSTER MEANING: "see to us."

TRANSCENDENT MEANING: hidden reservoirs of powerful life energy buried within you.

Calcite

KEY WORDS: COMMON; VARIED; FLUORESCENT; TRANSLUCENT; CRYSTALLINE; HEALING; EMPOWERING; STRENGTHENING; OPENING; HAPPINESS; ILLUMINATION.

DESCRIPTION: Calcite, the mineral totem associated with illumination and the third Spirit Path stone of the East, is a crystalline calcium carbonate and a major component of the shells of sea beings. These shells over time make limestone and then marble. Calcite, one of the most common minerals in existence, is found throughout the world. It is fluorescent or translucent white, or colorless. Other mineral mixes can give it many color variations. When found in crystalline form, calcite has been purported to aid with healing and with magnifying energy.

COMMON MEANING: common truths; simplicity; the light within; potential healing.

TRICKSTER MEANING: Cal's (name) sight.

TRANSCENDENT MEANING: light that can cut through the darkness of ignorance; true power.

Candle

KEY WORDS: SLOW-BURNING; FIRE WITHIN; CONTAINED; CAUTIOUS.

DESCRIPTION: Candles in various forms have been used by humans for untold years to bring light to the darkness. They are a contained form of the element of fire. They are usually made of oil or wax with a wick.

COMMON MEANING: contained fire; slow and steady; fire serving man; working with fire elemental; glimpse of the radiant parts of your being.

TRICKSTER MEANING: can, meaning a container for food; slang for buttocks; can, slang for fire or discharge or dispense; the ability and knowledge to do something; permission to do something; dell, a small valley, usually in the forest; dell, slang for girl.

TRANSCENDENT MEANING: a light within the void; a ceremony; ceremonial protection; note the color and way of using any candle in a transcendent dream.

SEE ALSO: *Fire*

Canoe

KEY WORDS: TRAVEL; WAY OF GOING THROUGH LIFE; BOAT; BALANCE; POTENTIAL TO MOVE THROUGH EMOTIONS OR SPIRIT.

DESCRIPTION: A canoe is a lightweight, narrow boat that is propelled by using paddles. Earth peoples usually made canoes out of tree trunks or bark; more recently, they have been made of light metal or fiberglass.

COMMON MEANING: a desire to get into your emotions, your sensuality, but still keep a protective barrier between you and your emotional life; a way of moving through spirit; balance.

TRICKSTER MEANING: can, ooh; can do.

TRANSCENDENT MEANING: a pleasurable dream of enjoying sensuality, your vision, your path, your way of moving through life. To dream of steering the canoe with your own body is a dream of enjoyment of your own being and emotions.

Cardinal

KEY WORDS : RED; SWEET SONG; WEALTH; HEART; BLOOD; VITALITY; PROMINENCE.

DESCRIPTION : The cardinal, a scarlet songbird found in many parts of the world, has a beautiful song, and is an important bird for many Native people. The male wears the bright plumage, while the female has some scarlet feathers scattered among gray ones. The feathers of this bird were highly prized.

COMMON MEANING : communication; song; attitudes toward wealth; heart connection; blood; vitality.

TRICKSTER MEANING : cardinal as in a high-ranking member of the Roman Catholic clergy; also meaning the first, the most important.

TRANSCENDENT MEANING : a gift of vitality; an indication of something being very important to you.

Cardinal Directions—North

KEY WORDS : RENEWAL; PURITY; DORMANCY; PARADOXICAL POWER; NEW LIFE; DEATH; REST; COLD; INTERNAL GROWTH; WHITE BUFFALO; THE MYSTICAL REALMS; HEALERS; PSYCHIC POWERS; NEED GROUNDING; REJUVENATING; WABOOSE, SPIRIT KEEPER OF THE NORTH.

DESCRIPTION : The North represents the winter, the time both of old age and youth, the time of midnight, the time of death and of rebirth, the time when you have become an elder, a person of wisdom. This is the time when your physical prowess might not be as great as during youth, but your spiritual capabilities are greater than they may have ever been before.

The North has the power of renewal and purity. The power of the North is paradoxical; it is new life cloaked in death, rapid growth cloaked in rest. The white buffalo is associated with the North. The buffalo gave of itself so the people could live. White Buffalo Woman was said to bring the sacred pipe to the people. The major lesson of the North is the giveaway.

COMMON MEANING : physical health; relationship to the world; job; housing.

TRICKSTER MEANING : the paradox of winter.

TRANSCENDENT MEANING : understanding of the giveaway.

FOSTERS' TEACHING : adulthood; winter; incorporation.

SEE ALSO : *White Buffalo, Winter* and *Waboose, Spirit Keeper of the North*

—East

KEY WORDS : EAGLE; WISDOM; SPRING; NEW LIFE; DAWN; YOUTH; BIRTH; STRAIGHTFORWARD; ENLIGHTENMENT; AWAKENING; ILLUMINATION; WISDOM; CLARITY; MESSENGER; VITAL ENERGY; WABUN, SPIRIT KEEPER OF THE EAST.

DESCRIPTION : The East is the time of spring; the time of dawn; the time of youth; the time of new, high, fresh, and intense energy. This is the season in which the Earth seems to come alive from all directions. It is the time of day when the darkness dissipates and we see fresh beginnings, and the mystery of life continuing itself.

The power of the East is straightforward. It can help you find the illumination possible for all the earth's children. The animal associated with the East is the eagle. The colors are the red and gold of the rising sun.

COMMON MEANING: better communication; new beginnings; fresh philosophies; intense energy; messages from and about the different realms of creation; awakening; knowledge of childhood; dawn; mental life; thinking.

TRICKSTER MEANING: the Orient.

TRANSCENDENT MEANING: a revelation about what is most true for you.

FOSTERS' TEACHING: illumined one; springtime.

SEE ALSO: *Wabun, Spirit Keeper of the East; Spring,* and *Eagle.*

—South

KEY WORDS: GROWTH; TRUST; LOVE; SUMMER; MIDDAY; ACTION; TESTING; SEARCHING; MATING; LOVING; SEXUALITY; RELATIONSHIPS; COYOTE; TRICKSTER; HEALING; FRIENDLY; GREGARIOUS; HEARTFELT; SHAWNODESE, SPIRIT KEEPER OF THE SOUTH.

DESCRIPTION: The South is the time of summer, of midday. In human life it is the time of our adolescence and young adulthood, the time of rapid growth when instinct overcomes thought, when you must rely on your intuition because change is coming too quickly to be figured out by logic. The animal associated with the South is the coyote, the trickster who helps us to grow even in times when we don't want to. The colors of the South are the green of growth and the yellow of natural wisdom.

COMMON MEANING: rapid growth; relationship; love; the heart; fruitfulness; heat; passion.

TRICKSTER MEANING: the Southern Hemisphere.

TRANSCENDENT MEANING: the gift of love; better relationships.

FOSTERS' TEACHING: childhood; summer; severance.

SEE ALSO: *Shawnodese, Spirit Keeper of the South; Coyote,* and *Summer.*

—West

KEY WORDS: EXPERIENCE; INTROSPECTION; STRENGTH; AUTUMN; TWILIGHT; MATURITY; LEADERSHIP; HEALING; TEACHING; RESPONSIBILITY; KNOWING YOURSELF; IDEALISM; SELFLESSNESS; SUNSET; MOON RISE; GRIZZLY BEAR; SELF-HEALING; BRINGERS OF UNITY; MUDJEKEEWIS, SPIRIT KEEPER OF THE WEST.

DESCRIPTION: The West is the time of autumn, the time of twilight, the time when humans have reached their maturity and are ready to take their place as teachers, healers, and leaders of the people. It is a time of power, when all living things have experienced enough of life to know their direction, what works for them and what doesn't. The time of the West is a time of responsibility, a time to care both for the children and the old ones. The animal associated with the West is the grizzly bear, the animal who knows his own heart. The colors of the West are blues, merging into the blacks of night. The West is considered to be the home of the West Wind, father of all the winds.

COMMON MEANINGS: power; direction; leadership; responsibilities; teaching.

TRICKSTER MEANING: Europe and the United States.

TRANSCENDENT MEANING: deep knowledge of the sacred and your relationship with the Creator.

FOSTERS' TEACHING: adolescence; autumn; initiatory dreams.

SEE ALSO: *Mudjekeewis, Spirit Keeper of the West; Autumn, and Grizzly Bear.*

Carnelian

KEY WORDS: BLOOD; EMERGENCY; HEALER; HEART; LOVE; STRONG SUN MOON.

DESCRIPTION: Carnelian, the mineral totem for those born during the Strong Sun Moon (June 21–July 22), is a clear chalcedony, that ranges from pink to red to yellow. Carnelian is associated with the blood; it is considered to be an emergency stone, useful in accidents and particularly in stopping the flow of blood. The carnelian is also associated with the heart, and with love.

COMMON MEANING: emotions; heart energy; communication of feelings; healing of the emotions; love.

TRICKSTER MEANING: car; knee; lie on; lion.

TRANSCENDENT MEANING: deep understanding of what love means to you; knowledge of how to express love.

Cascara Sagrada

KEY WORDS: LAXATIVE; UNBLOCKING; FREE-MOVING ENERGY; SACRED.

DESCRIPTION: Cascara sagrada, a flowering tree also known as "sacred bark," is found in the western part of the United States and in other locations in the world. The young bark from the tree, aged for at least a year, has been used by both Native and non-Native people as a very effective laxative. Cascara is an important ingredient in many of the herbal laxative preparations that are sold in natural food stores today. It has also been utilized by pharmaceutical companies.

COMMON MEANINGS: elimination; removing old blockages; understanding blockages; free-moving energy; sacredness; healing of old hurts.

TRICKSTER MEANING: Cass (name); Cara (name); cara, meaning in romance languages *face* and *dear.*

TRANSCENDENT MEANING: understanding of what you need to remove in order to make your life work well and your energy flow freely.

Catnip

KEY WORDS: PLAYFULNESS; SENSUALITY; CALM; DIGESTIVE EASE; FELINE INTOXICANT; MINT.

DESCRIPTION: Catnip, a perennial herb with a subtle mint smell and white blossoms, has been used to cure mild gastrointestinal distress in humans. It is an herb that has been used for babies and is one of the major herbal remedies for colic. Our feline friends find catnip to have a slightly narcotic effect, and sometimes an aphrodisiac effect.

COMMON MEANINGS: what is eating at you; what is causing you distress; cure for long-standing problems; help for chronic discomforts; the feline part of your nature; your feminine; a playful part of you; a sensual part of you.

TRICKSTER MEANING: a cat bite.

TRANSCENDENT MEANING: a playful solution to an old problem.

Cattails

KEY WORDS: REEDLIKE; NUTRITIONAL; NURTURING; STRENGTHENS; SUSTAINS; STIMULATES; BALANCES; PROVIDES GROUNDING; NURTURING; EARTH AND WATER; TURTLE CLAN.

DESCRIPTION: Cattails, the plants associated with the Earth or Turtle Clan position in the Center Circle of the Medicine Wheel, have been used by many Earth peoples for food as well as medicine. Cattail is said to strengthen a person, particularly the physical aspect. Cattails grow in wet areas throughout much of North America. It has swordlike leaves, long stalks, and seed heads that resemble miniature corncobs. It can grow as tall as nine feet. It has been called "wilderness supermarket" by many people. All parts can be eaten in the right season. The juice is purported to be a good antiseptic with anesthetic properties.

COMMON MEANING: the ways in which you can serve your relations on the earth; initial exploration of the waters of your own life; increasing your connection with earth's energy; a desire to nurture others.

TRICKSTER MEANING: the tail of a cat, or the tale of a cat.

TRANSCENDENT MEANING: the energy to go deeper into your dream; clear understanding of your earth connection.

Cave

KEY WORDS: WOMB; EARTH CONNECTION; PROTECTION.

DESCRIPTION: A cave is a naturally occurring opening in the Earth Mother. To many Earth people, a cave was considered to be a womb of the earth, and a very sacred place. In most ancient times, caves provided homes,

protection, and warmth for the people who dwelled in them.
COMMON MEANING: ancient beginnings; the void; emerging into the light; your deepest connection with Mother Earth.
TRICKSTER MEANING: the womb.
TRANSCENDENT MEANING: an opening leading to the underworld, or to other realms of creation.

Cedar

KEY WORDS: EVERGREEN; STRENGTH; NURTURING; SMUDGE; CLEANSER; PURIFICATION; PUNGENT; WISDOM; WEST.
DESCRIPTION: Cedar, the plant associated with the West, and with Mudjekeewis, the Spirit Keeper of the West, is an evergreen tree that grows throughout the world. Cedar plays an important role in the smudging ceremony; both the leaf and inner bark can be used for smudge, and the smoke produced is said to both cleanse and purify. In older times, Earth peoples used cedar in constructing homes, canoes, implements, clothing, and ceremonial items.
COMMON MEANING: the practical aspects of your spiritual nature; a realistic picture of your spiritual gifts; a purification.
TRICKSTER MEANING: see der ("see there"); or see Dar, as name or nickname.
TRANSCENDENT MEANING: a gift of ancient wisdom; strengthening within the dream state; help with an illness.

Chamomile

KEY WORDS: SWEET; PLEASANT; MILD; CALMING; RELAXING; COMFORTING; FEMININE; REFRESHING; INTROSPECTION.
DESCRIPTION: Chamomile, the plant associated with introspection, the second Spirit Path position of the West, provides humans with one of nature's sweetest, tastiest teas. It is also purported to have many medicinal aspects. Chamomile is said to calm, relax, comfort. It is known to be helpful with stomach problems. It has been used for childhood ailments, as well as for female problems. A salve made from chamomile keeps the skin healthy.
COMMON MEANING: looking inward; relaxing; evaluating; childhood.
TRICKSTER MEANING: came a mile; came a meal.
TRANSCENDENT MEANING: relaxation that allows you to experience deeper levels; releasing; understanding of childhood.

Chanting

KEY WORDS: COMMUNICATION; TRUE VOICE; OPENING; HEALING; SPEAKING TRUTH; REPETITION.

DESCRIPTION: Chanting is a form of singing that is often more repetitive and uses vocals as well as words. Chants are powerful ways to give the energy of your voice to the Earth Mother and her other children. Chants can also be powerful healing tools.

COMMON MEANING: opening your mouth; opening your voice; letting out your true sound; vocalizing your true message; receiving a message; receiving a healing. Listen carefully for words or vocals being expressed, as they may be important to the central part of your being.

TRICKSTER MEANING: enchanting.

TRANSCENDENT MEANING: a gift of sound that can bring healing, opening, or understanding. Again, listen carefully to chant being sung.

Chaparral

KEY WORDS: CURE; CLEANSER; BRUSH; DRY; TRANSITION ZONE.

DESCRIPTION: Chaparral, also known as dwarf evergreen oak, belongs to a group of *Artemesia* that grows in the transition zones around the deep deserts of the southwestern United States. It has a dark green stem and leaves, a very strong smell, and yellow flowers. In recent years, chaparral has become known as an old Indian remedy for cancer and many other maladies. It is thought to be a general internal cleanser for the body, and is mixed with many other herbs in preparations that can be obtained at natural food stores.

COMMON MEANING: transition; change; natural; wild; opening to long-suppressed emotions; deprived of water; volatile; cleansing.

TRICKSTER MEANING: chap is slang for man and a name for protective leggings; arral, or oral; an oral man.

TRANSCENDENT MEANING: going to the threshold place that helps you understand your true connection with the sacred; preparing for emotional release and healing.

Chicken

KEY WORDS: FOOD; FEATHERS; FLOCK; HOUSE; COOP.

DESCRIPTION: Chickens are a species of domesticated birds that lay eggs which are used for food; the flesh of chickens is also used for food. Chickens vary greatly in terms of size, coloration, and shape of feathers. They like to live in flocks. Roosters are quite verbal, and are known for waking people up in the morning.

COMMON MEANING: conformity; service; nurturing; waking up.

TRICKSTER MEANING: frightened; scared.

TRANSCENDENT MEANING: a deep understanding of what really frightens you; an understanding of the best ways in which you can serve others.

Chief

KEY WORDS: LEADERSHIP; POWER; MATURITY; SERVICE; LOVE OF HUMANITY; LOVE OF SELF; LEADERSHIP.

DESCRIPTION: The chief is one of the extra stones used in Earth stones or Earth cards; it appears in the western quadrant of the Medicine Wheel, the quadrant representing maturity, leadership, teaching, and healing. The chief is usually symbolized as being masculine, although leadership qualities can be found either within the masculine or feminine parts of your being.

COMMON MEANING: service; leadership; power hunger; powerful; maturity.

TRICKSTER MEANING: first or primary.

TRANSCENDENT MEANING: can represent the head of your personal dream council; a gift of leadership.

Childhood

KEY WORDS: CHILDLIKE; CHILDISH; EASY; BEGINNINGS; PLAYFUL; LEARNING.

DESCRIPTION: Childhood is a time of extremely rapid growth for the human species. It is when the brain reorganizes itself so it is capable of living in the culture with which it is surrounded. It is a time when we learn to talk, walk, think, and act in the ways normal to our society. Today, childhood can be a time when we lose a good bit of the knowledge that we are born with. In Earth cultures, people were encouraged to retain what they knew as children.

COMMON MEANING: a literal dream of your own childhood; a dream of your children; an opportunity for relearning; new ways of relating to the world; new beginnings.

TRICKSTER MEANING: hood is slang for a criminal; child hood, a criminal child.

TRANSCENDENT MEANING: understanding of your childhood, or childhood in general; a gift of new beginnings.

Chipmunk

KEY WORDS: CHATTERING; CHEERFUL; NATURAL; INADVERTENT PLANTER OF FORESTS; ZIPPY.

DESCRIPTION: Chipmunks are ground squirrels found in many parts of the world. These noisy small rodents seem always to have a strong opinion. Unlike the mouse, which often provokes the ire of man, the chipmunk seems to remind us of our relationship to nature and seems to bring out the playfulness in human nature. Because of their busy gathering and storing of seeds and nuts, they are often very helpful in bringing about new growth of forest areas.

COMMON MEANING: the mundane; your small-scale connection to nature; the chattering part of your mind; noisiness; annoyance; inadvertent help given or received.

TRICKSTER MEANING: chip is a small piece, or breaking off; monk, a person in a monastic order, or an abbreviated form of "monkey"; chip off the old monk, or chip off the old monkey; evolution; view of religion.

TRANSCENDENT MEANING: a view of the part of your mind that is difficult to silence; a message; help being offered or given without your knowledge.

Chrysocolla

KEY WORDS: SKY; EARTH; QUENCH; CONNECT; PURIFY; FROGS RETURN MOON.

DESCRIPTION: Chrysocolla, the mineral totem for those born during the Frogs Return Moon (April 20–May 20), is a hydrous copper silicate ranging in color from true green to greenish blue to true blue. Chrysocolla sticks to the tongue, while turquoise, which can look very similar, doesn't; this is often the way the two stones are distinguished. Chrysocolla can purify all levels of your being and help to bring balance between the elements of earth and sky, both within you and around you.

COMMON MEANING: balance; purification; beauty; adornment.

TRICKSTER MEANING: Chris (name); a cola.

TRANSCENDENT MEANING: a gift of connection; understanding of both elements of earth and sky.

Circle

KEY WORDS: WEB OF LIFE; SACRED; NATURAL SHAPE; FLOW; INTERCONNECTION; RELATIONSHIP; MEDICINE WHEEL, BASIC SHAPE.

DESCRIPTION: The circle is one of the natural shapes of life and a central symbol for most Earth people. It represents life without beginning or ending, life that continues. The circle encompasses everything in the universe, from the entirety of the universe itself to the smallest microbe found within. Earth peoples respected the circle as they respected life. When they came together to counsel they sat in a circle. In much of their construction they reminded themselves of the circle, and of the continuous flow of life. Today, physics is finding that much of the energy of life is circular or spiraling.

COMMON MEANING: coming back into the flow of life; accepting your place in the circle of life; increased harmony; understanding of all aspects of life and nature.

TRICKSTER MEANING: sir, kill.

TRANSCENDENT MEANING: a gift of greater harmony with all life; increased unity.

Clarity

KEY WORDS: TWO-EDGED; FREEDOM; PRISON; SIMPLIFY; CLEAR; DISCRIMINATING; AWARENESS; ONE QUALITY OF THE EASTERN SPIRIT PATH.

DESCRIPTION: Clarity is the Outer Stone in the Eastern Spirit Path of the Medicine Wheel. The mineral associated with clarity is mica; the plant, rosemary; animal, hummingbird; color, clear.

COMMON MEANING: looking at the totality; restricting yourself by your mental processes; simplifying your life; unblocking energy; spontaneity; direction or directness.

TRICKSTER MEANING: clear it.

TRANSCENDENT MEANING: a gift of vision or understanding.

Clay

KEY WORDS: FIRM; TOOLS; EARTH; HEALING; UNDERSTANDING; DRAWING; CLEANS-
ING; MALLEABILITY; EARTH MOTHER.

DESCRIPTION: Clay, the mineral that is connected with the Earth Mother
Stone in the Center Circle of the Medicine Wheel, is a firm, fine-grained
earth mainly composed of aluminum silicate. Clay can become hardened
when it is put in a fire and has been used to make bricks and pottery.
Some clays have also proven useful for healing. Some Earth peoples particularly valued red clay, while others particularly valued either green or
white clays that could be used for compresses that would both heal and
detoxify, and could also in some instances be taken internally.

COMMON MEANING: giving shape to your abilities or thoughts; drawing out
impurities; cleansing yourself; malleability.

TRICKSTER MEANING: a person's name.

TRANSCENDENT MEANING: a gift of direction, or of earth connection.

Cleansing

KEY WORDS: CLEAR OUT; DETACH; DISCHARGE; CATHARTIC; RID; SURRENDER; NORTH-
ERN SPIRIT PATH.

DESCRIPTION: Cleansing is the outer stone in the Northern Spirit Path of
the Medicine Wheel. Cleansing is a process of clearing out old ideas or
severing former ways of thinking. It also helps you to get rid of blocked
emotions as well as misunderstandings on the emotional levels. Cleansing is connected with surrender of old spiritual ideas. The mineral associated with cleansing is sodalite; plant, echinacea; animal, raccoon; color,
pale green.

COMMON MEANING: cleansing on the physical, mental, emotional, or spiritual level; new beginnings.

TRICKSTER MEANING: Clean and sing.

TRANSCENDENT MEANING: clearing out of old to prepare for new.

Clear

KEY WORDS: UNOBSTRUCTED; UNMISTED; INNOCENT; FREE; NOT CONFUSED; CER-
TAIN; CLARITY.

DESCRIPTION: Clear is the color associated with the clarity position, the
first stone of the Eastern Spirit Path of the Medicine Wheel. Something
that is clear is unblemished, undimmed, unobstructed, sparkling, lumi-
nescent.

COMMON MEANING: removing darkness; coming out of confusion or dull-
ness; letting go of guilt; having a sound that is distinct; removing yourself
somewhat from whatever you are seeing.

TRICKSTER MEANING: nonexistent, or freed from blame.
TRANSCENDENT MEANING: a gift of increasing understanding or sensory awareness.

Clown

KEY WORDS: HUMOR; LIGHTNESS; HAPPINESS; HEART; TRICKSTER; CONFUSER; SACRED; CEREMONY; MEDICINE WHEEL SOUTH.

DESCRIPTION: The clown is one of the extra positions used in Earth stones or Earth cards; the clown is placed in the southern quadrant and represents humor. Clowns were sacred beings to many Earth peoples. The clown teaches about humor and the important lesson of not taking yourself or life too seriously, even in sacred situations. For many tribal peoples, the clown was one of the most sacred of holy people who often played a very important part in the ceremonial life of a nation.

COMMON MEANING: humor; lack of humor; happiness; being tricked.

TRICKSTER MEANING: see and own.

TRANSCENDENT MEANING: a trickster; duality. Beware the clown in dreams; what the clown encourages you to do might be exactly the right thing, or exactly the wrong thing. Clown teaches you to trust your intuition.

Comfrey

KEY WORDS: DEEP-ROOTED; PROLIFIC; SPREADING; STRENGTH; HEALING; HEALS; REGENERATES; BINDS/KNITS BONES.

DESCRIPTION: Comfrey, the plant associated with the second Spirit Path position of the South, growth, is a prolific plant. Once you put the root in the ground, it will spread until it runs out of room. Comfrey is used as both food for the animal beings and as medicine for human beings. Internally or externally, it relieves pain. Comfrey is purported to be excellent as a compress that will help to reduce swelling and knit bones or muscles that have been sprained or wounded.

COMMON MEANING: rapid growth; fertility; being prolific; ease of service.

TRICKSTER MEANING: come free.

TRANSCENDENT MEANING: a healing of old wounds.

Copper

KEY WORDS: IMPLEMENT; ORNAMENTATION; TOOLS; PURIFICATION; CONDUCTS; SPREADS HEAT; MYSTICAL POWERS; FREEZE UP MOON.

DESCRIPTION: Copper, one of the mineral totems for the Freeze Up Moon (October 24–November 21), is found worldwide and has been used for tools and ornamentation. Copper is said to have special powers that can help purify the spirit and the blood. Copper conducts electricity and helps spread heat evenly. Copper is frequently used in combination with crystals, as it is said to have power to focus energies that are relatively unknown in modern times.

COMMON MEANING: finding new tools; transformation of physical looks or view of the world.

TRICKSTER MEANING: slang for policeman; also a name, and the name of a color; "cop" is slang for steal; her.

TRANSCENDENT MEANING: understanding of mystical powers, how you conduct yourself with them, and how they might change or change you.

Coral

KEY WORDS: SEA; LIVING; HOUSE; BLOCKAGE; RESIDUE; PROTECTION.

DESCRIPTION: Coral is formed by the hard skeletons of small marine animals; it is mainly composed of calcium carbonate, which hardens over time. Coral is most often red or white, although black coral is found in some parts of the world. Historically, coral was purported to protect one from diseases, including diseases of the mind.

COMMON MEANING: parts of your emotional body that may have atrophied; blockages; residues; knowledge about what may be keeping you from fulfilling your highest potential.

TRICKSTER MEANING: a name; corral or fence in.

TRANSCENDENT MEANING: a gift of protection; knowledge of how you are keeping yourself from your spiritual goals. Coral can be a protector stone in dreaming.

Corn

KEY WORDS: NURTURANCE; BALANCE; EARTH CONNECTION; HEALTH; SHARING; FEMININE BLESSING; HARVEST; THE ETERNAL MOTHER; GUARDIAN; ASSOCIATED WITH THE EARTH; EARTH MOTHER.

DESCRIPTION: Corn is one of the plants associated with the Earth Mother position in the Center Circle of the Medicine Wheel, along with beans and squash. Corn, or maize, is cereal that grows in kernels on ears and originated in the Americas. Corn provided a staple food for the people of the Americas; corn, beans, and squash were referred to as the "three sisters." There are quite a number of legends about how the three sisters came to the people. One tells of the death of First Woman, a sacred woman, in childbirth, and of her burial by her good son, who had been born a fully grown human. After a period of time, the son came back and from the mother's body had grown the three sister crops, and from her forehead sprang the sacred tobacco plant. So it is said that Spirit Woman, the First Woman, gave her body into the Earth Mother so that people could be fed throughout the millennia.

Another story tells how the three crops were always grown together to remind people that harmony is much more important in the world than disharmony. It is said that the three plants, by helping each other to grow, inspire humans to also help each other. Corn, beans, and squash complement each other as they're growing, and they also provide a balanced meal when eaten together. The three sister plants were also recognized as giving spiritual gifts. Corn particularly was used as a ceremonial offering, most frequently ground into meal. All three were used in medicine bags to bring a good earth connection to the person wearing them.

COMMON MEANING: what brings you nurturance; what you wish to nourish; a desire for harmony; a guide to find more harmony.

TRICKSTER MEANING: trite humor; an old suffix meaning horned, as in "unicorn"; an often painful thickening of the skin on a toe.

TRANSCENDENT MEANING: a revelation about your connection with the Earth Mother; a gift given or received.

Cougar

KEY WORDS: FIERCE; NOBLE OF SPIRIT; ELUSIVE; PROTECTIVE; BIG WINDS MOON.

DESCRIPTION: The cougar, the animal totem for those born during the Big Winds Moon (February 19–March 20), is also known as the mountain lion or the ghost cat. They are the largest felines on the American continent, growing up to nine feet and three hundred pounds. Cougars used to be found all across the United States. They are the best climbers of all felines, swift runners, and are very protective of their individual territories. The cougar is an elusive animal that seems to evoke a sense of mystery and wildness within people.

COMMON MEANING: mystery; wildness; a primitive part of your being; a ferocious aspect of your nature; your own territoriality; a part of you that runs swiftly either toward or away from something.

TRICKSTER MEANING: coo, as in make loving sounds; gar, as in growl.

TRANSCENDENT MEANING: knowledge of the hunter within you; the dream hunter.

Cows

KEY WORDS: DOMESTIC; MILK; MEAT; PASSIVE; HERD ANIMAL.

DESCRIPTION: Cows are animals that are easily domesticated, and in recent times have been providers of both milk and meat for humans. The cow is normally a passive animal who obeys whoever is providing her with food. They like to herd and generally have a placid nature.

COMMON MEANING: the part of you that goes along with the crowd; your passive nature; a lack of questioning.

TRICKSTER MEANING: cowed, threatened, or pushed down; conforming against your better judgment.

TRANSCENDENT MEANING: an understanding of the part of you that can easily surrender to the collective consciousness.

Coyote

KEY WORDS: WILD; WILY; SACRED; PROFANE; SINGER; SURVIVAL; ENDURANCE; ADAPTABILITY; SWIFT; HOWLING; SHAWNODESE.

DESCRIPTION: Coyote, the animal associated with the South and with Shawnodese, Spirit Keeper of the South, has been an important symbolic figure for many peoples of the earth. The coyote is a relative of the wolf found in western North America. Coyote has a wild, eerie, and unforgettable song, and the ability to survive in almost any situation. It is omnivorous and a very important part of the ecosystem, since a large part of a coyote's diet consists of rodents. Because the territory of coyotes has expanded in recent years, in some parts of the country people who fear all coyote is and represents are again trying to pass laws that would allow hunters to shoot them. If such laws are passed, the coyote, like the buffalo, could well become an endangered species.

Coyote has been an important symbolic figure for many Earth peoples. Most often coyote is considered to be a trickster, sometimes a clown, who is portrayed as both sacred and profane.

COMMON MEANING: needing to be tricked in order to grow; being tricked to help your growth; the trickster aspect of your own nature; the natural world prevailing over man; a view of what is natural within you; the survivor.

TRICKSTER MEANING: coy; tea or tee.

TRANSCENDENT MEANING: coyote can be a trickster, a symbol of duality. Be cautious of this symbol. Like the clown, what the coyote encourages you to do might be either what you need to do or the exact opposite of what you need to do.

MEDICINE EAGLE'S TEACHING: trickster; adaptability; fools us into seeing.

Crab

KEY WORDS: PINCH; CLAWS; SHELL; SEA; HOLDING ON; CANCER.

DESCRIPTION: A crab is a crustacean with a round body, a short tail, and pincers that are sharp and quite capable of holding on. Many varieties of crab are edible and considered to be delicacies.

COMMON MEANING: areas in which you are holding on; things that you need to release; things that are no longer of service to you; tenacity; endurance, even against great odds.

TRICKSTER MEANING: complaining; sour; sour-tempered; a form of louse; the fourth sign of the Zodiac; a name used in the dice game.
TRANSCENDENT MEANING: a gift of endurance within the dream, or an indication of endurance in life.

Crab Apple

KEY WORDS: TART, SWEET FLOWERS; BITTER FRUIT; DECEPTIVE.
DESCRIPTION: Crab apples are small, very sour apples that either grow wild or are cultivated. The apple is used for making jellies and preserves.
COMMON MEANING: something that is bittersweet; something deceptive; bitterness hiding as sweetness; something sweet that could become bitter.
TRICKSTER MEANING: see *Crab;* a sour fruit.
TRANSCENDENT MEANING: an unexpected benefit from a bitter experience.

Cranberries

KEY WORDS: THANKSGIVING; RED; ROUND; EDIBLE; SOUR.
DESCRIPTION: Cranberries are red berries that are edible but sour, the fruit of a particular variety of *Vaccinium* that grows in bogs or marshes. In the United States, cranberries are associated with Thanksgiving celebrations.
COMMON MEANING: that which you are thankful for; that for which you should give thanks.
TRICKSTER MEANING: cram berries.
TRANSCENDENT MEANING: an understanding of thanks giving.

Crane

KEY WORDS: PATIENCE; WATER; EMOTIONS; CONNECTION WITH EARTH, SKY, AND WATER; LEADERSHIP; GRACEFUL; CONTEMPLATION.
DESCRIPTION: Cranes are long-legged migratory birds that live in and near the water. They can fly high and have a trumpeting call that can be heard before they can be seen. Like its smaller relative, the great blue heron, for which the crane is often mistaken, these birds seem to have an unending supply of patience, which allows them to wait in water for fish, frogs, seeds, or whatever else it is they want to eat. To some Earth peoples, the crane represented leadership; the silence and the gentleness that should be part of leadership.
COMMON MEANING: your ability to be patient; your willingness to enter your own emotions; a desire to find what truly nurtures you; mature parts of your being; comfort with power; contentment with emotions; grounding on the earth.
TRICKSTER MEANING: to stretch in order to see what is around you; a piece of heavy equipment.

TRANSCENDENT MEANING: a reconnection with earth, sky, and water; a newfound ability to expand your horizons and understanding.

Cricket, see Grasshopper

Crescent Moon

KEY WORDS: BEGINNING OR COMPLETING EXPLORATION OF FEMININE, OF SHADOW, OF DREAMING.

DESCRIPTION: The moon appears to be a crescent in the first quarter when it is waxing, and in the last quarter when it is waning.

COMMON MEANING: the beginning or completion of exploration into the feminine aspects of being; beginning or completion of your understanding of dreaming; a tentative first step.

TRICKSTER MEANING: crest; scent; to "moon" is to expose your posterior.

TRANSCENDENT MEANING: a revelation about aspects of yourself long hidden from your conscious mind.

SEE ALSO: *Full Moon, Dark Moon, Grandmother Moon, Thirteenth Moon, Half Moon,* and *Menstruation.*

Crow

KEY WORDS: MAGIC; VERBAL; MESSENGER; SHAPE-SHIFTER; TEACHER; CONNECTOR; GUARDIAN; ALLY; CLEVER; SLY; MISCHIEVOUS.

DESCRIPTION: Crow, like raven, is a bird associated with duality. The crow is also a bringer of magic of all kinds. Crow is the slightly smaller brother of the raven who lives in places that the raven would spurn, like fields, suburban areas, and even cities. Crow is a large bird with glossy black feathers and a loud *caw.* Crows can be taught to talk. Consequently, they are considered to be messengers who can verbalize the secrets of the universe. In many traditions, crow was considered to be a guardian and an important ally for people who followed various Earth ways. Some traditions attribute the crow with the gift of shape-shifting. Others say that many shape-shifters would often take on the form of the crow. These birds were often associated with witches and witchcraft by some Native tribes. To other Earth peoples, the crow also represents the wisdom of the old Earth religions. Crow is also the name given to a Siouan tribe that lives in the upper basins of the Yellowstone and Big Horn rivers.

COMMON MEANING: a message about your gifts and talents; aspects of yourself you prefer to keep in darkness; teachings that you might have ignored; ancient wisdom.

TRICKSTER MEANING: to exult or to boast; a tool; to make the noise of a rooster; to eat crow is to admit you are wrong.

TRANSCENDENT MEANING: some aspect of your own magic may have to do with your ability to shift your shape or your way of relating to the world; another dream symbol of duality with which you should use caution; a gift of magic.

SEE ALSO : *Raven.*

Crystal

KEY WORDS : AMPLIFIER; RECEIVER; TRANSMITTER; POWER; EARTH RENEWAL MOON, QUARTZ CRYSTAL; HARVEST MOON, AMETHYST CRYSTALS; BUTTERFLY CLAN, AZURITE CRYSTALS; PURITY, HERKIMER DIAMOND; GROWTH, FLUORITE; FATHER SUN, GEODES CONTAINING QUARTZ OR AMETHYST CRYSTALS.

DESCRIPTION : Crystals are minerals with identical, internal, periodically repeated atomic arrangements, often with external planes. People used the word *crystal* to refer to anything with a crystallike appearance, most often stones of the quartz family. Quartz crystals are powerful forms of crystals that receive, transmit, and amplify the life energy. Various other forms of minerals in crystalline form are also amplifiers of energy. They each may have more specific sorts of energies with which they help.

COMMON MEANING : a time of power; understanding of the flow of life; better communication skills; rigidity; hardness; can be a warning to reevaluate your views and let in new information.

TRICKSTER MEANING : a person's name; to make hard; a protective shield; clear.

TRANSCENDENT MEANING : the gift of power; a revelation about how you see the world; the ability to perceive things differently.

SEE ALSO : *Quartz, Amethyst, Azurite, Herkimer Diamonds, Fluorite,* and *Geodes.*

Dance

KEY WORDS : MOVEMENT; CONNECTION; FLUIDITY; GRACE; DIGNITY; UNITY; ONE-NESS.

DESCRIPTION : Dance was a very critical part of the ceremonial life of most Earth peoples. To dance was to allow one's entire body to merge with the heartbeat of the Earth Mother. It was to bring one's physical being into harmony with the sacred web of life. To dance was also a way to express joy and to take yourself into a state of ecstasy. Dance was one of the most sacred movements of many Earth peoples.

COMMON MEANING : how you are relating to the web of life. The way in which you are dancing tells you about your relationship with life at any given time, as in the following examples: fluid and graceful, fluid and graceful living; jerky, disharmonious living; flowing as one, a unity between your being and the web of life; with dignity, self-respect, respect for the web of life; with joy, feeling happiness; trance dance, ecstasy.

TRICKSTER MEANING: Dan's, belonging to Dan (name).
TRANSCENDENT MEANING: a gift of knowledge of yourself and your connection with the universe.

Dandelion

KEY WORDS: COMMON; ROOTED; TENACIOUS; HEALING; BUDDING TREES MOON.
DESCRIPTION: Dandelion, the plant totem for people born during the Budding Trees Moon (March 21–April 19), is one of the most common wild plants, one with very deep roots and the ability to propagate itself easily. The dandelion has a yellow flower that, when gone to seed, becomes a white puff, the separate seeds from which appear to be carried by a feathery parachute. Dandelion has been used as a tonic and as an edible green. It is purported to have abilities to renew and revitalize the body.
COMMON MEANING: finding the source of your own strength; discovering your rootedness upon earth; discovering the foundation of your own life; discovering your source of power; associated with the power of the wind.
TRICKSTER MEANING: dandy lion; tooth of the lion.
TRANSCENDENT MEANING: the ability to go gently from one phase of life to another.

Dark of the Moon

KEY WORDS: PREPARATION FOR EXAMINING FEMININE; CONTEMPLATING WORK ON SHADOW SIDE OF BEING; CHANGE; RESISTANCE TO CHANGE; FEAR OF CHAOS; FEAR OF FEMININE.
DESCRIPTION: The dark of the moon is the time when we are not able to see any aspect of the moon shining in the night sky. To dream of the night sky where the light of the moon is not visible but you feel its presence means that you are dreaming of the dark of the moon.
COMMON MEANING: examining fear of your feminine nature; examining fear of the void or of chaos.
TRICKSTER MEANING: to "moon"; to expose what you perceive as underlying darkness.
TRANSCENDENT MEANING: a gift of courage to examine that which you have heretofore avoided.
SEE ALSO: *Moon, Full Moon, Half Moon, Crescent Moon, Thirteenth Moon, Menstruation,* and *Grandmother Moon.*

Datura, see Jimsonweed

Death

KEY WORDS: CHANGE; TRANSFORMATION; REBIRTH.

DESCRIPTION: Death is an ending of one phase of life and a beginning of another.

COMMON MEANING: rarely, literal death of self or another; more usually, change; leaving behind an aspect of your life that you have outgrown; allowing transformation; welcoming rebirth.

TRICKSTER MEANING: fear of literal death when dream is of figurative death.

TRANSCENDENT MEANING: help with leaving an outmoded way of being; traveling into a new aspect of life.

Deer:

KEY WORDS: SENSITIVE; GRACEFUL; FAST-MOVING; INTUITIVE; CLEVER; RESOURCEFUL; CREATIVE; COMMUNICATING; CORNPLANTING MOON.

DESCRIPTION: The deer, the animal totem for the Cornplanting Moon, May 21–June 20), is an animal that does well in the civilized world, being able to adapt to many of the environments that have been created by man. Deer are sensitive, graceful, fast-moving, alert. They are also clever, resourceful, and creative. The three most common species of deer are white-tailed, black-tailed, and mule. Deer live in herds with others of their own sex, except during the mating season. Bucks have antlers that they lose every year and then regenerate.

COMMON MEANING: exploring your creativity; coming in touch with your adaptability; increased sensitivity to change; major shifts in your life; lessons about your intuition.

TRICKSTER MEANING: dear. If you dream of a male deer, "buck" can mean money or to go against.

TRANSCENDENT MEANING: an increase in healing abilities or intuitive knowledge.

WOLF CLAN TEACHING: hearing; clan animal for May.

HUICHOL TEACHING: Lord of the Dream; cultural hero; intermediary between people and the gods; one's higher self. If you see a deer, you are trying to learn something, or a spirit is trying to teach you.

Diamond

KEY WORDS: COMMITMENT; GREED; HARDNESS.

DESCRIPTION: Diamond, which is carbon in crystalline form, sometimes pure, is the hardest substance known. Diamonds are brilliant and can refract light. They are found in various parts of the world. Historically, diamonds, though not as popular as they are today, were associated with lightning and were purported to give a person both strength and courage.

COMMON MEANING: fear of change; hardness; greed; desire for or fear of commitment.

TRICKSTER MEANING: a figure; a suit in a deck of playing cards; a baseball field.

TRANSCENDENT MEANING: a gift of strength; revelations about the level of your courage.

Dog

KEY WORDS: FRIEND; LOYAL; PROTECTIVE; ANIMAL OUTCAST; HERO; ALLY; LOVING NATURE.

DESCRIPTION: This domesticated relation of both coyote and wolf has long been considered a great friend to humankind. Throughout many millennia, dog has given protection as well as love and loyalty to its human friends. Some legends say that dog is an outcast from the animal world because of his loyalty to the two-leggeds, who often mistreat the animal beings. Nonetheless, the history of humans and dogs seems to be closely interwoven, and in many cases dogs have given humans their only experience of loving a member of the animal kingdom. As such, they might well be the true heroes of the animal world, not the outcasts.

COMMON MEANING: your connection with the animal kingdom; your connection with the animal inside you; loyalty; friendship; protection.

TRICKSTER MEANING: a pejorative name for a person, as in "You dog!"; also slang for an unattractive person; very or completely, as in "dog tired"; to hunt or follow; to deteriorate, as in "go to the dogs"; elegance, as in "put on the dog."

TRANSCENDENT MEANING: an important ally; a guide in the dream world.

Dolphin

KEY WORDS: ANCIENT; INTELLIGENT; PLAYFUL; COMPASSIONATE; COMFORTABLE IN BOTH AIR AND WATER; GREGARIOUS; COMMUNICATORS; PLAY; HARMONY; PURITY.

DESCRIPTION: The animal associated with the third Spirit Path position of the North, purity, is the dolphin. The dolphin is a very old mammal of the sea who is purported to have intelligence that we humans do not yet fully understand. Dolphins have the ability to communicate with their own kind; in some instances, to communicate with humans as well as other creatures of the sea. Dolphins are found in warm and mild waters. In recent years, too many dolphins have been killed, trapped in the nets of tuna fishermen. It's important to be sure you only eat tuna that is dolphin-safe. In this way we help to protect our elder brothers and sisters of the water, who have often extended protection to two-leggeds.

The dolphin, like the whale, is a sea mammal, one who needs to breathe air while living in the watery expanse of the world's oceans and rivers. Dolphins are social animals and like to live in groups, which protect and care for each other. Some people feel the dolphin is a link with the gods, or those who dwell in different realms.

COMMON MEANING: a part of you that playfully swims in the waters of life; the child within; your capacity for play; compassion; love.

TRICKSTER MEANING: doll, as in a toy or a beautiful woman; fin, slang for five; also fin on a fish. There is also a species of swift marine fish that is called dolphin; this is a game fish that is eaten in several parts of the world.

TRANSCENDENT MEANING: a messenger; a gift of literal lessons from other realms.

Doves

KEY WORDS: SPEED; SONG; PEACE; LOVE.

DESCRIPTION: Doves and their close relatives, pigeons, are prevalent in many parts of the world. The dove is a bird with very strong wings that make a very notable rushing sound as the doves flies, sometimes at speeds up to forty miles an hour. Doves are seed eaters who require water once a day in order to digest the seeds they have eaten. Some Native people thought the dove could help to bring the rains. The dove's sweet cooing song often inspires thoughts of love and peace. The most familiar dove is the rock dove, also called the domestic pigeon. Another common dove is the mourning dove, which is the most common of wild doves.

COMMON MEANING: softness; strength; peace; relationships; love interest.

TRICKSTER MEANING: peaceful people.

TRANSCENDENT MEANING: a gift of peace; an understanding of the strength it takes to retain a peaceful outlook.

Dragonfly

KEY WORDS: IRIDESCENT; ILLUSORY; INSPIRES THE IMAGINATION; GENTLE; SKILLED FLIERS.

DESCRIPTION: The dragonfly is a long, narrow insect with two pairs of iridescent wings. Like the hummingbird, the dragonfly tends to inspire the imagination of humans. Their gentle, nonthreatening presence is often a natural reminder that can pull man from his thoughts into the world that exists around him. Dragonflies, when they've just hatched, live on pond bottoms and eat many other insects. The adult dragonfly is quite an aerial acrobat who, like the hummingbird, can hover, fly forwards, backwards, up and down. They use their skills to catch insects that aren't quite as acrobatically inclined.

COMMON MEANING: inspiration; earth connection; seeing through illusions; becoming aware of the light.

TRICKSTER MEANING: a dragon that flies.

TRANSCENDENT MEANING: a messenger from the Earth Mother.

• • •

Drum

KEY WORDS: EARTH BEAT; HEARTBEAT; EARTH CONNECTION; HEALING; CENTERING; POWER.

DESCRIPTION: The drum is a percussion instrument that is made from a hollow cylinder with a membrane at one or both ends. This instrument, which is played either with the hands, sticks, or sometimes with bones, was central to most Earth peoples. The beat of the drum is considered to be the beat of the Earth Mother, and can help people come into harmony with this heartbeat. The drum has also been used by many Earth peoples to induce trance states.

COMMON MEANING: coming to know yourself; attaining more power; knowledge of the deep earth energy; knowledge of your own deep emotional nature.

TRICKSTER MEANING: a part of the ear; to expel.

TRANSCENDENT MEANING: help with going deeper into the dream state; a healing from music; deep understanding of the universal energy.

Eagle

KEY WORDS: MESSENGER; HIGH-FLYING; INSPIRING; PREDATOR; STRONG WINGS; KEEN SIGHT; ALOOFNESS; COURAGE; PRESCIENCE; FORESIGHT; WABUN, SPIRIT KEEPER OF THE EAST.

DESCRIPTION: Eagle, the animal associated with Wabun, Spirit Keeper of the East, is a large, powerful raptor who flies high and sees far. The eagle has long touched the imagination of humans and won their respect. Eagle feathers were a badge of honor in many Native societies and are still highly valued today. The head bonnets of chiefs were usually made of eagle feathers. The eagle has been used as a symbol or emblem both by the Roman empire and by the United States. There have been coins called eagles. Because of overhunting, eagles almost became an extinct species. They are now protected and are making a comeback in the ecosystem.

COMMON MEANING: your ability to fly high; your strength; clear sight; seeing things keenly.

TRICKSTER MEANING: a golf score; the name of a satellite that landed on the moon; a reference to the Hopi prophecy "the Eagle has landed."

TRANSCENDENT MEANING: a messenger of the Creator who can direct you; knowledge of the mysteries both of earth and of air.

WOLF CLAN TEACHING: the East, or lofty ideals.

HUICHOL TEACHING: the breath of life.

MEDICINE EAGLE'S TEACHING: high-flying; far-seeing; vision; illumination; connecting with Spirit; bringing Spirit energy to nest on earth.

SEE ALSO: *Wabun, Spirit Keeper of the East* and *Cardinal Directions—East.*

Earth (element of), see Turtle Clan

Earth mother

KEY WORDS: NURTURING; FERTILITY; LOVING; FECUNDITY.

DESCRIPTION: The Earth Mother is the name given to the planet Earth by many Native peoples. In the Medicine Wheel, the Earth Mother stone is the first stone placed in the Center Circle. The color for the Earth Mother is forest green; the element is earth; the mineral is clay; corn, beans, and squash are the plant totems; the great tortoise is the animal totem. The Earth Mother position is one in which people can feel their connection to the earth more strongly.

COMMON MEANING: understanding of parenting; increased fertility; lushness; rapid growth; solace; understanding of the condition of life on Earth.

TRICKSTER MEANING: mother of the earth, a mother made of earth; a dirty mother.

TRANSCENDENT MEANING: a revelation about your connection with the planet.

Earth (the planet), see Earth Mother

Earthworm

KEY WORDS: NARROW; LONG; REGENERATIVE; TRANSFORMING; OXYGENATING; ENRICHING; RENEWAL.

DESCRIPTION: Earthworm is the animal associated with the second Spirit Path position of the North, renewal. This small being has a large importance in the continuation of life. Rarely thicker than a small finger, earthworms are found worldwide. They can grow to be very long, and they have the ability to regenerate. The digestion of the earthworm gives us that most important building block of life, new soil. Worms don't have vision or eyes, but they go underground when they sense light. They aerate the soil as they move and eat, which allows bacteria to decompose and enrich the soil. Earthworms have both male and female sex gonads in separate parts of their body. If part of the earthworm is torn off, the rest can regenerate that missing part.

COMMON MEANING: regeneration; how you can help the earth; how you can best serve life; how even small actions have large consequences.

TRICKSTER MEANING: parasite; a person who is an object of contempt, as in "You Worm!"; to insinuate yourself or ingratiate yourself into or out of something.

TRANSCENDENT MEANING: transformation.

• • •

Echinacea

KEY WORDS: PURIFYING; HEALING; STRENGTHENING; CLEANSING.

DESCRIPTION: Echinacea is the plant associated with the first Spirit Path position of the North, cleansing. Echinacea grows wild in many prairie areas of the United States. It is a plant that is purported to have many healing properties. Foremost among these is the power to disinfect, strengthen, and cleanse. Echinacea has been said to help with snake bites and with many illnesses that come from problems with the blood or the lymphatic system.

COMMON MEANING: a deep cleansing; an aspect of yourself that needs to be strengthened; a weakness in your immune system; a weakness in your ability to fight off external forces; cleaning out.

TRANSCENDENT MEANING: a gift of deep cleansing; a gift of understanding of those things that block you.

Elder

KEY WORDS: OLDER; RESPECT; ESTEEM; WISDOM.

DESCRIPTION: In Earth societies, the time when one was an elder was a time when one had achieved the pinnacle of respect within the community. Because an elder had succeeded in living through all the experiences that life brought to him, he was considered to have a great deal to teach the rest of the community.

COMMON MEANINGS: the power of experience; yourself as an older person; your own grandparents; your ancestors.

TRICKSTER MEANING: a tree; one who holds a superior position; ancient times; leaders in a church organization.

TRANSCENDENT MEANING: yourself in your full power, with the wisdom and illumination that might come to you as a result of living your life the best way you can.

Elder Tree

KEY WORDS: HEALING; NUTRITIOUS; BEAUTIFYING; HELPFUL.

DESCRIPTION: Elder, or elderberry, is a shrub that grows throughout the world. It can reach from five to twelve feet in height and blooms in early summer with clusters of fragrant flowers, usually white. The flowers are replaced in the fall by purplish-black berries. The entire elder shrub has been used medicinally and as a food and drink by Earth peoples around the world. It is said to heal many maladies. It also provides a tasty and nutritious jam or wine. Herbalists use the elder in cosmetics for both beautifying and healing the skin. The leaves and roots of the elder tree are poisonous. The berries, before they have turned purple or black, can also be toxic, inducing diarrhea or vomiting. The fresh flowers can be dipped in a batter and fried.

COMMON MEANING: ancient knowledge; healing; nourishment; nurturing from nature.
TRICKSTER MEANING: the older tree; the elder energy within you.
TRANSCENDENT MEANING: a gift of beauty and nurturing.

Elementals

KEY WORDS: PRIMAL; FIRST KINGDOM OF CREATION; EARTH, AIR, FIRE, AND WATER.
DESCRIPTION: The elements—earth, water, fire, air—can exist without plants, animals, and humans. They need nothing besides themselves. Earth people considered the elementals to be the first, the primary people, and thus gave them great respect. It is possible to dream of the elementals either as one force of nature or in their separate components: earth, air, fire, and water.
COMMON MEANING: your relationship with the elements, either as a whole or individually; the elemental or primary part of your own being.
TRICKSTER MEANING: being elemental; being primary, primitive.
TRANSCENDENT MEANING: a gift from one of the four elements, or from the entire elemental kingdom.

Elk

KEY WORDS: IMPOSING; PERSISTENT; PLAYFUL; DANCERS; QUICK; HIGH-JUMPING; TRUMPETING; COMMUNICATIVE; TEACHER OF OTHER TEACHERS; LONG SNOWS MOON.
DESCRIPTION: Elk is the animal totem for people born during the Long Snows Moon (November 22–December 21). The elk is a member of the deer family, also called *wapiti*. The males, who can reach a weight of seven hundred and fifty pounds, have antlers that can resemble the branches of a tree. Elks live in the woodlands, going to the high country in summer, and eat grass, leaves, twigs, and bark. Like deer, elk live in same-sex herds except during mating season. At that time, the bull tries to bring as many females as he can into a "harem." Elk seem to dance together at times, forming a big circle in which they prance around. They are fast animals with an ability to jump very high. They have few natural enemies. Before 1900, most of the elk in the United States were slaughtered by European hunters who often only wanted two of their teeth to make into jewelry.
COMMON MEANING: exploration of the strong, vital, communicative part of your being; introduction to your playful nature; knowledge of your capacity for joy.
TRICKSTER MEANING: not applicable.
TRANSCENDENT MEANING: a gift of inspiration, mystery, and beauty.

Experience

KEY WORDS: CONCRETE SKILLS; BODY MEMORY; EDUCATION; EXPERTISE; DOING;

LEARNING; REMEMBERING; STABILITY; COMPETENCE; TEMPERING; INTEGRATING; FOCUSING; WISDOM; WESTERN SPIRIT PATH.

DESCRIPTION: Experience is the outer Spirit Path stone of the West. The mineral associated with experience is hematite; plant, olive tree; animal, whale; color, steel gray. Experience is what you have actually lived through, observed, and thus made part of you, or the skills and knowledge that result from having lived life.

COMMON MEANING: a review of your life; knowledge that you have learned your lesson; accepting knowledge offered; maturity; increasing abilities.

TRICKSTER MEANING: ex-peer; peer.

TRANSCENDENT MEANING: a gift of deep understanding of your experience of life or of some particular aspect of your life.

Fasting

KEY WORDS: ABSTAINING FROM FOOD AND/OR WATER; CLEANSING; RITUAL PREPARATION.

DESCRIPTION: Fasting is doing without food and/or water for a period of time, usually in preparation for a ceremony, particularly a ceremony of the threshold such as a vision quest. Some Earth people would refer to what we now call the vision quest as fasting, as dreaming, or as a fasting quest. Fasting from food and/or water was thought to move one closer to the spirits, who have need of neither food nor water. It is a ritual sacrifice of these pleasures that allows you to have a deeper connection with the gods or the spirits. A fast can also be a voluntary abstinence as a token of grief, sorrow, or repentance.

COMMON MEANING: abstention; feelings of deprivation; feelings of sacrifice; feelings of giving away in anticipation of spiritual experience.

TRICKSTER MEANING: fast moving; sting; quick sting, either meaning an insect sting or a dishonest maneuver.

TRANSCENDENT MEANING: a dream of preparation for an important spiritual event in your own life.

Father Sun, see Sun

Feasting

KEY WORDS: CELEBRATION; RICH MEAL; SPECIAL TREAT; DELIGHT.

DESCRIPTION: A feast followed most important ceremonies in the Earth religions and, in their own way, were a part of the ceremony. After a sweat lodge or a sauna, after a marriage or a naming, after a change of season celebration or a funeral, there would usually be a feast. The feast would consist of the best foods that were available to the people who were sponsoring the celebration. A feast is a symbol of prosperity, abundance, joy, and gratitude.

COMMON MEANING: abundance; increasing prosperity; celebration; joy; delight in sharing; entertainment.

TRICKSTER MEANING: fee, as in payment; sting; the payment stings.

TRANSCENDENT MEANING: a gift of pleasure, entertainment, and enjoyment in a dream; celebration of an important spiritual event; deep understanding of what fulfillment means to you.

Feather

KEY WORDS: BIRD NATION; LIGHT; HEALING; CEREMONIAL; MESSAGE; GIFT.

DESCRIPTION: Feathers played and still play an important role in the ceremonial life of many Earth peoples. To these people, feathers are respected as gifts from the winged ones or the bird nations. A feather is considered to carry some of the power of the bird from which it came. Consequently, if a feather comes from a bird with healing abilities, the feather carries these same healing abilities; from a bird who is a messenger, the feather has the capacity to bring messages.

COMMON MEANING: a message; a message from the bird nations; a message from the spirit beings; a healing; announcement of a ceremony. It is important to ascertain as much as possible about the feather in your dream state.

TRICKSTER MEANING: something or someone very light, either surrounded by light or lightweight.

TRANSCENDENT MEANING: a gift from an ally or spirit who has come to work with you.

Fetish

KEY WORDS: MEDICINE TOOL; POWER; HEALING; SUPERNATURAL; MYSTERIOUS; CHARM.

DESCRIPTION: A fetish is literally any object that is regarded with feelings of awe. Such objects are considered to have supernatural powers, since they represent some powerful part of the Great Mystery. Some cultures believed that the spirit of the being represented actually resided in a fetish.

Monotheistic cultures tend to view the fetishes of animistic cultures with disdain while denying their own artifacts are also fetishes.

COMMON MEANING: dreaming, once removed, of the being represented by the fetish; beginning to prepare yourself to work with whatever the fetish represents; fear and desire for what is represented by the fetish; something that is an object of mystery to you; inspirational or full of awe.

TRICKSTER MEANING: something to which you are abnormally or excessively devoted; something or someone to whom you give your love without discrimination; a common nonsexual object that arouses sexual feelings in the viewer; a charm used by an "uneducated" culture.

TRANSCENDENT MEANING: a gift of power given by the object that is being represented, or the kingdom from which that object comes.

Fire

HUICHOL TEACHING: wisdom.
SEE ALSO: *Thunderbird.*

Firefly

KEY WORDS: ILLUMINATING; RADIANT; LIGHT-FILLED; MIRACULOUS; THE LIFE FORCE.

DESCRIPTION: The animal that represents illumination, the third Spirit Path position of the East, is the firefly, which is also known as the lightning bug. Fireflies are small beetles that emit light through an organ that contains a light-producing chemical called luciferin. Fireflies have a radiant, though short, life span. Their illumination is part of their mating dance.

COMMON MEANING: increasing light coming into your life; if in difficult circumstances, an indication of help.

TRICKSTER MEANING: a flame is leaving; fire is flying; a pants fastener that is hot, either stolen or passionate.

TRANSCENDENT MEANING: an indication of the direction in which you should be heading.

Fire Opal

KEY WORDS: HOPE; MAGIC; FIRE; SUN.

DESCRIPTION: Fire opal is the mineral totem for people born during the Budding Trees Moon (March 21–April 19). Fire opal is considered to be a symbol of hope and a stone with many magical properties, including the ability to render its wearer invisible at times. The fire in this stone is often associated with the sun or the moon, and also with the powers of fire and water.

COMMON MEANING: your ability to hope and believe; indicating a magical time of life; work on your male and female balance; sun connection; moon connection; willingness to work with your feelings.

TRICKSTER MEANING: fire; oh, pal; a friend to fire; a salutation to a friend.
TRANSCENDENT MEANING: a gift of hope and of light coming at a time that might appear dark.

Fireweed

KEY WORDS: HEALS; REVITALIZES; BEAUTIFIES; NUTRITIOUS; REGENERATING.

DESCRIPTION: Fireweed is the plant associated with the Fire or Thunderbird Clan position in the Center Circle of the Medicine Wheel. Fireweed describes a variety of plants. The one associated with this position, *Epilobium angustifolium,* is a tall plant with purple spikes that, in flower, can be said to resemble fire. This is one of the first plants that grows in areas that have been damaged by fire; in this way, it helps to regenerate the earth itself. Fireweed has been used by Earth peoples for food and also for tea.

COMMON MEANING: true healing; a healing path upon the Earth Mother; regeneration of yourself or your environment.

TRICKSTER MEANING: we'd fire; fire weed; light up a smoke.

TRANSCENDENT MEANING: a gift of healing to parts of you that may have been burned by your desire for too rapid spiritual experience, or too rapid transformation.

First Woman

KEY WORDS: SPIDER WOMAN; CHANGING WOMAN; WHITE BUFFALO WOMAN; SPIRIT WOMAN; THE GREAT MOTHER; THE CREATOR; COPPER WOMAN; THOUGHT WOMAN; MORNING STAR WOMAN; DAYBREAK STAR WOMAN; THE FEMININE.

DESCRIPTION: First Woman is considered by some Earth peoples to be the Creator of all. She is known by many names, including Spirit Woman, Morning Star Woman, Daybreak Star Woman, Spider Woman, Changing Woman, White Buffalo Woman, Copper Woman, Thought Woman. To some Native people, she is the one who nurtures life both through food and ceremonies.

COMMON MEANING: your view of the Earth Mother; a view of the deepest part of your feminine nature; harmony with your feminine.

TRICKSTER MEANING: primary woman; the woman is first; the woman is primary; the primary feminine.

TRANSCENDENT MEANING: a guide or ally to help you discover your deepest connection both with the earth and with all feminine aspects of being.

Flicker

KEY WORDS: COURAGE; RELATIONSHIP; DRUMMING; COMMUNICATING; LOVING; GIFT-BRINGER.

DESCRIPTION: The Flicker, the animal totem for people born under the

Strong Sun Moon (June 21–July 22), is a woodpecker. There are two kinds of flickers in the United States, one with yellow underwings, the other with red underwings. Flickers spend quite a bit of time on the ground, and will perch upright on limbs as songbirds do. They are drummers who play their song on dead limbs, tin roofs, and wooden houses. During mating they put on a particularly magnificent display of their musical talent. In legend, the flicker is considered to be a bird of courage; some legends say that he has red underwings because he went too close to a fire, and the flame from it colored his wings and tail. Flickers are valued because of their drumming. Their feathers were used in many religious articles and ceremonies by Native American people.

COMMON MEANING: finding your own special song; discovering your special place in the world; improved communications; intense desire for relationship; concern about your nest or home; a time for beautifying yourself and your environment.

TRICKSTER MEANING: to waver rapidly; flick her.

TRANSCENDENT MEANING: understanding of your own desire for relationship; understanding of how relationship forms and colors all of life.

Flies

KEY WORDS: COMMON; PERSISTENT; ANNOYING; TENACIOUS.

DESCRIPTION: Flies are any one of a large group of insects that have two transparent wings. Flies, like mosquitoes, have a very adversarial relationship with humans, sometimes seeming to be a plague upon humankind. Flies carry disease and can be quite annoying. Some of them bite, attempting to eat human flesh as well as anything else they can find. Flies have large eyes, which give them the ability to see all around themselves. Like the mosquito, the fly is very good at getting your attention, thus focusing your attention on nature.

COMMON MEANING: a view of the persistent, tenacious part of you; understanding of an annoying aspect of your nature.

TRICKSTER MEANING: to move through the air; swift; rushing; to run from; the fastener in pants; the door of a tent; part of spinning. There are also several pun meanings that can be associated with fly, mainly having to do with the actual act of flying.

TRANSCENDENT MEANING: an attempt by part of you to reconnect all of you with nature, the earth, and what is natural.

Fluorite

KEY WORDS: CRYSTAL; GLASSY; LUSTROUS; MULTICOLORED; FLOW; FLUX; MELD; MELT; ALTER; STRENGTHEN.

DESCRIPTION: Fluorite is the mineral totem associated with growth, the second Spirit Path position of the South. Fluorite is a crystal with a glassy luster that comes in both cubical and octahedral shapes. It can range in color from colorless through yellows, greens, blues, purples, blacks. Fluorite melts easily and is often used in smelting. Fluorine is a main component of fluorite, and it is purported to help the human body be strong in both teeth and bone.

COMMON MEANING: your ability to flow, to melt, to mix, to meld; a synthesis; an opportunity to be more varied or broader of philosophy.

TRICKSTER MEANING: flow right; right flow.

TRANSCENDENT MEANING: the ability to be fluid in the dream state; the ability to perceive the source of things occurring in your dreams.

Flying

KEY WORDS: RAPID; GOAL-ORIENTED; TRANSCENDENT; SPIRITUAL; ETHERIC; FORMLESSNESS.

DESCRIPTION: Flying is moving rapidly. In dreams, this can be in your own body, in some other sort of body, or just as energy rapidly moving. In dreams of yourself flying as a bird or flying with a bird, it is important to note the kind of bird, then either see the entry for that bird or study the habits of that bird to better understand the dream.

COMMON MEANING: literally having an out-of-body experience.

TRICKSTER MEANING: see *Flies*.

TRANSCENDENT MEANING: traveling in your etheric or spiritual body; a pleasant dream in which you feel free and without limits.

HUICHOL TEACHING: traveling to spirit places.

Fox

KEY WORDS: SURVIVOR; CUNNING; SLY; WILY; ADAPTABLE; INVISIBLE AT WILL; CONTRARY; RESOURCEFULNESS.

DESCRIPTION: The fox, like the coyote and the opossum, is a survivor, an animal that even today can be found in parks in some major cities. The fox has a reputation of being wily, sly, and cunning. In reality, the fox has the ability to adapt himself so well that he does not allow himself to be seen unless he wants to.

Foxes tend to be nocturnal, and anxious around humans. They are omnivorous, preferring vegetation when it's available and small birds, rodents, and insects when it is not. It's possible the fox is cautious rather than cunning, having learned to exercise extreme caution whenever two-leggeds are around.

COMMON MEANING: the sly and cunning aspect of your nature; the adaptable part of your being; the survivor; understanding of your visibility; knowledge of your resourcefulness.

TRICKSTER MEANING: a good-looking person; a tricky person.
TRANSCENDENT MEANING: in dreaming it is a lesson, either in invisibility or in other spiritual work.

Foxglove

KEY WORDS: BEAUTIFUL; BELL-LIKE; HEART; HEALING.

DESCRIPTION: Foxglove (*Digitalis purpurea*) is a plant that originally came from Europe but has spread throughout the United States. It is a beautiful biennial plant that grows from two to five feet tall. It has spikes of bell-like flowers, generally purple, although some can be white. Foxglove is a source of digitalis, a poison if taken incorrectly but a medicine for relieving heart problems if used properly.

COMMON MEANING: a healing of the heart; caution in matters of the heart; be cautious about too much of a good thing.

TRICKSTER MEANING: a good-looking glove; a good-looking love.

TRANSCENDENT MEANING: a gift of healing from old hurts; a gift of love.

Frog

KEY WORDS: CHANGING; DEEP FEELINGS; DEPTH; REFLECTION; ADAPTABILITY; LOVING; REGENERATING; WATER CLAN.

DESCRIPTION: In the Medicine Wheel system, the Frog Clan is the clan associated with the element of water. People of the Big Winds Moon (Cougar), Strong Sun Moon (Flicker), and Freeze Up Moon (Snake) are all members of the Frog Clan. Water is a flowing, changing, renewing element, and also a transforming one. The frog itself represents transformation, beginning life as a tadpole and then over a period of time becoming the frog. The frog is a small, four-legged animal with long, powerful hind legs that allow it to leap. Frogs have webbed feet and no tail.

The Water Clan is the clan of the emotions, the heart, deep feelings, empathy, reflexivity. Frog Clan people bring new life and feelings into a project. They can also bring healing, both physically and emotionally. They tend to be very creative people, who sometimes allow themselves to change more frequently than would be best for them. They feel emotions so deeply they sometimes dam all of them up.

COMMON MEANING: exploration of your emotions; change; working with your feminine nature; working with your sexual nature; releasing emotions.

TRICKSTER MEANING: a derisive term for a Frenchman.

TRANSCENDENT MEANING: a revelation about your emotional life; indication of a deep change or a transformation.

• • •

Full Moon

KEY WORDS: TOTAL IMMERSION IN SHADOW SIDE; ABILITY TO FULLY EXAMINE FEMININE; SENSUALITY; SEXUALITY; EMOTIONAL ENERGY; INTENSITY.

DESCRIPTION: The full moon is the moon clearly seen as a circular orb of light in the sky.

COMMON MEANING: readiness to be influenced by the moon; examination of the feminine; willingness to explore the shadow side of your being; understanding of the emotional; respect for your sensual nature.

TRICKSTER MEANING: to "moon" is to expose one's posterior; to expose one's bottom; to find out what is at the bottom; to be melancholy.

TRANSCENDENT MEANING: a gift from Grandmother Moon.

SEE ALSO: *Moon, Dark of Moon, Thirteenth Moon, Half Moon, Crescent Moon,* and *Menstruation.*

Garden

KEY WORDS: EARTH CONNECTION; MANIPULATION; BEAUTY; NURTURING; SUSTENANCE; PLANTING; HARVESTING.

DESCRIPTION: A garden is a place where humans make a special connection with the Earth Mother and with the beings in the mineral and plant kingdoms, as well as the water spirits. Usually a garden is grown for food, spice, or pleasure.

COMMON MEANING: reconnection with the earth, but unwillingness to immerse yourself in the earth energy; closeness without manipulating your connection.

TRICKSTER MEANING: guard in; in guard; guarded.

TRANSCENDENT MEANING: understanding of a secret part of your nature that has always remained deeply connected with the energy of the earth.

Garnet

KEY WORDS: CRYSTAL; HEART; BLOOD; STIMULANT; BALANCER OF SEXUAL ENERGIES; RIPE BERRIES MOON.

DESCRIPTION: Garnet is the stone for people born during the Ripe Berries Moon (July 23–August 22). Garnet is a silicate crystal with a resinous luster. There are six types of garnet minerals, which run in color from red to brown, green, yellow, black, and white. They can be found in many parts of the world. Red garnet is most often associated with sturgeon people and with the heart and the blood. Garnet was believed to help stimulate the heart and balance sexual energies.

COMMON MEANING: balance of sexual energies; stimulation of your heart; deep-felt beliefs; love.

TRICKSTER MEANING: guard; net; guard the net.
TRANSCENDENT MEANING: a gift of love.

Geode

KEY WORDS: ROUND; SURPRISING INTERIOR; FATHER SUN; WARMTH; CREATIVITY.
DESCRIPTION: Geodes, the mineral totem for the Father Sun position in the Center Circle of the Medicine Wheel, are round hollow stones lined with mineral; most often of the quartz family, sometimes amethyst. Geodes are plain-looking on the outside but spectacular on the inside. Geodes are reputed to have various uses in bringing rain and in healing.
COMMON MEANING: a plain facade masking flamboyance; sun connection; relationship to masculine energies.
TRICKSTER MEANING: gee; ode, or a lyric poem or sung poem.
TRANSCENDENT MEANING: understanding of your connection with Father Sun and other stars.

Giveaway

KEY WORDS: CLEARING AWAY, GENEROSITY, SHARING, TRANSMITTING JOY, TAKING CARE OF THE PEOPLE; NORTH.
DESCRIPTION: Many Earth peoples practiced something that is referred to as a time of giveaway. This was a time when a person would give gifts to others to honor something positive that had happened in his own life. It was believed that such gifts would help other people to share in the joy that the person arranging the giveaway felt. Giveaways would also be done at the time of death to allow others to remember the deceased person through the gifts they received in the giveaway. The giveaway is associated with the energy of the North, and it is a major lesson of the North. For contemporary people, the idea of the giveaway is frequently frightening, since society places so much emphasis on obtaining and maintaining goods.
COMMON MEANING: divesting yourself of goods; sharing your knowledge; clearing space for new energies, new gifts to come to you.
TRICKSTER MEANING: a way to give.
TRANSCENDENT MEANING: revelation about your spiritual abundance; a deep desire to share.

Goat

KEY WORDS: OMNIVOROUS; HAIR; HORNS; BUTTING; LECHERY; HORNED GODS; EARTH RELIGIONS.
DESCRIPTION: Goats are horned four-leggeds found throughout the world. The males have beards. Goats are valued both for their hair and, in some parts of the world, for their milk and flesh. They are relatively easy to do-

mesticate, and like to be with others of their species. They enjoy butting, or pushing others around with their horns. They will eat almost anything and are very difficult to fence in.

COMMON MEANING: the freedom-seeking part of you that feels confined by the pressures of convention; a part of you willing to fight for whatever you desire.

TRICKSTER MEANING: a lecherous person; an old man; a randy man; a person forced to take blame, as in scapegoat; irritating, as in "get your goat."

TRANSCENDENT MEANING: an ally who, with his sureness of movement, can help you find whatever it is you are seeking.

Gold

KEY WORDS: VALUE; CONNECTION; LIFE FORCE; SUN; EAST; WABUN, SPIRIT KEEPER OF THE EAST.

DESCRIPTION: Gold as a color is associated with the East and with Wabun, Spirit Keeper of the East. While gold is often associated with greed today, this color and mineral have both been valued throughout the ages for their beauty. Gold is the color of sunrise and sunset; consequently, of new beginnings. Golden rays coming from the skies are associated with the idea of illumination or enlightenment.

COMMON MEANING: value; insight; connection with the life force; enlightenment.

TRICKSTER MEANING: as in archery, the center of a target.

TRANSCENDENT MEANING: understanding of what you value most; the color of the cords that attach some humans to the sacred web of life.

Goldenseal

KEY WORDS: ANTISEPTIC; ANTIBIOTIC; HEALING; REVITALIZING.

DESCRIPTION: Goldenseal is a perennial herb found in eastern North America. The yellow root yields a greenish yellow powder that has been used by Native peoples for treating wounds and ulcers. It has been used in modern times as an antiseptic and tonic; it has even been said to have some antibiotic properties.

COMMON MEANING: a part of you needing healing; a part of you capable of giving healing; help for old wounds.

TRICKSTER MEANING: literally, the golden seal on a letter or document; a golden seal swimming in the waters.

TRANSCENDENT MEANING: a gift of intense healing.

Goose

KEY WORDS: PRUDENT; RESPECTFUL; TRADITIONAL; COMMUNITY.

DESCRIPTION: A goose is a long-necked bird with webbed feet that re-

sembles a large duck. They can be wild or domestic. The male is called a gander. The goose is a bird that shows respect for tradition, hierarchy, and authority, as demonstrated in its flight patterns and its social structure.
COMMON MEANING: a realization of your views toward bureaucracy, hierarchy, authority; insight into your ability to cooperate with others; your feelings toward community.
TRICKSTER MEANING: to startle from behind; to pinch; a silly person; to hiss. Gander also means to look at.
TRANSCENDENT MEANING: inspiration; direction.
SEE ALSO: *Snow Goose.*

Gourds

KEY WORDS: HARDENED; USEFUL; ADAPTABLE; CEREMONIAL; MUSICAL.
DESCRIPTION: Gourds are the fruit of various species of cucumber and melons that harden after they are dried. Earth people used gourds to make bowls, dippers, and rattles. As rattles, gourds are filled with pebbles, shells, beads, or beans to make a noise.
COMMON MEANING: your ability to use the gifts nature has given you; how you see your own usefulness; your musical talent; to dream of a healing, particularly of your ability to communicate.
TRICKSTER MEANING: the slang phrase "out of your gourd" means slightly crazy.
TRANSCENDENT MEANING: a ceremonial tool; the ability to make music.

Grandmother/Grandfather

KEY WORDS: NEAR ANCESTORS; ELDERS; SPIRIT FORCES; ANCIENT KNOWLEDGE.
DESCRIPTION: Your grandparents are the parents of your parents. Many Earth peoples used the terms *Grandmother* and *Grandfather* to show respect for their elders, whether or not related by blood. The Grandmothers and Grandfathers were also considered to be special spirit forces that carry much of the ancient knowledge.
COMMON MEANING: a literal dream of your own grandparents or ancestors; a dream of yourself as a grandparent; a special kinship with an elder; a possible teacher.
TRICKSTER MEANING: great mother or great father.
TRANSCENDENT MEANING: a revelation from the ancient spirit forces.
FOSTERS' TEACHING: unknown sacred ancestors.

Grandmother Moon, see Moon

Grasshoppers

KEY WORDS: EAT; SING; MATE.

DESCRIPTION: Grasshoppers are an ancient species of insect. They, along with their close relation the cricket, seem to live to eat and sing. The songs, which come from the males, are actually mating calls to the females. Both grasshoppers and crickets love to eat grasses and other plants. Grasshoppers can be annoying when they devastate a garden. If any of these insect species experience a lack of food or overpopulation, they can become locusts, turning very dark, which allows them to take in more sunlight. Then they swarm, eating everything in sight.

COMMON MEANING: the male aspect of your being that loves to express itself in song, that appreciates the feminine, and that desires to attract a woman or the feminine energy; in the locust form, a feeling of deprivation, of famine, of desolation, of earth changes.

TRICKSTER MEANING: hops in the grass.

TRANSCENDENT MEANING: a gift of song or food for your soul; a prophetic dream about times of famine; the meaning of life summed up in their actions.

Gray

KEY WORDS: EXPERIENCE; PURPOSE; MYSTERY; ANCIENT KNOWLEDGE; INTEGRATION.

DESCRIPTION: Gray is a color made by mixing black and white or other complementary colors. Steel gray is the color associated with the experience position in the Western Spirit Path of the Medicine Wheel. Gray is the color of twilight, the color of the mysterious time between full light and full darkness.

COMMON MEANING: mystery; service; perspective.

TRICKSTER MEANING: dull or dreary; gray-haired or old; murky.

TRANSCENDENT MEANING: a gift of ancient wisdom and understanding.

Great Spirit

KEY WORDS: CREATOR; GREAT MYSTERY; SOURCE OF LIFE.

DESCRIPTION: Great Spirit is a short version of the name for the Creator utilized by many Natives of the Americas. Great Mystery is also another such name, as are the tribal names for the Great Mystery in the languages of the people addressing this force. The Great Spirit is the Creator, the force that is within all things and around all things, equivalent in importance to the dominant society's God.

COMMON MEANING: understanding of your conception of what is sacred.

TRICKSTER MEANING: grate, or grating, hence annoying, spirit.

TRANSCENDENT MEANING: a direct connection with the source of all life. Such a dream is transcendent by its very essence. It is imperative to pay particular attention to whatever follows in this dream state.

• • •

Green

KEY WORDS: VERDANT; GROWTH; NEW ENERGY; REJUVENATING; RESTORING; DEEP HEALING; EARTH MOTHER; FROG CLAN; CORNPLANTING MOON; CLEANSING; RENEWAL; WISDOM.

DESCRIPTION: Green is the color associated with a number of positions of the Medicine Wheel. Forest green represents the Earth Mother; blue-green represents Frog Clan; green and yellow represent the South; white and green represent the Cornplanting Moon, the deer totem; pale green represents cleansing; dark green represents renewal; jade green represents wisdom.

Green is a predominant color in the Medicine Wheel because it is a predominant color upon the earth. Green is the color of the plant people growing and one of the colors that predominates in pictures of the earth taken from space. Often we think of this as the blue-green planet. The green comes from the forested areas of the planet, from the verdant, rich parts of the Earth Mother that are covered by trees and shrubs and undergrowth. From these areas come water, and from these areas come the clear air and oxygen that are necessary for life on the planet to continue. These green areas are threatened today because man is cutting down so much of the planet's forest.

COMMON MEANING: the rich, primal, watery parts of your own nature; the earth coming alive; yourself coming alive; new growth; new beginnings; rejuvenation.

TRICKSTER MEANING: money; envy; sick; untrained.

TRANSCENDENT MEANING: understanding your own healing abilities; foreknowledge of a healing coming to you.

Grizzly Bear

KEY WORDS: POWERFUL; PRIMITIVE; HUGE; SOLITARY; PROTECTIVE; MALIGNED BY SOME HUMANS; HEALING; CAUTIOUS; DISCRIMINATING; STRENGTH; COURAGE; SHAPE SHIFTER; MUDJEKEEWIS, SPIRIT KEEPER OF THE WEST.

DESCRIPTION: Grizzly bear is the animal associated with the West and with the Spirit Keeper of the West, Mudjekeewis. The grizzly bear is one of the larger and more powerful members of the *Ursus* family, growing sometimes to weigh more than nine hundred pounds and to stand taller than eight feet. Grizzlies often inspire fear in man. Sometimes such bears will be accused of attacking man, but it is rare that they will do so unless they are attacked first or fear for the lives of their young. Grizzlies are largely extinct in North America because of being overhunted. You only find them in national park areas and farther north.

COMMON MEANING: the mature, powerful aspect of yourself; your own strength; a wild streak; yourself as a protector; yourself offering protection.

TRICKSTER MEANING: a shade of gray; someone having gray hair; slang for particularly disgusting, as in "a grisly crime." Bear; bare.

TRANSCENDENT MEANING: a messenger telling you about your spiritual strength; a messenger indicating the ability to travel in spirit form; one who gives the gift of changing your shape.

SEE ALSO: *Brown Bear* and *Mudjekeewis, Spirit Keeper of the West.*

Growth

KEY WORDS: CHANGE; DEVELOPMENT; UNFOLDING; FLOWERING; EXPANDING; MA-

TURING; BROADEN; DEEPEN; ENRICH; HARVEST; EVOLUTION.
DESCRIPTION: To grow is to increase in size, experience, or maturity. Growth is the quality associated with the outer Spirit Path Stone of the South in the Medicine Wheel. The mineral associated with growth is fluorite; in plants, comfrey; in animals, rabbit; in colors, violet.
COMMON MEANING: change; expansion; maturation.
TRICKSTER MEANING: a protuberance somewhere in or on the body.
TRANSCENDENT MEANING: a gift of readiness that will allow new universal knowledge to come to you.

Half Moon

KEY WORDS: INCREASING UNDERSTANDING OF FEMININE, OF SHADOW; BEGINNING TO EMBRACE CHANGE AND FLOW.
DESCRIPTION: The half moon is when the moon appears as a half circle in the night sky.
COMMON MEANING: taking steps toward understanding parts of your being you might have previously feared exploring; growing understanding of the feminine; increased understanding of the shadow; embracing your own intensity.
TRICKSTER MEANING: exposing half of your posterior to the world; almost seeing what is at the bottom of situations or problems.
TRANSCENDENT MEANING: a gift of moon energy; a gift of the feminine.
SEE ALSO: *Moon, Full Moon, Dark of Moon, Crescent Moon,* and *Menstruation*

Hawk

WOLF CLAN TEACHING: seeing; clan animal for April; the "little eagle."
SEE ALSO: *Red-Tailed Hawk.*

Hawthorn

KEY WORDS: STRONG; HEALING; VULNERABILITY; HEART; CALMING.
DESCRIPTION: Hawthorn trees, the plant associated with love, the third Spirit Path position of the South, can grow to thirty feet or more in height. The tree has scalloped leaves and small, circularly petaled flowers. Both shrubs and trees have berries. Hawthorn is purported to be helpful both internally and externally. Healers in old times used it to relieve hardening of the arteries and circulation problems. It is said to promote sleep and reduce anxiety.
COMMON MEANING: your heart's true desire; your willingness to love; your ability to love.
TRICKSTER MEANING: ha!; thorn; surprise at finding a thorn.

TRANSCENDENT MEANING: a gift of loving energies, either from yourself, the universe, or another person.

Healing
KEY WORDS: CURE; MAKE WELL.
DESCRIPTION: Healing is a process by which a being recovers from a wound or an illness, whether physical, mental, emotional, or spiritual.
COMMON MEANING: literally, a gift of healing; closing up or finishing something; another chance.
TRICKSTER MEANING: heel, part of a shoe or foot; a stupid human.
TRANSCENDENT MEANING: a literal gift of healing.

Hematite
KEY WORDS: POLISH; PAINT; RECORDER; SOLID GROUNDING; STRENGTHENING; BALANCING; EXPERIENCE.
DESCRIPTION: Hematite, the mineral totem associated with experience and the first Spirit Path stone of the West, is ferric oxide, which comes in iron ore. In Greek, hematite means "bloodlike." Hematite ranges from gray to red and black. Like Herkimer diamonds, hematite is considered to be a recorder stone that can hold the memory of other times and impart these memories to humans. Hematite is also purported to be an excellent stone for grounding energies solidly on the earth plane.
COMMON MEANING: growing strength; increasing calm; better connection with the Earth Mother.
TRICKSTER MEANING: him a tight; he's tight; tight him.
TRANSCENDENT MEANING: a revelation from the collective consciousness; a gift of grounding; a good stone to ground you while dreaming.

Herkimer Diamond
KEY WORDS: PURITY; RELEASE OF NEGATIVITY; HEALING; RECORDER STONE; PAST MEMORIES; PROPHECY.
DESCRIPTION: Herkimer diamonds, the mineral associated with purity and the third Spirit Path stone of the North, are very clear quartz crystals that are only found in Herkimer County, New York State. They have a clear, sparkling beauty and need little polishing. They have been used by Earth peoples for communication, for transmitting and receiving strong forms of energy. It is said to be a recorder stone with impressions from the past and the ability to see into the future.
COMMON MEANING: understanding your past; releasing negativity; contemplating or planning for your future; healing of past memories.
TRICKSTER MEANING: her diamond.

TRANSCENDENT MEANING: understanding of past lives; help with psychic and/or prophetic abilities; seeing your own past lives.

Heron

KEY WORDS: PATIENT; AT HOME IN OR NEAR THE WATER; TRUMPETING.

DESCRIPTION: Herons are either medium or large birds that wade, have long necks, and are often mistaken for the crane, which is a larger and stockier bird. Herons are found around the globe. Most of them have a basic coat of gray feathers, with other colors around the head and/or stomach.

COMMON MEANING: a part of you comfortable with the waters of the earth, or the waters of life; a part of you ready to speak out about whatever it is you believe in.

TRICKSTER MEANING: her on; on her.

TRANSCENDENT MEANING: a gift of emotional understanding; a gift from the element of water.

WOLF CLAN TEACHING: love, or food; clan animal for July.

SEE ALSO: *Crane*.

Hops

KEY WORDS: SLEEP; RELAXING; CALMING; DREAMING.

DESCRIPTION: The hop plant is a perennial that figures prominently in commercial crops because it is one of the major ingredients used to make beer. In older times, hops in the form of tea was used for treating many conditions, foremost among them being nervousness or wakefulness. Hops is sometimes used in pillows to induce sleep, and it is one of the plants most often used in dream pillows. Consequently, hops is a good helper for your dream life.

COMMON MEANING: help with sleeping and dreaming; indication of problems with your sleeping and dreaming; increasing calmness; release of anxiety.

TRICKSTER MEANING: to hop is to jump; to jump from one thing or person to another.

TRANSCENDENT MEANING: literal help with the dream state.

Horse

KEY WORDS: FAST; FLEET; INSPIRING; POWERFUL; BALANCE; MASCULINE; HERO; OLDER BROTHER.

DESCRIPTION: The horse is a large four-legged animal with a flowing mane and tail who runs swiftly. The beauty and power of the horse have long inspired the imagination of two-leggeds. By domesticating the horse, slow and lumbering humans gained the ability to become fast moving. The horse teaches many people about the strong power of the animal kingdom. The horse has long played an important part in mythology and is sometimes represented as the creature that humans can use to ride beyond the earthly realm.

COMMON MEANING: the power of your natural being; sensuality; speed; fleetness; swiftness; the ability to work more efficiently; the sexual nature; doing battle; improving abilities.

TRICKSTER MEANING: losing your voice; something built to support something else.

TRANSCENDENT MEANING: an ally who can take you to other realms.

Horsetail

KEY WORDS: BRUSHY; SPIKY; CLEANSING; ABRASIVE.

DESCRIPTION: Horsetail, which is also known as shave grass and bottle brush, is a perennial spiky plant that most often grows in areas where water is nearby. The stems have been used for cleaning and scouring pots. A tea made from it has also been used as both an astringent and a diuretic. Horsetail contains a lot of natural silica, so it is useful in treatments of the eyes and the skin.

COMMON MEANING: an abrasive part of you; something that is irritating you.

TRICKSTER MEANING: the tail of a horse; the tale of a horse; acting like a horse's tail or in a foolish manner.

TRANSCENDENT MEANING: a gift of cleansing, physically or emotionally.

Hugging a Tree

KEY WORDS: PLAYFUL; POSITIVE; BALANCING.

DESCRIPTION: Hugging a tree is just what it sounds like, the activity of embracing a tree. This activity is fun and is also a good way for many people to increase their connection with the earth and the sacred web of life.

COMMON MEANING: the importance of your connection with nature; a more playful aspect in your nature; reconnecting with the web of life.

TRICKSTER MEANING: hugging a tall, slender person.

TRANSCENDENT MEANING: a positive step toward harmony with all life.

Hummingbird

KEY WORDS: RAPID; BEAUTIFUL; FEISTY; MUSICAL; SACRED; MYSTERY; HEALING; JOY; ENDURANCE; CLARITY.

DESCRIPTION: Hummingbird is the animal associated with clarity, the first Spirit Path position of the East. Hummingbirds are small and beautiful birds that eat both insects and nectar they obtain through thrusting their long beaks into flowers. This action helps the plants to reproduce. Hummingbirds' wings can flap ninety times per second, making a humming sound. Hummingbirds can fly forwards, backwards, up, and down, as well as hover. The iridescence of the hummingbird's wings can be thought to resemble the rainbow. The hummingbird has not only speed but also endurance. Hummingbirds and humans enjoy each other; humans often feed them sugar water, while the birds feed humans their beauty and inspiration.

COMMON MEANING: your ability to thrust your energy into something; taking negativity from a situation; making things cleaner and clearer than previously; getting to the heart of the matter.

TRICKSTER MEANING: a bird that hums.

TRANSCENDENT MEANING: a healing, particularly of an old wound or abscess; a gift of sewing up divergent elements within a person or between people; a messenger that can introduce you to other realms.

Illumination

KEY WORDS: ENLIGHTENMENT; SACRED ENERGY; CREATOR; TRUTH; DEEP UNDERSTANDING; INTUITIVE KNOWING; EASTERN SPIRIT PATH.

DESCRIPTION: The inner Spirit Path Stone of the East in the Medicine Wheel represents illumination. The mineral associated with illumination is calcite; plant, wild American ginseng; animal, firefly; color, fluorescent blue. To illuminate is to light up.

COMMON MEANING: coming into harmony with life; understanding your own creativity and the way to express it; the capacity to be radiant; the ability to communicate to others truths that you have learned.

TRICKSTER MEANING: ill you.

TRANSCENDENT MEANING: a gift of deep understanding; a step toward enlightenment.

Infancy

KEY WORDS: BIRTH; NEW BEGINNING; HEALING OF CHILDHOOD HURTS; A DREAM OF BABIES.

DESCRIPTION: Infancy is the time when you are coming from the dreamtime into the society that now exists upon the Earth Mother. It is a time of learning new skills and forgetting many truths with which you are born. In a healthy society, it is a time of love, intimacy, and care, a time that allows the being to make a gentle transition into life upon the Earth Mother.

COMMON MEANING: a new part of you being born; a dream of birth; a literal dream of yourself as an infant; a dream of your present or future children as infants.

TRICKSTER MEANING: in fancy; fancy in; fancy inn.

TRANSCENDENT MEANING: a revelation about rebirth; deep emotional understanding or healing of hurts from infancy.

Introspection

KEY WORDS: LOOK WITHIN; RETREAT; SOLITUDE; CONTEMPLATION; SYNTHESIZING; TAKING STOCK; INTEGRATION; REEVALUATION; MEDITATION; WESTERN SPIRIT PATH.

DESCRIPTION: Introspection is the middle Spirit Path Stone of the West. The mineral associated with introspection is lapis lazuli; plant, chamomile; animal, mouse; color, royal blue.

COMMON MEANING: a willingness to examine yourself; a time of reflection or reevaluation; a willingness to mature.

TRICKSTER MEANING: internal inspection, as in examining both literal and figurative parts of your inner being.

TRANSCENDENT MEANING: a gift of meditative or contemplative time or ability.

Iron

KEY WORDS: HARD; RESILIENT; CHANGING CULTURES; TECHNOLOGY; SURVIVAL; HEALTH; CENTRALITY; TEMPER; RIPE BERRIES MOON.

DESCRIPTION: Iron, the mineral totem, along with garnet, for the Ripe Berries Moon (July 23–August 22), is one of the hardest of minerals. It is the mineral that changes cultures, bringing them to the edge of the technological age because of the tools that can be made from it. Iron is also the central ion in the hemoglobin molecule upon which human blood, and therefore the human, depends. The earth's core is composed of iron.

COMMON MEANING: examination of your strength, your hardness, or your resiliency; new tools to explore; new ways of relating to your own culture and traditions; a caution that you need to balance the amount of iron in your diet.

TRICKSTER MEANING: I run; ire on.

TRANSCENDENT MEANING: increased resiliency in your ability to dream; a thorough understanding of how you need to temper your life; of how life might be tempering you.

Jade

KEY WORDS: WISDOM; REVERED; PAST LIFE; PRAYER; INTERPRETATION; TRANQUILLITY; STAMINA; SERENITY.

DESCRIPTION: Jade, the mineral totem associated with the second Spirit Path Stone of the East, wisdom, is a glassy-looking stone that generally ranges from shades of green to black. Jade has been considered a sacred stone by many people around the earth, particularly revered in the Orient. Artifacts, both tools and ornamentations, made of jade are found in many burial sites.

COMMON MEANING: the wisest part of you; the knowledge you have gained through experience; increasing courage and clarity.

TRICKSTER MEANING: a name; to have a sullied view of something, a jaded viewpoint.

TRANSCENDENT MEANING: a gift of finding your correct spiritual path; literal help with prayer and/or meditation.

Jaguar

KEY WORDS: SOLITARY; SWIFT; DEEP FEMININE.

DESCRIPTION: The jaguar, a large feline that can be tawny-colored with black spots or nearly black with black spots, is found in Central and South America. Jaguars are very powerful and need a large territory. Unlike many other felines, they like the water. They tend to be solitary animals, except when raising their young. They can roar loudly. In Central and South America the jaguar was very sacred, and representations of the jaguar are found at many archaeological sites as well as in the textiles and basketry from the Earth peoples there. The jaguar was considered to be an ally to a very strong, protective, emotional, sensual aspect of the feminine nature.

COMMON MEANING: coming into contact with the deep aspect of feminine nature just described; seeing yourself as a hunter; seeing yourself as a protector; the aggressive feminine part of your nature.

TRICKSTER MEANING: jag you are; you are on a jag, which is a drunken celebration; you are cutting something; a kind of car.

TRANSCENDENT MEANING: an ally who can help you understand that deep, feminine part of your nature that connects you with the energy both of Earth Mother and Grandmother Moon.

MEDICINE EAGLE'S TEACHING: the black jaguar symbolizes the feminine; deep, unconscious realms of the dark; the richness of the nighttime.

Jasper

KEY WORDS: TREASURED; MAGICAL; EMPOWERS IN THE SPIRITUAL REALM; BRINGS BLESSINGS; ATTRACTS EARTH ENERGY; DUCKS FLY MOON.

DESCRIPTION: Jasper, the mineral totem for people born under the Ducks Fly Moon (September 23–October 23), is a cryptocrystalline quartz that can come in many colors—brown, reddish brown, black, blue, yellow, green, and combinations that are called picture jasper. The form most directly connected with the people of the Ducks Fly Moon is the bloodstone, which is green with red spots, and is also known as heliotrope.

Heliotrope in particular, and jasper in general, have many magical properties attributed to them. Ancient peoples in many parts of the world treasured heliotrope as an amulet because they believed it had the power to give forth the heat of the sun and, placed in water, would cause the water to boil. They also believed it had the power to stop bleeding, make the owner invisible, ensure a long life, restore lost eyesight, and draw poison from snakebite. Heliotrope was used until quite recent times to stop hemorrhaging. It was also believed to give the owner the ability to turn away bad spirits. All forms of jasper are considered to give a blessing to their owner, and to both possess and attract earth energy.

COMMON MEANING: receiving a blessing; increased understanding of the earth; a possible healing; heating up of a situation or a relationship.

TRICKSTER MEANING: a person's name; chintzy, as in "get blood from a stone."

TRANSCENDENT MEANING: a direct blessing, possibly one from the earth.

Jimsonweed

KEY WORDS: NARCOTIC; DREAM INDUCER; HALLUCINOGEN.

DESCRIPTION: Jimsonweed, also known as stinkweed or *Datura stramonium*, is a member of the nightshade family and can be found growing along roadsides or on land that has been ill-used. Jimsonweed is an annual that can grow to over four feet and has white or purple flowers and a hard capsule that yields the actual datura. Datura is a narcotic that has been used as a hallucinogenic agent and also as a dream enhancer. Used incorrectly, datura can be fatal.

Datura was used by Native people in the Americas to bring on hallucinations and to heal the pain or swelling of rheumatism. Some Indian people are reported to have taken datura to diminish the pain of childbirth. It was also used to provide relief during simple operations, the cleaning of wounds, or the setting of bones.

COMMON MEANING: seeing your desire to enter more fully into the dreamtime; a readiness to have more colorful and intense dreams than in the past; a relief from pain of some sort.

TRICKSTER MEANING: Jim's son; we'd.

TRANSCENDENT MEANING: a plant ally that can help you with your actual dreaming. However, as with any hallucinogenic agent, things might not be as they seem; so it is important to be sure that the plant is there to help you rather than trick you.

Killdeer

KEY WORDS: GUARDIAN; SENTINEL; PROTECTIVE; DECEPTIVE.

DESCRIPTION: Killdeer is a common plover, a small North American wading bird. It builds its nest on the ground. Its cry sounds like *killdeer;* it can also trill and has several other sounds. It is reported that a killdeer will feign a broken wing to draw a predator away from its nest and its young. Because of this, Earth peoples respected the killdeer as a guardian and a good protector of future generations.

COMMON MEANING : a part of you that would deceive others to protect your children or the child within you; a part that is always on guard.

TRICKSTER MEANING : kill a deer; kill a dear; the famous television doctor, Dr. Kildare.

TRANSCENDENT MEANING : a guardian spirit that can protect your dreams and your work in the dream world; a sentinel between your waking life and your dream life.

Kinnikinnick, see Bearberry

Kite

KEY WORDS : GRACEFUL; PREDATORY; GRASPING.

DESCRIPTION : A kite is a small graceful bird of prey that is a member of the hawk family. Kites eat large insects, reptiles, and rodents and are generally found in the south. They seem to glide when they fly.

COMMON MEANING : a small part of you that is aggressive, has keen sight, and flies smoothly from situation to situation; a predatory part of you; a part of you that glides.

TRICKSTER MEANING : a rogue who is greedy and grasping; a child's toy that flies high in the sky; to float a financial transaction with no money to back it up, as in "kite a check."

TRANSCENDENT MEANING : the ability to see and attack your own habits or small patterns of thought that you no longer wish to have.

Lapis Lazuli

KEY WORDS : CONTEMPLATION; MEDITATION; PSYCHIC POWER; SPIRITUAL GROWTH; INTROSPECTION.

DESCRIPTION : Lapis lazuli, a blue-tinted calcite mineral, is the totem associated with the second Spirit Path position of the West, that of introspection. Lapis lazuli has been used by Earth peoples all over the world to make the holder of the stone more receptive to the voice and powers of Spirit. Its magical uses and properties were known and valued throughout recorded history in many parts of the world. Lapis has also been used in intricate work and for jewelry.

COMMON MEANING : a thorough examination of your life, particularly emphasizing your spirituality and connection with the Creator.

TRICKSTER MEANING : lap is; lazy.

TRANSCENDENT MEANING : increased receptivity to the voice of Spirit; help with reaching deeper levels of dream work; increased power in the psychic realms.

• • •

Lark

KEY WORDS: MUSICAL; SPRING; SONG.

DESCRIPTION: A lark is a small songbird best known for its very beautiful and recognizable song. The lark in various species is found worldwide; most common in this country is the meadowlark, which is brown with a white and yellow breast.

COMMON MEANING: spring fever; a time to play; music you enjoy; increased ability to sing or make music.

TRICKSTER MEANING: to go on a spree; to frolic; to make fun of; to play a prank.

TRANSCENDENT MEANING: a gift of song.

Lava Rock

KEY WORDS: MOLTEN; FLOWING; DEPTH; INTENSITY; FIRE; EARTH CONNECTION; TRANSFORMATION; THUNDERBIRD CLAN.

DESCRIPTION: Lava rock is the mineral totem for the Thunderbird Clan (Fire Clan) position in the Center Circle of the Medicine Wheel. Lava flows in molten form from a volcano, and makes its way to the surface of the earth where it cools and solidifies. Lava rock varies greatly in color and density, from small Apache tears to the stone that forms the foundation of the Hawaiian Islands.

COMMON MEANING: the fire within; intensity; the depth of your earth connection; ridding yourself of emotional or spiritual debris.

TRICKSTER MEANING: the name of a soap; rock is a form of music and dance.

TRANSCENDENT MEANING: a gift from the elemental of fire or from the deep earth; leashing or unleashing the volcano within you.

Leaf

KEY WORDS: GREEN; STRETCHING; CHANGING.

DESCRIPTION: Leaves are any of the organs that grow from stems or blades of a plant, although usually the word refers to a bladelike leaf or a petal leaf. The leaves of hardwood trees make a spectacular color change each autumn, and then fall from the tree, drawing people's attention to nature.

COMMON MEANING: something that is growing from a deep part within you; temporary turn in your life path; transformation; the beauty of nature.

TRICKSTER MEANING: the leaf of a table; a leaf of paper; to turn pages, as in "leaf through."

TRANSCENDENT MEANING: a gift of an experimental new beginning.

Leech

KEY WORDS: PERSISTENT; CLINGING; PARASITIC; BLOOD.

DESCRIPTION: The leech is a bloodsucking worm that usually lives in water or mud. Leeches were used in medicine to bleed patients as an attempt to heal them.

COMMON MEANING: something you feel is draining you; something or someone you feel is taking your vital energy; an attempted healing.

TRICKSTER MEANING: a physician; a person who clings to get what they want from someone else.

TRANSCENDENT MEANING: understanding of things that rob you of energy.

Lepidolite

KEY WORDS: ECSTASY; DEPRESSION; MALLEABLE; ASTRAL TRAVEL; CALM; TRUST.

DESCRIPTION: The mineral associated with trust, the first stone of the Southern Spirit Path, is lepidolite. This stone ranges from pink to all shades of purple. A derivative of lepidolite, the element lithium, has recently been given to people as a medication to aid with manic-depression. Lepidolite is often used in medicine and spiritual tools as well as jewelry. Lepidolite, a soft silver-white alkali, has many of the properties of quartz crystal, but unlike quartz it is purported only to be usable for the good of all concerned.

COMMON MEANING: your ability to receive and transmit the common energies of the universe.

TRICKSTER MEANING: lite; light.

TRANSCENDENT MEANING: a revelation about the powerful positive aspects of your being; a stone that can help with out-of-body travel, including the dream state; a strong grounding to the earth that can be used in out-of-body travel.

Lightning

KEY WORDS: DANGER; FEAR; POWER; EMPHASIS.

DESCRIPTION: Lightning is a way the atmosphere discharges electricity, either from one cloud to another or from a cloud to the earth. This electrical discharge produces a bright flash. Throughout the ages lightning has inspired both fear and joy in humankind. Lightning is thought to be a messenger of the gods; a director of the energy of the sun; an emphatic punctuation to a point being made by realms beyond those of the everyday.

COMMON MEANING: messages from other realms; your connection with fire; releasing tension.

TRICKSTER MEANING: to make lighter; to reduce weight; to illuminate; lightning speed.

TRANSCENDENT MEANING: a message from the thunder beings; unexpected illumination; energy bolts that can feel as if they're either helping you or testing you.

Lizard

KEY WORDS: REPTILE; LONG-LIVED; ADAPTABLE; PROTECTIVE; REGENERATIVE; FATHER SUN.

DESCRIPTION: The lizard is the animal associated with the Father Sun position in the Center Circle of the Medicine Wheel. The lizard is a member of the reptile family, and like the snake it avoids contact with humans. Approximately four thousand species of lizards inhabit the earth, ranging from the chameleon, which changes the color of its skin to blend with its surroundings, to the gecko, of which there are eight hundred species worldwide. Lizards live on earth and sometimes in water. They blend with the earth, and they love to bask in the sun. Lizards can break off their tails to escape enemies, but they can grow a replacement tail, and this replacement has no vertebrae.

COMMON MEANING: an adaptable part of you; a protective aspect of your being; a part of you that knows about the old Earth ways; a part of you that can deceive to protect; a part of you not afraid of leaving things behind if the necessity arises.

TRICKSTER MEANING: Liz (name).

TRANSCENDENT MEANING: a positive omen; a messenger; regenerative power.

Lobelia

KEY WORDS: EMETIC; DUAL; STIMULATING; RELAXING.

DESCRIPTION: Lobelia, which is also known as wild tobacco, is a genus that contains more than two hundred plants, either annuals or perennials, that belong to the bellflower family and are found worldwide. It was used as an emetic, a stimulant, and a relaxant. The plant tends to be of dual nature—a small dose stimulates, a large quantity relaxes. A small species of lobelia is frequently seen today as an ornamental plant with a very pretty blue flower.

COMMON MEANING: something you need to get rid of in your life; understanding of parts of your environment that both stimulate you and irritate you.

TRICKSTER MEANING: a lobe is a round protuberance; an ear lobe.

TRANSCENDENT MEANING: a gift of relaxation coming from letting go of unneeded ideas, situations, or people.

Loon

KEY WORDS: WILD; EERIE; INSPIRATIONAL; GREGARIOUS; VOCAL; TRANSFORMING; MAGIC; FIDELITY; GRANDMOTHER MOON.

DESCRIPTION: The loon, the animal associated with the Grandmother Moon position in the Center Circle of the Medicine Wheel, is a ducklike bird who eats fish and dives. It has an eerie song that has inspired poets for years. The loon has the ability to wail, yodel, and almost sound like it's laughing. Some Earth peoples considered the loon to be a symbol of transformation, new birth, creation, and the Great Mystery.

COMMON MEANING: the creative part of you; transformation in your life; a part of you not in synch with the society around you.

TRICKSTER MEANING: someone who is crazy; someone who is stupid; a person of low class.

TRANSCENDENT MEANING: the sound of the loon in a dream can help you travel between the different realms; a revelation about the mysteries of life; a symbol of true transformation.

Love

KEY WORDS: PLEASURE; AFFECTION; SEXUAL ENERGY; ORGASM; SENSUALITY; UNION; PARENTING; MATING; CHERISH; DEVOTION; TENDERNESS; COMPASSION; DELIGHT; JOY; ECSTASY; PASSION; TRANSCENDENCE; BLENDING; SOUTHERN SPIRIT PATH.

DESCRIPTION: Love is a word with as many meanings as there are people who say them. Love is the inner stone of the Southern Spirit Path in the Medicine Wheel. The mineral for love is the rose quartz; plant, hawthorn; animal, wolf; color, rose.

COMMON MEANING: pleasure; preparing to open yourself to one of the many forms of love, from individual, romantic, sensual, sexual, or unconditional to love of community, Creator, ideas, philosophies, or concepts; a positive sign; love being given can mean you will love yourself more; love being taken away, areas in which you need to learn to love yourself more.

TRICKSTER MEANING: as many as there are people having dreams of love.

TRANSCENDENT MEANING: a direct gift from the Creator.

Lynx

KEY WORDS: FIERCE; TERRITORIAL; INDEPENDENT; SILENT; PATIENT; SILKY.

DESCRIPTION: Lynx is a small feline by wild standards, but quite large by domestic standards. In temperament, the lynx is close to its larger brother the cougar. Lynx are territorial and like to keep to themselves. They don't like to be seen. They feed on whatever animals they can get. Lynx is a tawny feline with blackish hairs; its short tail has a black tip. Lynx rest by day, sometimes on the ground, sometimes in trees. Silent and speedy, they are one species of feline that can swim.

COMMON MEANING: a part of you that is silent, stealthy, and capable of being patient to obtain whatever it is you are hunting; a territorial part of your nature; a part of you that protects itself, personal objects, or people you consider to be your territory; a measure of independence.

TRICKSTER MEANING: links, a connection; a part of a fence; golf links.

TRANSCENDENT MEANING: understanding your attitudes toward independence and dependence; guardians that will ferociously fight to keep people from entering realms where they have not been invited; can tell you about your masculine energy, and how to make it more harmonious with the feminine.

Magpie

KEY WORDS: COMMUNICATION; SCAVENGING; SOCIABILITY.

DESCRIPTION: The magpie is a relatively large black and white bird with iridescent greenish patches and a long tail. Magpies are scavengers who are happy to partake of the garbage humans leave behind. They are noisy birds with a somewhat quarrelsome sound. There have been reports of magpies learning to say human words. Like his larger relation, the vulture or peace eagle, the magpie helps to keep the balance of nature. They are social birds.

COMMON MEANING: the social part of you; the part of you that is willing to take other people's leftovers; the part of you that has lessons in communication; to give or to learn.

TRICKSTER MEANING: Mag's pie.

TRANSCENDENT MEANING: the understanding of your limits in relation to other people.

Malachite

KEY WORDS: MALLEABLE; ORNAMENT; SENSITIVITY; COMMUNICATION; SUBTLE ENERGIES; PSYCHIC POWERS; FREEZE UP MOON.

DESCRIPTION: Malachite, the gemstone for people born under the Freeze Up Moon (October 24–November 21), is a copper carbonate, bright green in color. It has been used in jewelry and has been carved into vases and statues. Malachite is said to have particular spiritual powers and to help a person be more sensitive to spirit. It is said to increase receptivity to subtle energies and increase psychic powers.

COMMON MEANING: a period of increased psychic ability; the sensitive aspect of your nature; receptivity to Spirit.

TRICKSTER MEANING: mail or male; a kite; mail a kite or male, a kite. (See *Kite*.)

TRANSCENDENT MEANING: a gift of psychic awareness.

Manatee

KEY WORDS: HUMANLIKE; MERMAIDS; MATERNAL; SOCIAL; AFFECTIONATE.

DESCRIPTION: Manatees are large mammals shaped almost like cylinders that live in coastal waters or rivers. They have forelegs that resemble arms. The mothers hold their babies in their arms and press them to their breasts.

They are social animals who like to congregate and play together. They embrace and press their lips together. They have a wide variety of sounds. Manatees are slow and not cautious, so they have been increasingly injured by boats. Often manatees have been called mermaids or sirens, and have been thought to have a resemblance to humans.

COMMON MEANING: the nurturing parts of your nature; your desire to give and receive affection.

TRICKSTER MEANING: a golfer about to tee off.

TRANSCENDENT MEANING: a revelation about your watery beginnings, either in your mother's womb or at some other developmental point; a look at the part of you that, while human, remembers your connection to the animal kingdom and to the elemental water.

Maple Tree

KEY WORDS: BEAUTY; SWEETNESS; BALANCE.

DESCRIPTION: The maple species has about a hundred different types of trees, and they are frequently used for ornamentation. The sugar maple, if tapped for its sap, can yield up to six pounds of syrup annually. This syrup is one of the best sweeteners humans can ingest. The inner bark and leaves of the maple have been used as an astringent, and they are purported to be a tonic that also soothes the nerves.

COMMON MEANING: your sweetness.

TRICKSTER MEANING: Mabel (name); sugary sweet; sappy; may pull.

TRANSCENDENT MEANING: help with strengthening your connection to the earth and to the sky.

Masks

KEY WORDS: DIFFERENT VIEW; HIDING; EMPOWERING; DUALITY OF EXISTENCE; OTHER SELVES.

DESCRIPTION: A mask is a covering for the entire face and head or part of the face and head. A mask is used either to conceal and disguise or to allow the person wearing it to take on the energy of the being the mask represents. To work behind a mask is to utilize another power along with your own vital energy.

COMMON MEANING: a disguise; a concealment; a likeness of you; the false face you wish to project to the world; the power of another being mixing with your own.

TRICKSTER MEANING: ask.

TRANSCENDENT MEANING: a gift of different views and different powers. If you dream of a mask, it is good to make or obtain one similar to the mask in your dream, and to observe your experience utilizing it.

• • •

Maturity

KEY WORDS: EXPERIENCE; RESPECT; TEACHING; HEALING; LEADING.

DESCRIPTION: To mature is to become ripe, fully grown, or developed—perfect. In natural societies maturity was a time when a person had great responsibility and great respect. Because a mature person had the gift of experience, they were given the honor of teaching the young ones at the same time as they helped to support the elders. Maturity was a time of leadership, teaching, and healing abilities.

COMMON MEANING: to dream of what you can be when you are fully developed; to perceive your own ripeness; to get a glimpse of your perfected state.

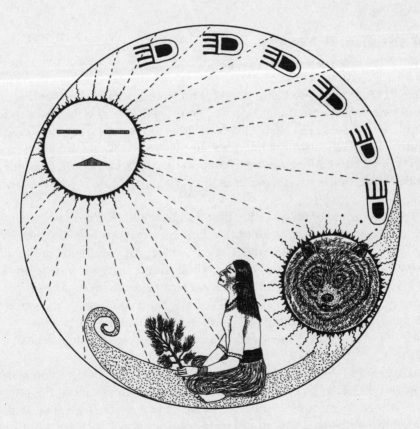

TRICKSTER MEANING: Ma, tour it.
TRANSCENDENT MEANING: a revelation of where your vision can take you.

Meadowlark, see Lark

Medicine Bundle

KEY WORDS: MEDICINE GIFTS; POWER, SYNTHESIS; INTEGRATION.
DESCRIPTION: A medicine bundle was a container usually made of leather or cloth in which a person kept their objects of power.
COMMON MEANING: a gathering together of your power; the ability to utilize the powers you have obtained; a time of synthesis and integration.
TRICKSTER MEANING: medicine, as in an allopathic prescription; bundle, to wrap together or to put on a lot of clothing.
TRANSCENDENT MEANING: the ability to utilize the powers that your life has brought to you.

Medicine Wheel

KEY WORDS: SACREDNESS; CONNECTION; CIRCLE; WHEEL; ALL OF YOUR RELATIONS; LIFE PATH; HARMONY; UNDERSTANDING.
DESCRIPTION: The Medicine Wheel is an Americanized term for the sacred wheel, the web of life. In other Earth cultures, what we refer to as Medicine Wheels are called Circles of Power, Mandalas, Sacred Circles, and Wisdom Wheels. Contained within this Sacred Circle are all the aspects of creation. All beings travel around the Medicine Wheel, beginning in the place of their birth and ending in the place of their passage from body.

For a human to fulfill his or her destiny, he should pass around the Medicine Wheel, experiencing all of the different positions as many times as is right during his or her lifetime. Not all aspects of your being are in the same position at the same time, which accounts for your having an attraction to many different animals, plants, or minerals simultaneously.
COMMON MEANING: the sacred wheel of life, the sacred circle, the web of life; your connection with all of your relations in all the kingdoms.
TRICKSTER MEANING: medicine, as in allopathic prescription; wheel, as in tire.
TRANSCENDENT MEANING: information about the place where you stand now in relation to your spiritual path. When you dream about the Medicine Wheel, try to observe where you are or where you are going on the wheel. Also observe any other beings on the wheel with you. Both of these pieces of information will help you ascertain where you are now located on the Medicine Wheel.

Menstruation

KEY WORDS: MOON TIME; BLEEDING; FLOWING; SACRED; EMOTIONAL; CLEAR CONNECTION WITH SPIRIT; THE FEMININE; THE SHADOW; DEEP UNDERSTANDING; THIN VEIL BETWEEN THE WORLDS; MOON LODGE.

DESCRIPTION: Menstruation is the time in a woman's cycle when she releases the blood she was holding in her womb for the previous part of her cycle. To many Earth peoples the time of a woman's bleeding was the time that indicated her strong connection with the energy of the earth. In many traditions this is considered to be a very sacred time for a woman, a time when she is very receptive to dreams and visions of all kinds.

COMMON MEANING: an acceptance of the totality of your femininity; indication of the readiness to explore your feminine nature, or your shadow; a literal dream of coming into menarche for girls, or coming into Moon Time for women.

TRICKSTER MEANING: men's ration.

TRANSCENDENT MEANING: a lifting of the veil between the worlds; a clear connection with Spirit; a gift of vision.

SEE ALSO: *Moon, Crescent Moon, Dark of Moon, Full Moon, Thirteenth Moon,* and *Half Moon.*

Mica

KEY WORDS: TRANSLUCENT; PAPER-THIN; HIGHER REALMS; WINDOW; SCRYING; PSYCHIC ABILITIES; CLARITY.

DESCRIPTION: Mica is the mineral totem associated with clarity, the first Spirit Path Stone of the East. Micas are translucent mineral silicates arranged in layers that allow you to shave off paper-thin sheathes. Mica is common throughout the world. Earth peoples considered mica a window to higher realms, and they also used mica as a scrying stone.

COMMON MEANING: clear knowing; intellectual reliance; lack of intuition.

TRICKSTER MEANING: a name.

TRANSCENDENT MEANING: a warning that mental clarity has limitations as well as gifts.

Milkweed

KEY WORDS: NURTURING; CARING; CLINGING; ELIMINATING.

DESCRIPTION: Milkweed, or *Asclepias syriaca,* is a family of perennial herbs with beautiful white or purplish white flowers and capsulated pods. When you pull a leaf from one of these herbs, a white liquid that resembles milk comes to the surface. Milkweed is an emetic. The plant fibers have been used to make rope.

COMMON MEANING: the part of you desiring to nurture self and others; a maternal part of your nature that can be both caring and clinging; a possibility that you are only giving because of what you wish to receive.

TRICKSTER MEANING: weeds in milk; we'd milk it; to "milk" something for all it's worth.

TRANSCENDENT MEANING: a gift of nurturance; the ability to sail into other realms of creation.

Minnow

KEY WORDS: BAIT; FOOD.

DESCRIPTION: Minnows are very small fish found in fresh water. They may belong to several different species. Humans most often use them as bait to catch larger fish. Larger fish feed on them.

COMMON MEANING: a part of you that feels tiny and vulnerable; a part of you that is afraid of being "eaten" or encompassed by another; a part of you that is food for the rest of you.

TRICKSTER MEANING: Min (name); no; Min, now; to bait someone; someone small.

TRANSCENDENT MEANING: bait offered either to help you go further in dreaming, or to trick you to go into areas for which you are not prepared.

Mint

KEY WORDS: SOOTHING; AGREEABLE; HELPFUL; TASTY.

DESCRIPTION: There are many plants known as mint. The best known are spearmint and peppermint. Mints are perennials, generally having small, purplish blossoms. Mint provides an herb tea that many people enjoy and is safe for children. It is a mild relaxer that also cleanses, strengthens, and stimulates the system.

COMMON MEANING: an agreeable, pleasant part of your nature; a part of you that enjoys helping others; a part of you that either wishes to be soothed or is capable of soothing.

TRICKSTER MEANING: candy; to print money; a place where money is coined; something that's in its original condition.

TRANSCENDENT MEANING: a gift of a common item that has value you don't initially realize; a gift of health.

Mole

KEY WORDS: VISIONLESS; SUBTERRANEAN; SHADOWY; EARTH CONNECTION; SEES BELOW THE SURFACE; KEEPER AND CARRIER OF THE SUBCONSCIOUS.

DESCRIPTION: The mole is an underground animal that has very poor vision. There are a dozen species in the United States, including one that is not only sightless but also furless. Although they are the bane of gardeners, they also help in gardens because they eat insects that would otherwise eat plants.

COMMON MEANING: the instinctive part of you that has burrowed into the Earth Mother and understands your relationship with her; an understanding of the true meaning of ecology and the natural ways for you to live a more balanced life.

TRICKSTER MEANING: a spy (as a double agent) who establishes a cover long before beginning espionage; a pigmented spot or small protuberance on the body.

TRANSCENDENT MEANING: can help you to see what would otherwise be hidden.

Monsters

KEY WORDS: LARGE; FEARFUL; UGLY; VICIOUS; SILLY.

DESCRIPTION: There are as many forms of monsters as there are people imagining or seeing them. Monsters of various kinds have been reported all over the world from the earliest times. Many of them are featured in a variety of Earth legends; others are the core of a genre of contemporary entertainment.

COMMON MEANING: that which you fear, whether real or imaginary; often fears of the mind.

TRICKSTER MEANING: mons is a part of the female genitalia; ter is slang for her; her mons, her genitals.

TRANSCENDENT MEANING: monsters often bear gifts for the dreamer. The best way to work with them is to face them and ask what it is they have to teach you or to give you. They will then either give you a gift or disappear.

Moon

KEY WORDS: SHADOW SIDE; DREAMS; VISIONS; INTUITION; PSYCHIC ABILITIES; SENSUALITY; SEXUALITY; THE FEMININE NATURE.

DESCRIPTION: To many Earth peoples the moon represents one part of the feminine nature of life. This part is the intense, emotional shadow side of the feminine. The moon was considered to be like women because she, too, had a cycle; she was often referred to as Grandmother Moon and as the leader of feminine life. The menstrual time was referred to as Moontime by many Native people. The influence of Grandmother Moon can be felt particularly strongly by a woman who is flowing. It is said that a man can best understand the energy of the menstrual cycle of a woman by exposing himself to the energy of the moon, preferably while he is abstaining from sleep.

COMMON MEANING: understanding of your psychic abilities; working with your sexuality; understanding the feminine side of your being, and/or the shadow part of you; exploration of your emotions; reconnecting with the moon and the energy of the moon.

TRICKSTER MEANING: to "moon" is to expose your posterior; getting to the bottom of a problem; moony or lovesick.

TRANSCENDENT MEANING: a vision or a dreamtime revelation. Dreams of the moon often come to women during their menstrual cycle, and these can be very powerful dreams.

SEE ALSO: *Full Moon, Half Moon, Crescent Moon, Thirteenth Moon, Dark of Moon,* and *Menstruation.*

Moonstone

KEY WORDS: CEREMONIAL; MOON CONNECTION; SACRED; REFLECTIVE; PEARLESCENT; FEMININE ENERGY; GRANDMOTHER MOON.

DESCRIPTION: Moonstone is the mineral associated with the Grandmother Moon position in the Center Circle of the Medicine Wheel. Moonstone is a form of the mineral alvite, a sodium feldspar. Moonstones can range from white to gray to bluish silver. Throughout the world moonstone has been used to heighten one's connection with the moon.

COMMON MEANING: exploring your connection with the moon emotionally and ceremonially; increased intuition; increased consciousness of the feminine.

TRICKSTER MEANING: stoning the moon; being stoned or under the influence of psychedelics with the moon or under the moon; feeling like you are under the influence of psychedelics from the energy of the moon; a rock from the moon.

TRANSCENDENT MEANING: a gift of intuition.

Moontime, Woman's, see Menstruation

Moose

KEY WORDS: DEER; LARGE; POWERFUL; STRONG; BELLOWING; WISE; ANCIENT.

DESCRIPTION: The moose is the largest member of the deer family, a very strong and speedy animal. Like the elk, the moose has the ability to be heard at great distances. His bellow, like the elk's trumpeting, will warn others of his species about any problems that might be coming toward them. Moose tend to be solitary when it's warm. When insects bother them, many submerge themselves under water to get a coat of mud that will give them some protection.

COMMON MEANING: your own strength and power; your ability to communicate clearly.

TRICKSTER MEANING: a name; a member of a fraternal organization.
TRANSCENDENT MEANING: a gift of strength; strength to continue your dream work.
WOLF CLAN TEACHING: the North, or wisdom.

Mosquito

KEY WORDS: REMINDING; DISTRACTING; NATURAL; ANNOYING; BLOOD-SEEKING; WARMTH-FINDING.

DESCRIPTION: Mosquitoes are found worldwide, with over three thousand species known to exist. The female mosquito drinks blood as part of her diet, while the male survives on plant juices. The female finds her meals by seeking out warmth. The bite of a single mosquito can be annoying; the bite of multiple mosquitoes can be quite painful. Mosquitoes also carry diseases, such as malaria, yellow fever, and encephalitis. There are Native stories that say that the mosquitoes used to help humans until humans forgot to help other parts of the web of life. From that time on, the mosquito has had a stinger to remind humans of their imbalance.

COMMON MEANING: life's little problems; minor annoyances; a conglomeration of annoyances that might be proving painful.

TRICKSTER MEANING: taking your attention from the matter at hand in your dream.

TRANSCENDENT MEANING: pay attention; you might observe something you thought was small or inconsequential but which you need to know.

Moss Agate:

KEY WORDS: HEALING STONE; LINKS HUMAN, MINERAL, PLANT KINGDOMS; CORNPLANTING MOON.

DESCRIPTION: Moss agate, the mineral totem for those born during the Cornplanting Moon (May 21–June 20), is a fibrous form of chalcedony or cryptocrystalline quartz. The "moss" is made of manganese oxide, iron, or other minerals. Most moss agate is found as translucent white quartz with green, blue, or black "moss" inside. Moss agate is purported to be a healing stone, particularly beneficial for the eyes. It also can help you to connect with both the mineral and plant kingdoms. Ancient peoples believed it had the ability to help the rain to come.

COMMON MEANING: seeing your connection with the mineral and/or plant kingdoms; receiving a healing.

TRICKSTER MEANING: Moss (name); a small, velvety plant that grows on rocks, trees, and moist ground; agate, a gate; a mossy gate or an unused gate.

TRANSCENDENT MEANING: a gift of clear vision.

• • •

Mouse

KEY WORDS: LIMITED; SMALL; FORAGING; INNOCENCE; TRUST; EVERYDAY WONDERS; INNER STRENGTH; SCRUTINY; COMPARTMENTALIZE; INTROSPECTION.

DESCRIPTION: The mouse, the animal associated with introspection and the second Spirit Path position of the West, is small and keeps within a relatively tiny territory. A mouse does not have long-range vision, but only sees what's right before its eyes. Mice, part of the rodent family (the largest family of mammals), are found throughout the world. Most mice, which are nocturnal, have long had an adversarial relationship with humans. The mouse is a forager who will eat anything it finds: food, crops, clothing, books. They also provide some service to the web of life by feeding on insects and the seeds of weeds.

COMMON MEANING: seeing that which is right in front of you; seeing the truth in a more simple way; looking within.

TRICKSTER MEANING: a timid person; slang name for a young woman; also a term of endearment; a shiner, or a bruise under the eye, usually caused by a blow.

TRANSCENDENT MEANING: mouse is a teacher who can show you both your strong and weak points, and teach you to know the obvious before you reach beyond.

Mudjekeewis, Spirit Keeper of the West

KEY WORDS: GRIZZLY BEAR; HARVEST; EXPERIENCE; INTROSPECTION; STRENGTH; COURAGE; ABILITY; MATURITY; FATHER OF THE WINDS.

DESCRIPTION: Mudjekeewis is the name Sun Bear was given for the Spirit Keeper of the West in his vision of the Medicine Wheel. The West is the time of autumn, the time of twilight, the time when humans have reached their maturity. It is a time of power, a time of responsibility, a time to care both for the children and the old ones. The element associated with Mudjekeewis is fire; the mineral is soapstone; the plant is cedar; the animal is the grizzly bear; the colors are blue and black.

COMMON MEANING: power; your time of maturity; your strengths.

TRICKSTER MEANING: mud; you; Jew; key; wuss, a person who is an impotent fool.

TRANSCENDENT MEANING: a gift from the West.

SEE ALSO: *Cardinal Directions—West*

Mud Puppy, see Salamander

Mugwort

KEY WORDS: DREAMING; PROTECTION; CALMING; HEALING; GRANDMOTHER MOON.

DESCRIPTION: Mugwort, the plant associated with the Grandmother Moon position in the Center Circle of the Medicine Wheel, is officially called *Artemisia vulgaris,* which indicates that the plant can be found almost anywhere. Mugwort has had many historical uses as tea, tonics, poultices, and as a smudge. It is used in Chinese acupuncture and is purported to help with problems in menstruation and labor pain. Mugwort is calming. It helps you to dream, and so it is important as you learn to work with your dreams. Mugwort is a major component of dream pillows, often used with roses, lavender, and chamomile. It is helpful in working with the moon energy, and is said to be a plant that grants protection.

COMMON MEANING: help with your dreaming; strengthening the feminine part of your being; work with the emotional and shadow nature.

TRICKSTER MEANING: mug, as in face; wart; a wart on the face.

TRANSCENDENT MEANING: a major gift of protection; deep understanding of the powers of Grandmother Moon.

Mullein

KEY WORDS: HELPFUL; VERSATILE; VELVETY; WOOLEN; IRRITATING; SOOTHING; CALMING; DUCKS FLY MOON.

DESCRIPTION: Mullein, the plant totem for those born under the Ducks Fly Moon (September 23–October 23), is a helpful and versatile plant that can grow five or six feet in height and is topped with a spikelike central column from which its small flowers grow—usually yellow but sometimes red, purple, or brownish red. Mullein is found throughout the United States and in many other countries of the world. The leaves can be made into a tea that soothes mucous membranes, and it is purported to help with bladder, kidney, and liver problems as well as nervous conditions. Mullein has been reported to be helpful for problems of the lungs and heart. Native people of North America smoke the leaves of the mullein and also burn them as an incense to help with lung congestion. Oil made from the mullein flowers can be used as eardrops, as well as to relieve the pain of bruises, sprains, and chapped skin.

COMMON MEANING: exploration of the smooth, soothing, velvety aspect of your personality; also exploration of the irritating, annoying, woolen part of you; extremes; vacillating between irritability and joy.

TRICKSTER MEANING: mull, or think; on; think on.

TRANSCENDENT MEANING: a gift of soothing, calming, and understanding.

Mushrooms

KEY WORDS: FOOD; MEDICINE; PSYCHEDELIC; POISON.

DESCRIPTION: Mushrooms are fungi that grow rapidly and generally have a cap. There are many varieties. Some are food. Some are medicines. Some are psychoactive. And some are deadly poison. As food, mushrooms are considered to be among the world's delicacies. As medicine, they have been used to heal a wide variety of ills, including those of the mind. As psychoactive substances, they have also been used as both healers and trance-inducers. The psilocybin mushrooms are a commonly used hallucinogenic agent.

COMMON MEANING: rapid growth; rapid growth in darkness; a delicacy or a treat; having to do with opinions of use of psychedelics; going into unfamiliar realms. A mushroom cloud is a hallmark of a nuclear explosion, so a dream of a mushroom can be prophetic about nuclear accidents or can mean extremely rapid change in yourself or a situation.

TRICKSTER MEANING: mush is a cereal or an imperative meaning "to hurry," usually given to sled dogs in Alaska; sentimentality; a room full of cereal; a rapid room; a room full of sentimentality; spreading rapidly.

TRANSCENDENT MEANING: mushrooms are allies that can help you go deeply into the dream world. They should only be used with caution even in the dreamtime, since they can easily mislead, overwhelm, or confuse the dreamer.

Necklace

KEY WORDS: GIFT; HEART; THROAT; MESSENGER; COMMUNICATION; LOVE; RELATIONSHIP.

DESCRIPTION: A necklace is an ornament that is worn around the neck. It can hang to either throat or heart level.

COMMON MEANING: working with the energy of the throat, or communication, or of the heart, of love. When in a dream it is good to note the kind of necklace and its composition, because these clues will either tell you of the areas upon which you need to work on your body or on your life, or they will tell you of the gifts that are coming to help you with that work. For example, to dream of a piece of turquoise on a thong that hung down close to your heart would mean that you are now either receiving healing power directly to your heart, or that you are prepared to give healing power to others from the energy of your heart. See the stones included in this dictionary for more specific information.

TRICKSTER MEANING: less neck; lace around the neck; necking means sensual foreplay, so it can also mean less sensuality.

TRANSCENDENT MEANING: increased understanding of love or communication.

Nettle

KEY WORDS: STINGING; HEALING; IRRITATING; NUTRITIOUS; BALANCING; ATTENTION; DISCRIMINATION; STRENGTH.

DESCRIPTION: Nettle is the plant associated with the third Spirit Path position of the West, strength. The common name for this plant, which tells a lot about it, is "stinging nettle." Nettle grows in many places, and you often come upon it most unexpectedly when you become entangled in its stems. If you have encountered nettle in this way, you know that it certainly does sting. While the plant can be irritating, it can also be a powerful healer. Nettle is very rich in vitamins and minerals, and can be delicious once cooked. It has been used to help with skin disorders and blood disorders. It is commonly used in skin and hair care products.

COMMON MEANING : areas of your life in which you are not paying enough attention; the need for centering.

TRICKSTER MEANING : to annoy; to net, or to encase.

TRANSCENDENT MEANING : a guardian plant that can help you to avoid paths not conducive to your spiritual growth. Always pay attention to nettle in your dreams.

Night Hawk

KEY WORDS : TRICKY; NOISY; DECEIVING; MAGIC; CHANGE.

DESCRIPTION : The night hawk is a gray-brown bird with slim wings and bare white circles said to resemble the full moon. The night hawk flies very high. When hunting, the male dives, then zooms sharply upward, causing the wings to make a deep whirring sound, often taken to be a growl. The night hawk has two calls, one of which almost sounds like a growl. Consequently, night hawks are sometimes mistaken for bears and other large animals. Earth peoples associated night hawk both with hunting and the moon. The growl was also associated with thunder, so the bird was said to help bring rain as well as work with the moon.

COMMON MEANING : the courageous hunter within you; knowledge about your feminine energy and moon connection; a clear passage through your own shadow; the possibility that something you fear as a large problem might be a minor irritation that makes a big noise.

TRICKSTER MEANING : to hawk is to sell.

TRANSCENDENT MEANING : an ally that can help you hunt out information that you need.

SEE ALSO : *Full Moon.*

Oak Tree

KEY WORDS : STRENGTH; ENDURANCE.

DESCRIPTION : The oak is one of the strongest and most enduring of trees upon the earth. It has been considered a sacred tree by people all across the world, throughout the ages. The seed of the oak, the acorn, is a symbol of strength and hope coming from a small beginning.

Oak trees belong to the beech family. Acorns provide a very important food source for many Native people. The wood of oak is prized, as is the bark, which is used for tanning. White oak is the most commonly used medicinal oak. Its bark acts as an astringent and antiseptic.

COMMON MEANING: your own strength and endurance; information about the parts of your life built upon a firm enough foundation that they will not be disturbed by external events.

TRICKSTER MEANING: yolk, as in egg; yoke, a heavy load to carry; joke.

TRANSCENDENT MEANING: endurance in the dreamtime; strength to reach new heights of understanding.

SEE ALSO: *Acorn*.

Obsidian

KEY WORDS: SHINY; TRANSLUCENT; DEEP EARTH ENERGY; RAZOR-SHARP; PROTECTING; GROUNDING; CUTS THROUGH; LONG SNOWS MOON.

DESCRIPTION: Obsidian, the mineral totem for the Long Snows Moon (November 22–December 21), is a volcanic glass, chemically identical to granite. It comes from volcanic magma pouring rapidly onto the earth and cooling quickly. Obsidian is usually black and translucent, although it can be found in a variety of colors. Obsidian has been used throughout the world as a tool, a mirror, jewelry, and a carving medium. It is hard and can be razor-sharp. Obsidian is said to ground people to the earth energy. It is used for scrying, or seeing the future.

COMMON MEANING: reconnecting with the earth energy; finding new tools; seeing a part of you that is razor-sharp or sharp-witted; exploring a decorative or ornamental aspect of you or your personality.

TRICKSTER MEANING: obstinate; insidious.

TRANSCENDENT MEANING: a gift of the ability to see into the future. If you see obsidian in a dream, always look closely at any images contained within it.

Ocean

HUICHOL TEACHING: white foam on the ocean means love, creation; walking on water means trying to re-create something.

SEE ALSO: *Water*

Ochre

KEY WORDS: EARTHY; DECORATIVE; CEREMONIAL; SACRED.

DESCRIPTION: Ochre is an earthy clay, usually red or yellow in color, that contains iron ore. In contemporary times, it is used to color paint. In older times, Earth people considered it to be a sacred clay and would use it for ornamentation and in ceremonies.

COMMON MEANING: seeing where you can enhance some aspect of your being.
TRICKSTER MEANING: oak, her; she is an oak; ogre.
TRANSCENDENT MEANING: a gift of ceremonial knowledge.
SEE ALSO: *Clay*

Olive

KEY WORDS: ANCIENT; DELICACY; OIL; HEALING; MATURITY; UNDERSTANDING; BEING; EXPERIENCE.
DESCRIPTION: Olive trees, the plants associated with the first Spirit Path position of the West, experience, have been on the earth for many millennia. They are medium-sized trees with fruit that is considered a delicacy. Oil from olives has been used both internally and externally, in cooking and in healing.
COMMON MEANING: an ancient part of your being; help in understanding experiences; preparation for new experiences.
TRICKSTER MEANING: oh, live!; a name; a color of skin.
TRANSCENDENT MEANING: a gift of old powers that can come to you either as outright allies or as allies that can be won if you pass a test.

Opossum

KEY WORDS: TRICKSTER; DEVIOUS; TRANSFORMATION; REBIRTH; ABILITY TO FEIGN DEATH.
DESCRIPTION: The opossum is in its own way as much of a trickster as coyote. The opossum, which likes to sleep hanging by its tail in trees, relies upon its ability to play dead as its foremost means of protection. The opossum can even mimic the musk smell of death to convince an enemy that there is no more reason to fight. The opossum is nocturnal and solitary. If it feels threatened it feigns death, which is the origin of the phrase "playing possum." It also will try and strike fear in the heart of its attacker by opening its mouth to show all of its teeth.
COMMON MEANING: transformation; rebirth; being tricked into thinking of death; the part of you that will be devious in order to protect yourself.
TRICKSTER MEANING: "playing possum," as in playing dead.
TRANSCENDENT MEANING: radical transformation of your spiritual nature; help with understanding near-death experiences.

Orange

KEY WORDS: HARVEST; GLOW; VITALITY; FREEZE UP MOON.
DESCRIPTION: Orange is the color associated with the Freeze Up Moon, Snake (October 24–November 21). Orange is a color of harvest, a color

that describes many fruits when they have reached their full development.
COMMON MEANING: what you may harvest; an indication of your stage of development; maturity.
TRICKSTER MEANING: oh, range, as in open spaces or a kitchen appliance.
TRANSCENDENT MEANING: a gift of integration.

Osprey

KEY WORDS: FISHERMAN; DIVER; WATER/SKY CONNECTOR; FAR-SEEING.
DESCRIPTION: The osprey has quite a bit in common with its larger brother, the bald eagle: a snowy head, a white breast, and a black mask. However, the osprey is a more skilled diver and fisherman, at home both in the sky and near the waters of the earth. The osprey is the only raptor that will go plunging headlong into the water. Ospreys are large, with a wingspan that can measure six feet.
COMMON MEANING: the masculine aspect of yourself that is also comfortable with emotions; the part of you willing to explore the waters within and without; the part of you willing to hunt in whatever medium you need to.
TRICKSTER MEANING: I'll pray; I'll prey.
TRANSCENDENT MEANING: clear understanding of your emotions; a gift from the water or sky beings.

Otter

KEY WORDS: SWIMMER; PLAYFUL; FAMILY-ORIENTATION; ENJOYMENT; REST AND CLEANSING MOON.
DESCRIPTION: The otter, the animal totem for those born during the Rest and Cleansing Moon (January 20–February 18), is a curious, noble, and very playful animal. They enjoy the company of other otters, and they enjoy being in the water. They have a large appetite and a warm and friendly family life.
COMMON MEANING: learning how to play; making contact with the child within; allowing your curiosity to guide you; increased sociability; increased social life.
TRICKSTER MEANING: utter, as in *say;* an exclamation of approval, meaning completely, as in "It's utterly divine!"
TRANSCENDENT MEANING: a gift of communication; newfound harmony with your inner child.

Owl

KEY WORDS: NIGHT-FLYING; SILENT; HEARS WELL; MESSENGERS; ANCIENT KNOWLEDGE; STRENGTH; FEMININE; WISDOM; PARADOX; MAGIC; MYSTERY; BRINGER OF THE DREAM.

DESCRIPTION: The animal for the second Spirit Path position of the East, that of wisdom, is the owl. This nocturnal predator flies noiselessly and has exceptional hearing, so much so that some people suggest that they hunt by sound rather than sight. The human has long considered the owl to be rich in symbolism, and like the raven, the owl is a bird of duality. Some people think of the owl as a very positive messenger; others fear the owl as a negative messenger.

These birds were often associated with witches and witchcraft by some Earth people, who believed that witches could take the form of this bird. To other ancient ones, the owl also represents the wisdom that once came from all Earth religions.

COMMON MEANING: your deep wisdom; your feminine attributes, your intuition, your vulnerability, and the strength that can come from all of these; magic, either good or bad; the mystery of night and the unknown; the mystery of silence; paradox; duality.

TRICKSTER MEANING: a person who likes to stay up at night; a person who resembles the bird.

TRANSCENDENT MEANING: understanding of the unknown; a messenger of magic or wisdom.

Parrot

KEY WORDS: RAIN; SUN; COLOR; VITALITY; FERTILITY; BEAUTY; IMITATION.

DESCRIPTION: Parrots come from Central and South America, where their feathers have been used by Native people for untold numbers of years in dress, ornamentation, and the making of sacred objects. Because of their vibrant colors, parrots were considered to be messengers of the sun, bringers of light. Many Earth people also associated them with the rain, perhaps because they came from areas in which the rain was abundant.

COMMON MEANING: exploration of your own beauty and flamboyance; understanding the part of you that seeks beauty in life.

TRICKSTER MEANING: to echo what another person has said without understanding; to imitate the actions of another person without understanding.

TRANSCENDENT MEANING: a deepening understanding of beauty in the sacred web of life.

Perch

KEY WORDS: VARIED; POWERFUL; STRONG; SPINY.

DESCRIPTION: There are many species of fish both fresh and saltwater that are called perch. They have in common powerful dorsal fins and spines that are both strong and sharp.

COMMON MEANING: an old part of you that was strong in the waters either of the earth or of your life; the ability to swim strongly through the currents of life; a part of you that protects itself through its strength and ability to scare off potential attackers.

TRICKSTER MEANING: to sit, or roost; to sit on a limb; to be on a limb; purchase.

TRANSCENDENT MEANING: perch is a messenger of the beings of the waters of the earth.

Peridot

KEY WORDS: OVERWHELMING; STRONG; REBIRTH; SPIRITUAL PURPOSE; INTEGRATOR; RENEWAL.

DESCRIPTION: Peridot is the mineral associated with renewal, the second Spirit Path Stone of the North. Peridot is a form of olivine, which is usually green or transparent yellow-green. Peridot is said to be a powerful stone, revered since ancient times. On a psychic level, peridot can sometimes be overwhelming. It is purported to bring intense clearness and to help with healing the spirit as well as the body.

COMMON MEANING: work on the psychic level; deep understanding; working with negative images of the Creator; synthesis of knowledge.

TRICKSTER MEANING: Perry (name); Dot (name).

TRANSCENDENT MEANING: a gift of integration.

Petrified Wood

KEY WORDS: PRESERVATION; DETAIL; VARIETY; MESSENGER; PERSEVERANCE; UNDERSTANDING OF THE EARTH'S CYCLE; STABILITY; LINKING; BRIDGING; TURTLE CLAN.

DESCRIPTION: Petrified wood is the mineral totem for the Turtle Clan position (the Earth Clan) in the Center Circle of the Medicine Wheel. Wood becomes petrified when its structure is altered by dramatic changes upon the earth. Petrified wood comes in many colors. It is considered to be a special stone because it honors both the plant kingdom and the mineral kingdom, since it is literally a plant that becomes a stone. Slices of petrified wood contain a variety of pictures that were sometimes considered to hold messages from the ages in which the stone was still a tree.

COMMON MEANING: exploring your relationship with plant and mineral beings; exploring ancient knowledge.

TRICKSTER MEANING: would be petrified.

TRANSCENDENT MEANING: the ability to link yourself with both the mineral and plant kingdoms.

Peyote

KEY WORDS: SACRED; PSYCHOACTIVE; CACTUS FRUIT; CLEANSING.

DESCRIPTION: Peyote is the crown of a mescal cactus that grows in the southwestern United States and in Mexico. Peyote is considered to be a very sacred plant to the Native peoples of these areas. Its use as a sacrament has now spread throughout much of the United States. Part of the spirituality of the southwestern Native people is based upon respect for this sacred plant, which they believe can take them back to paradise. Ever since they first came to the Americas, Europeans have objected to the Native people's use of peyote. This is a battle that is being fought on the legislative front even today. And it is a fight in which you can make your voice heard, to allow Native people to keep this important sacrament.

COMMON MEANING: your deep relationship to the Creator and creation; your true desires; what you need to cleanse to achieve them; the core of your creativity.

TRICKSTER MEANING: pay, oh tea.

TRANSCENDENT MEANING: peyote is an ally plant that can help you to go to the heart of life to reexperience paradise.

Pig

KEY WORDS: DEEP EARTH CONNECTION; NURTURING; SELFISHNESS; BAD MANNERS; GREEDINESS.

DESCRIPTION: A pig is a domesticated animal that has a thick, heavy body covered with bristles and a long, broad snout. Pigs are best known for the meat and hide they give to humankind. They were considered to be much more sacred creatures in some eras of Celtic mythology. While pigs have a bad reputation, they are in fact quite neat and organized animals who really enjoy their connectedness with the Earth Mother, be she wet or dry.

COMMON MEANING: a desire for a deeper earth connection; a wish to play around in the dirt; the selfish, inconsiderate, greedy part of you.

TRICKSTER MEANING: a person with bad manners, or who is messy; an overweight person; slang for a law enforcer.

TRANSCENDENT MEANING: clear understanding of how it feels in your body to be connected with the earth.

Pigeon

KEY WORDS: QUICK-FLYING; SQUAWKING; COMMON.

DESCRIPTION: The pigeon is a dove, usually gray in color, with a plump body, a small head, and the ability to fly quickly.

COMMON MEANING: a part of you that is always hungry; an aspect willing to squawk in order to achieve what it wants to.

TRICKSTER MEANING: a sucker; a victim; a term of endearment; a stool pigeon.

TRANSCENDENT MEANING: finding natural treasures in everyday life.

SEE ALSO: *Dove*

Pillbug

KEY WORDS: PROTECTIVE; ARMORED.

DESCRIPTION: Pillbug refers to any of a number of crustaceans that have flat bodies and can roll themselves into a ball when they perceive danger.

COMMON MEANING: the part of you that is armored; the part of you that is quick to protect.

TRICKSTER MEANING: bug, to tap or listen to something without authorization; bug, to annoy; pill, a common form of allopathic medication.

TRANSCENDENT MEANING: unexpected protection.

Pine

KEY WORDS: PEACE; SOOTHING; CONNECTOR.

DESCRIPTION: Pines are tall evergreen trees with multiple branches, scaly bark, and needles that usually come in twos or fives. They have egg-shaped cones. Many parts of pine trees are edible, and the needles are high in vitamin C. Pine nuts or seeds are a delicacy. Other gifts of the pine are pitch, amber, and pine oil. Being around pine has a very calming and soothing effect, and helps to alleviate guilt.

COMMON MEANING: seeing your connections with the earth and the sky; experiencing a soothing, peaceful environment.

TRICKSTER MEANING: melancholy; to suffer for someone or something.

TRANSCENDENT MEANING: understanding or an experience of the eternal now.

Pink

KEY WORDS: BEAUTY; UNCONDITIONAL LOVE; HEALING; CONNECTION WITH CREATOR; UNDEVELOPED FEMININE; CUTENESS; STRONG SUN MOON.

DESCRIPTION: Pink is the color associated with the Strong Sun Moon (Flicker). Pink is a color with dual meanings in the dominant culture. Pink is considered to be the color of young girls, of purity, of undeveloped femininity, of cuteness. Yet pink is also considered to be the color of unconditional love, the sort of love that requires a great deal of maturity.

COMMON MEANING: your undeveloped feminine nature, or your capacity for unconditional love.

TRICKSTER MEANING: in the pink, meaning in good health; pinko, someone with Communist leanings.

TRANSCENDENT MEANING: a healing of the feminine; a stronger connection with the Creator.

Pipe

KEY WORDS: SACRED; CONNECTOR; CHANNEL; WHOLENESS; PEACE; UNITY; UNDERSTANDING; PRAYER; HARMONY; ALTAR.

DESCRIPTION: The pipe was sacred to many Earth people. It is said to represent the universe. The bowl, which is made of clay or stone, represents the elemental people, also the feminine energies. The stem, which is made of wood, represents the plant kingdom and also the masculine energy. The stem is often decorated with fur, feathers, or leather, representing the animal kingdom. When the pipe is joined together by a human who uses it to pray and talk to Spirit, all of the kingdoms of the earth are brought together. The pipe was the cauldron of change, the cathedral, the Grail for many Native people.

COMMON MEANING: the most sacred part of your own being; connecting the masculine and feminine; connection with the web of life.

TRICKSTER MEANING: a channel for the passage of gas, water, and so on; pay the piper.

TRANSCENDENT MEANING: understanding your own connection with all of life; can be an indication that you are drawn to the way of the pipe.

SEE ALSO: *Pipestone*

Pipestone

KEY WORDS: MALLEABLE; EASILY CARVED; SACREDNESS; PRAYER; CEREMONY; COMMUNICATION; PEACEMAKING; TRUTH-SAYING; WABUN, SPIRIT KEEPER OF THE EAST.

DESCRIPTION: Pipestone, the mineral totem associated with Wabun, the East, is known as catlinite. It is a stone made of fine-grained clay, usually red or red with white, or gold, that can be easily carved. Native people in the Americas used pipestone to carve the pipes that were central to their religious practices. It was also used to carve fetishes and figures.

COMMON MEANING: increased understanding of your connection with life.

TRICKSTER MEANING: a channel made of stone.

TRANSCENDENT MEANING: understanding the way of the pipe.

SEE ALSO: *Pipe*

Plantain

KEY WORDS: HEALING; SOOTHING; COOLING; BIG WINDS MOON.

DESCRIPTION: Plantain, the plant totem for those born during the Big Winds Moon (February 19–March 20), is a common herb found throughout the world. The leaves are dark green, and the flowers are white. Plantain has many medicinal uses, both internal and external. Generally, it soothes and cools.

COMMON MEANING: understanding the part of you that is well connected with the earth and always ready to serve; the ability to find healing in commonplace things.

TRICKSTER MEANING: plant in, implant; in plant; a fruit similar to banana from a tropical tree.

TRANSCENDENT MEANING: a gift of relaxation; a gift of soothing.

Plants

KEY WORDS: SECOND PEOPLE; CONNECTED TO EARTH AND SKY; NOURISHING; HELPFUL; SERVING; HEALING.

DESCRIPTION: There are four different categories of plant people: the grasses, the trees, the fruits, and the flowers. Earth people considered the plants to be a little more dependent than the elementals, because the plants need the help of the elementals for their lives to continue. They need the earth in which to root, the water to feed them, the air, the winds, the sun to nourish them, and the fire in the form of heat from Father Sun to give them growth. Plants were used by Earth people for food, for medicine, sometimes for clothing and building, and often for ceremony.

COMMON MEANING: your connection with the plant people.

TRICKSTER MEANING: to set in place; to mislead; a person put in a situation for an ulterior and misleading motive.

TRANSCENDENT MEANING: a gift from the plant kingdom.

Porcupine

KEY WORDS: PROTECTION; GENTLENESS; LUMBERING; NONAGGRESSION; VALUE; VULNERABILITY; INVINCIBILITY.

DESCRIPTION: A porcupine is a small, slow-moving creature covered with an impressive array of protective quills. If you can observe a porcupine lumbering gently through the forest, you'll see this animal has no desire to hurt others. Although porcupines have thirty thousand quills, they have soft underbellies. The quills are appendages used when necessary for protection. Porcupines have to be close to a target in order to embed their quills in it. Once in, quills are hard to get out. The quills of the porcupine have been used by many Earth people to make ornaments of various kinds, as well as baskets.

COMMON MEANING: to see clearly how you protect yourself from real or perceived threats.

TRICKSTER MEANING: pork, you pine; an overweight person who is melancholy.

TRANSCENDENT MEANING: a gift of apparent invincibility; understanding of your vulnerability.

Pouch

KEY WORDS: CONTAINER; SPIRITUALITY; MEDICINE; GIFT.

DESCRIPTION: A pouch is a small container usually made of cloth or leather and worn around the neck or on the waist. It often contains power objects or practical objects that a person desires to have on a daily basis.

COMMON MEANING: a gift of understanding or spirituality coming to you. In a dream of a pouch, try to ascertain the contents, as this will help you understand what the gift is.
TRICKSTER MEANING: in slang, a fat belly is sometimes referred to as a pouch.
TRANSCENDENT MEANING: a gift of power.

Prairie Dog

KEY WORDS: VOCAL; SOCIAL; COMMUNITY.
DESCRIPTION: The prairie dog lives in towns that can often cover more than a hundred acres. The towns are divided into neighborhoods, and these are divided into family areas. Prairie dogs are extremely vocal and have up to nine calls. They are social and protect one another. If one prairie dog sounds an alarm, all the others dive for safety.

Prairie dog towns once covered a lot of the area of the great plains. When the buffalo were killed off, the prairie dogs had a population explosion and became the object of an extermination campaign that eventually led their numbers to be reduced by more than ninety percent. Now farmers realize that prairie dog towns can help to improve the range land.
COMMON MEANING: your search for community; your social nature; your ability to vocalize.
TRICKSTER MEANING: an unattractive person from the prairies; prayer dog, a dog that prays; a dog that preys; praying or preying like a dog.
TRANSCENDENT MEANING: a revelation about what community really is.

Praying Mantis

KEY WORDS: PRAYER; COMMUNICATION WITH THE CREATOR.
DESCRIPTION: Praying mantis is the name for a long, slender insect with spiny front legs that are used for grasping the other insects it eats. Between meals, the front legs are often held together as though the insect is praying.
COMMON MEANING: a part of you that makes time for communication with the Creator.
TRICKSTER MEANING: man t'is praying; man who is praying; a man who is preying.
TRANSCENDENT MEANING: a revelation about the nature of what prayer is.

Pumpkin

KEY WORDS: HARVEST; HALLOWEEN; DESSERTS.
DESCRIPTION: A pumpkin is the fruit of a specific kind of melon that is gourdlike, orange, and has an edible interior underneath the rind. It is frequently used in food, particularly in desserts or breads. In contemporary

society, pumpkins are often carved for Halloween, which is the modern equivalent of the cross-quarter festival known as All Saints' Eve.

COMMON MEANING: thanksgiving; abundance; connection to Earth religions; connection to the earth; sweet and pleasurable.

TRICKSTER MEANING: a term of endearment.

TRANSCENDENT MEANING: a deep understanding of the philosophies of the Earth religions.

Purity

KEY WORDS: WHOLESOME; PRISTINE; INNOCENT; SPONTANEOUS; RECEPTIVE; NORTHERN SPIRIT PATH.

DESCRIPTION: Purity is the inner Spirit Path Stone of the North. The mineral associated with purity is the Herkimer diamond; plant, trillium; animal, dolphin; color, white. Purity is the ability to look at the world with the eyes of a child—that is, with freshness and innocence.

COMMON MEANING: looking at the world with fresh eyes; a return to innocence; the ability to be enthusiastic; cleansing out misconceptions or sarcasm.

TRICKSTER MEANING: virginal; pour it tea, or pour the tea; purr it.

TRANSCENDENT MEANING: a gift of integrity and of balance.

Purple

KEY WORDS: CEREMONY; FLAMBOYANCE; THE PATH OF THE SPIRITUAL SEEKER; THE PATH OF THE INITIATE; THE COLOR OF THE MAGICIAN; HARVEST MOON.

DESCRIPTION: Purple is the color associated with the Harvest Moon (Brown Bear); in its violet shade, with the growth position in the Southern Spirit Path of the Medicine Wheel; and in its lavender shade, with the trust position, which follows the position of growth. Purple, violet and lavender are all colors that evoke an image of flamboyance in this culture. In older cultures, they were colors associated with serious ceremony and with a person versed in ceremonial practices.

COMMON MEANING: understanding of the importance of ceremony or magic in your life. The deeper the purple, the stronger your current connection. Lighter shades indicate an opening up to ceremony.

TRICKSTER MEANING: people; purr, as in the sound a happy cat makes; overly flowery speech or writing, as in "purple prose"; royalty.

TRANSCENDENT MEANING: a gift of magic; an initiation.

Quaking Aspen Tree

KEY WORDS: PLEASANT; MUSICAL; HARMONY; HEALING; REST AND CLEANSING MOON.

DESCRIPTION: Quaking aspen tree, the plant totem for those born during the Rest and Cleansing Moon (January 20–February 18), is a gentle, mu-

sical tree. The sound of the breeze blowing through the leaves makes them sound like tiny bells ringing. It is from this that the tree received its name of quaking or trembling aspen. Quaking aspen has been used as a tonic and a relaxing agent. It is also purported to help congestion and hay fever.
COMMON MEANING: learning to hear gentle messages; being able to perceive more subtle energies; the ability to sway gently with the winds of change.
TRICKSTER MEANING: quaking, as in shaking from fear; asp, a small poisonous snake, in.
TRANSCENDENT MEANING: a gift of music; something that can help you go deeper into the dream state.

Quartz
KEY WORDS: COMMON AMPLIFIER AND TRANSMITTER OF ENERGY.
DESCRIPTION: Quartz, the mineral totem for those born under the Earth Renewal Moon (December 22–January 19), is silicon dioxide, which is a brilliant crystalline mineral that is found in most parts of the world. Although it's most commonly colorless and transparent, when it is colored it is often considered to be a semi-precious stone. The crystallized form of quartz is most often associated with the Earth Renewal Moon. Quartz is a power stone that amplifies, transmits, and receives energy.
COMMON MEANING: understanding and amplification of power.
TRICKSTER MEANING: courts of law; court someone you love; a measurement of liquid, quart.
TRANSCENDENT MEANING: a gift of power or of earth energy.
SEE ALSO: *Crystal*

Quail
KEY WORDS: FAMILY; GAME BIRD.
DESCRIPTION: Quail is the name of several varieties of game birds found throughout the world. They are usually small plump birds that spend more of their time on the ground than in the air. In the wild, you often see a mother bird being followed by all of her babies walking single file.
COMMON MEANING: the importance of family to you; the aspect of you that can be victimized, or can give good chase to anything that is hunting you.
TRICKSTER MEANING: to lose courage.
TRANSCENDENT MEANING: deep understanding of either your family of origin or your family of choice.

Rabbit
KEY WORDS: PROLIFIC; GROWTH; CUTE; SMALL; INNOCENT; FERTILE; SUSTAINING; PLEASURE.

DESCRIPTION: Rabbit, the animal that is associated with growth and the first Spirit Path position of the South, is a rodent that burrows and has long ears, soft fur, and a short tail. The rabbit is known for its keen hearing, its speed, and its ability to reproduce. There are seventy species of rabbits found around the world. They have long provided sustenance for human beings. Some people believe that one of the reasons rabbits reproduce so quickly is because they can be the victim of almost any other animal. For this reason, people associate the rabbit with fear. If this is the case, then the rabbit proves that it is through growth that we overcome our fears.

COMMON MEANING: a period of rapid growth; examining the innocent part of your nature; examining any tendencies to be victimized.

TRICKSTER MEANING: rabid, as in having rabies, or vicious; welsh rarebit is a cheese dish served over toast; rapid.

TRANSCENDENT MEANING: an ally who can help to speed up your dream journey and bring quick growth along your spiritual path.

Raccoon

KEY WORDS: CLEAN; SURVIVING; WILY; THIEF; BANDIT; CLOWN; MISCHIEVOUS; TRICKY; MASKED; HUMOR; SURVIVAL; CLEANSING.

DESCRIPTION: Raccoon is the animal associated with cleansing, the first Spirit Path position of the North. The raccoon literally is a clean animal, one that washes off its food whenever it can find the water to do so. Raccoon is also a strong survivor. Because of his masked face, many people feel that the raccoon is a little thief, but he most often takes what others would consider to be waste. The raccoon has adapted well to living with man. Some people say the raccoon is similar to the coyote in its adaptability and its ability to trick and be mischievous. Raccoons have been known to outwit humans in many situations.

COMMON MEANING: the wily, humorous aspect of you; a part of you not afraid to take what it wants; a clean part of you; the need to put on or take off a mask.

TRICKSTER MEANING: rack coon, or rack on; on the rack, or torture; a framework; torment, as in wracked by sobs.

TRANSCENDENT MEANING: a gift of cleansing; understanding of adaptability.

Rainbow

KEY WORDS: SACRED; BLESSING; HEALING; REJUVENATING; BEAUTEOUS.

DESCRIPTION: The rainbow is an arc or circle that is composed of all the colors of the spectrum arranged in bands. The rainbow is formed by reflection of rays of light from drops of rain. It usually appears in the sky opposite the sun. The rainbow is considered to be a very sacred symbol by most people who live close to the earth, both in ancient times and today. The presence of the rainbow is often considered to be an indication of the presence of Spirit. The rainbow is considered to be a blessing to those who observe it from whatever parts of creation, and to those over whom it arcs.

COMMON MEANING: a blessing; rejuvenation; healing.

TRICKSTER MEANING: reign, or rule; beau, a gentleman friend; bow, to lower the head as a gesture of respect; the rule of a gentleman friend, or to bow to a ruler; rainbow warrior; *Rainbow Warrior*, the Greenpeace ship.

TRANSCENDENT MEANING: a direct blessing.

Rattle

KEY WORDS: SHARP; SHORT; RAPID; HEALING.

DESCRIPTION: A rattle is a percussion instrument made from a hollow tube or ball in which is placed stones or other objects that produce sharp, short notes when shaken. Rattles, like drums, have many ceremonial uses for Native people, including healing.

COMMON MEANING: a healing; a ceremony.

TRICKSTER MEANING: to confuse; to talk a lot; a noise made by a person who is dying.

TRANSCENDENT MEANING: an ability to heal; an ability to get attention; a gift of healing in the dream state.

SEE ALSO: *Drum*

Raven

KEY WORDS: OMNIVOROUS; CROAKING; WARY; GROUP-ORIENTED; BIRDS OF BALANCE; SYMBOL OF DUALITY; CONNECTED TO RAIN; CONNECTED WITH HUMANS; MAGIC; SORCERY; POWER; DUCKS FLY MOON.

DESCRIPTION: Raven, the animal totem for the Ducks Fly Moon (September 23–October 23), is an all-black bird with a wedge-shaped tail that can grow to be as large as a red hawk. Raven is a close relative to the crow, but is larger and prefers forest while crows will live anywhere. Ravens are found worldwide. They sing with a loud croak, are omnivorous and capable of riding the winds with much enjoyment. Although ravens can be aggressive, they are most often wary. They are intelligent birds, group-oriented, and defensive of their territory.

Ravens were particularly admired by Gypsy people for their loyalty to the tribe. It is said that ravens have tribal councils. Other Earth people thought of the raven as birds of balance between man and nature. Many tribes have a legend about the raven to explain why he is black. In all of these legends the raven begins as a white bird whose color is changed either because he did something wrong or tried to help man. These birds were often associated with witches and witchcraft. Raven also represents the wisdom of the old Earth religions.

COMMON MEANING: an exploration of community and relationships; able to soar skyward and plummet earthward rapidly; seeking balance; magic, sorcery, power.

TRICKSTER MEANING: rave (meaning to enthuse or babble crazily) in; rave inn; raving.

TRANSCENDENT MEANING: a gift of true balance.

SEE ALSO: *Crow.*

Red

KEY WORDS: POWER; FEARLESSNESS; ENERGY; SEXUALITY; PRIDE; STRONG WILL; CHALLENGE; THUNDERBIRD CLAN; WABUN, SPIRIT KEEPER OF THE EAST; RIPE BERRIES MOON.

DESCRIPTION: Red is the color connected with the Thunderbird Clan, the Clan of Fire. It is also associated with the East and Wabun, Spirit Keeper of the East, and with the Ripe Berries Moon (Sturgeon). Red is one of the predominant colors of fire. It is also a color that you see in your eyes after looking at the sun for a time. It is a color that is associated with warmth and promotes warmth. It is an action color, a color often associated with the life force itself in all of its aspects, including sexuality.

COMMON MEANING: warmth; activity; sexuality; leadership; excessive pride or will.

TRICKSTER MEANING: read; a Communist; an angry person; uncontrolled anger, as in "seeing red."

TRANSCENDENT MEANING: a gift from the element of fire; a warning to temper your pride or will.

Red Clover

KEY WORDS: CLEANSING; REGENERATING; HEALING; STRENGTHENING; SOOTHING; SEDATING; RENEWAL.

DESCRIPTION: Red clover is the plant associated with renewal, which is the second Spirit Path position in the North. Red clover is found in many parts of the world and is easily recognized by its beautiful red flower. It has been used for both food and medicine and is said to help regenerate any parts of the human body that have been depleted. It is a favorite plant for many of the animal beings.

COMMON MEANING: rebuilding; fixing what has become run down, either internal conditions or external circumstances.

TRICKSTER MEANING : read; clove is a spice.
TRANSCENDENT MEANING : a gift of revitalization.

Red Raspberry

KEY WORDS : SWEETNESS; BEAUTY; THORNS; CLEANSING; ASTRINGENT; HEALING; THE UTERUS; PREGNANCY; MENSTRUATION; BALANCE; RIPE BERRIES MOON.

DESCRIPTION : Red raspberry, the plant totem for people born under the Ripe Berries Moon (July 23–August 22), is a red, sweet perennial berry grown on canes that reach three to four feet or more in height. They have white flowers, thorns, and both a beautiful and delicious berry. Berries, leaves, and roots are all considered to be medicinal. The berries are cleansing and were believed to stimulate the urinary organs. The root is astringent, with some antibiotic and healing properties because of its tannic and gallic acid. The leaves are multipurpose, being reputed to help cure diarrhea, to remove cankers from mucous membranes, and to have a beneficial effect upon the uterus. A tea made from the twig has been used to help relieve colds, flu, and breathing difficulties.

COMMON MEANING : finding sweetness in your life; bringing sweetness to the life of others; preparation to cleanse out old ideas or habit patterns; awareness of the thorny aspects of your personality; increased fertility or knowledge of the feminine energy.

TRICKSTER MEANING : read; raspberry, to make a playful or contemptuous noise; to razz or tease.

TRANSCENDENT MEANING : sweetness in the dream state.

Red-Tailed Hawk

KEY WORDS : FAR-SEEING; HIGH-FLYING; MESSENGERS TO THE CREATOR; DELIBERATION AND FORESIGHT; LARGE SPIRITED HUNTERS; LIGHT AND DARK PHASES; FEARLESS; IMPATIENCE; BUDDING TREES MOON.

DESCRIPTION : The red-tailed hawk, the animal totem for those born during the Budding Trees Moon (March 21–April 19), is a magnificent flier who can create the desire to soar with the wind in many of the other beings upon the Earth Mother. The hawk is able to see far and clearly.

COMMON MEANING : realizing your own ability to soar; being able to see clearly and to see far; having keen sight and the ability to comprehend a large picture; the ability to inspire others with your beauty and grace.

TRICKSTER MEANING : red-tailed is the condition of a person who has been hit or spanked; hawk is to sell; also having read the tale of the hawk.

TRANSCENDENT MEANING : a message from the Creator; the ability to have foresight in the dream state.

• • •

Renewal

KEY WORDS : REPLENISH; REBUILD; REVITALIZE; RESTORE; NORTHERN SPIRIT PATH.

DESCRIPTION : Renewal is the middle stone of the Northern Spirit Path of the Medicine Wheel. The mineral associated with renewal is peridot; plant, red clover; animal, earthworm; color, dark green.

COMMON MEANING : help in viewing the world in a new way; new ways of thinking, or new ideas; restoration of your self-confidence or self-love; rebuilding anything that life has destroyed; beginning again or making new.

TRICKSTER MEANING : renew Al (name); renew all; all renew.

TRANSCENDENT MEANING : a gift of renewal.

River rocks

KEY WORDS : BRIDGING EARTH AND WATER; HEALING; CLEANSING; STABILIZING; CHANGE; FLOW; FROG CLAN.

DESCRIPTION : River rocks are the mineral totem for the Frog Clan (Water Clan) position in the Center Circle of the Medicine Wheel. River rocks are any kind of rocks found in a river, creek, or stream. Such rocks come in a variety of colors, weights, and shapes. They help both to channel the water and are worn away by the action of the water. They contain the energy of the earth and of the waters.

COMMON MEANING : your relationship with water; your feeling or emotional nature; blockages to your emotions.

TRICKSTER MEANING : to rock is to sway back and forth; a style of music; the river rocks, or the river dances, sings, and so on.

TRANSCENDENT MEANING : revelation about what is blocking your dreaming, or what is blocking your spiritual powers.

Roadrunner

KEY WORDS : STRONG; ENDURING; SPEED; COURAGE; MAGIC; CONFUSION ABOUT DIRECTIONS.

DESCRIPTION : The roadrunner, which has become a very popular symbol in the southwestern part of the United States, is a bird with short, rounded wings, which don't allow it to fly very high. The roadrunner likes to run, and can do so at great speed, with its head and tail seeming to be almost in line with the ground. Roadrunners live mainly in sagebrush flats in the Southwest, although some can be found in slightly higher elevations. The toes of the roadrunner are arranged almost in an X-pattern, so if you see its tracks it's hard to tell which direction the bird was running in. The roadrunner has great strength and endurance. It is also brave enough to take on rattlesnakes. Roadrunners are also purported to carry messages from one magician to another.

COMMON MEANING : increased strength and endurance; knowledge about your courage; what you are willing to stand up for and to.

TRICKSTER MEANING: one who literally runs along the road; riding on a runner, either a person running or a part of a sleigh.

TRANSCENDENT MEANING: a crossroads, a time when patience is necessary.

Robin

KEY WORDS: SPRING; HOPE; BEAUTY; SONG.

DESCRIPTION: The robin is a red or orange-breasted songbird found in many parts of the world. The robin has a beautiful song that makes humans stop whatever work they are doing to note the robin and, thus, the nature around them. The robin is often a symbol of spring and of hope.

COMMON MEANING: a new beginning; a song of beauty within or without; spring fever; increased musical talents or appreciation.

TRICKSTER MEANING: a person's name; robbing, as in theft.

TRANSCENDENT MEANING: a gift of hope.

Rose (color)

KEY WORDS: LOVE; HEALING; PASSIONS; JOY.

DESCRIPTION: Rose is the color associated with the quality of love in the Southern Spirit Path of the Medicine Wheel. Rose, a deeper shade of pink, shares many of the qualities of the lighter color, as well as the dualities. It is a color of maturing love and of passion within balance.

COMMON MEANING: romance; healing.

TRICKSTER MEANING: see *Rose (flower)*.

TRANSCENDENT MEANING: a gift of romantic love; a gift of passion, or of healing of the passions.

SEE ALSO: *Pink*.

Rose, Wild (flower):

KEY WORDS: WILD; THORNS; SCENT; PLEASURE; TRANSFORMATION; BEAUTY; HAPPINESS; STRONG SUN MOON.

DESCRIPTION: Wild rose is the plant totem for people born under the Strong Sun Moon (June 21–July 22). The wild rose is a prolific plant found in many parts of the Americas. The bush, flowers, and petals are similar to domesticated roses, but smaller. The flowers have five petals around a large yellow center and range from pale to bright pink. After the flowers disappear, the hips are formed; these are very high in natural vitamin C. Rose hips are used for colds, sore throats, and flu; rose petal tea is a slight astringent and was also used to scent less pleasant smelling herbs. It's been known to bring comfort to hay fever sufferers if used directly in the eye.

Cultivated roses generally have more petals and a smaller center than their wild relatives. They come in a variety of colors and are one of the flowers that humans prize highly.

COMMON MEANING: your wild nature; the intense part of your emotional being; what keeps you closed; what will allow you to open.

TRICKSTER MEANING: a name; lifted up, as "he rose from the chair"; in slang, can also mean an erection; to cause someone to blush; to perfume something or someone.

TRANSCENDENT MEANING: a gift of love in one form or another; changing your own feelings about love.

Rosemary

KEY WORDS: LEATHERY; OILY; HEALING; ASTRINGENT; STIMULATING; CALMING; SAVORY; CLARITY.

DESCRIPTION: Rosemary is associated with clarity, the first Spirit Path position of the East. Rosemary has slim, highly scented, slightly oily, leathery-looking leaves with blue flowers. Rosemary has been used medicinally to cure a variety of ills. It is purported to be astringent, stimulating, pain relieving, and very helpful for women experiencing female problems. Rosemary is also a popular cooking herb.

COMMON MEANING: adding spice to your life.

TRICKSTER MEANING: Mary got up; Mary with a rose; a name; rosary.

TRANSCENDENT MEANING: a gift of mental clarity.

Rose Quartz

KEY WORDS: LOVE; GOOD FOR CHILDREN; HEALS THE HEART; RELEASES COMPASSION; BALANCE; ALLEVIATES LONELINESS; UNCONDITIONAL LOVE; SELF-LOVE.

DESCRIPTION: Rose quartz is the mineral totem associated with the third Spirit Path Stone of the South, that of love. Rose quartz, like all quartz, is silicon dioxide, most often found in solid chunks or forms, not in crystalline pieces. As its name would imply, its color ranges from rose to pink. Rose quartz has been used by many Earth people to open the heart, to encourage the ability to love. It is a popular stone with children.

COMMON MEANING: your own ability to love; become more open and expansive; healing.

TRICKSTER MEANING: rose courts; Rose (name) in a court; Rose courts someone; quarts of roses.

TRANSCENDENT MEANING: the ability to transcend hurts that stem from childhood or more recent times.

SEE ALSO: *Quartz, Rose,* and *Crystal.*

Ruffed Grouse

KEY WORDS: CHANGE; SIGNALS FOUR WORLDS; DRUMMING.

DESCRIPTION: A ruffed grouse is a grouse with a ruff of feathers on each side of the neck. The grouse is a ground-dwelling, chickenlike bird that is larger than a quail. The male is a drummer, beating his tail to make the drumming sound. The male can display his tail feathers as a peacock or turkey does. Earth peoples thought that the banding pattern on the tail of the grouse symbolized the four worlds that the earth has been through since its creation.

COMMON MEANING: a change in your world; increased communication; understanding of your masculine nature.

TRICKSTER MEANING: rough; louse; rough grouch.

TRANSCENDENT MEANING: a gift of prophecy about the earth changes.

Sage

KEY WORDS: WISDOM; HEALING; STRENGTHENING; CALMING; SPICING.

DESCRIPTION: Sage is associated with the second Spirit Path position of the East, wisdom. Sage is also called *Salvia officinalis*. This is garden sage, and it is a member of the mint family. Sage has been used as both a condiment and a healer. It has been associated with the quality of wisdom for so long that the plant has become synonymous with the quality, as in "sage advice."

COMMON MEANING: your own wisdom; healing of the mind; mental strength; a change of mind.

TRICKSTER MEANING: a wise person; an abbreviation for Sagittarius.

TRANSCENDENT MEANING: revelation about your own deep wisdom.

Sagebrush

KEY WORDS: BUSHY; WILD; EARTH HEALING; SMUDGE; RELEASES NEGATIVE; TRANSFORMS; PUNGENT; STRONG; ROOTED; SHAWNODESE, SPIRIT KEEPER OF THE SOUTH.

DESCRIPTION: Sagebrush is the plant associated with the South and with Shawnodese, Spirit Keeper of the South. True sagebrush is a member, like mugwort, of the *Artemisia* genus. It is not of the *Labia* family, as are most types of culinary sage. Sagebrush is a shrub that grows wild in drier climates and desert areas. It is a plant that helps the earth by preserving some of the soil's dampness in the drier areas. Sagebrush was one of the most common smudges that Sun Bear taught people to use, along with sweet grass. It is said to have the property of allowing a person to transform negativity.

COMMON MEANING: a desire to release negative ideas, habits, or thought patterns; a release from limitations.

TRICKSTER MEANING: sage, as a wise person; brush, as an implement with which to clean or groom.

TRANSCENDENT MEANING: sagebrush in dreams offers protection from negative energies or spirits that might not be helpful to your development.

Salamander

KEY WORDS: FIRE SPIRIT; ELEMENTAL SPIRIT; MYTHOLOGICAL REPTILE; MUD PUPPY.

DESCRIPTION: The salamander is a lizardlike animal that has a tail and soft white skin; it is called a mud puppy in some parts of the United States. Salamander is also a mythological reptile that was supposed to be able to live in fire. Some Earth people refer to a spirit that lives in fire as a salamander.

COMMON MEANING: the part of you that desires the deep transformation of the fire elemental; a part of you that is comfortable with the element of fire, that enjoys the heat, the intensity of life. Sexuality, life energy; a part of you that likes the sun.

TRICKSTER MEANING: Sal (name); Amanda (name).

TRANSCENDENT MEANING: a gift from the element of fire.

Salmon

KEY WORDS: POWERFUL; DETERMINED; COURAGEOUS; STRONG; RESPECTING OF TRADITION; TRUSTING; FOLLOWING YOUR VISION.

DESCRIPTION: Salmon is the animal that represents trust, the second Spirit Path position of the South. The salmon is a very powerful swimmer who seems to be born with the knowledge that allows the species to continue. Salmon return each year to the same territory where others of their species have gone before to spawn, and then to die. Salmon will fight great odds to get back to their spawning ground. Sometimes they throw themselves over waterfalls, or even seem to fly out of the water for a period of time. They are found in several parts of the world, and provide a staple food for the people from these areas.

COMMON MEANING: your determination; searching for the truth about your own nature; lessons about your strength; knowledge of your instincts.

TRICKSTER MEANING: a color.

TRANSCENDENT MEANING: courage and strength to follow your own path, your own vision, no matter what the obstacles.

Scorpion

KEY WORDS: POWER; STING; POISON; DANGER; TRANSFORMATION.

DESCRIPTION: A scorpion is an arachnid that is found in the warmer parts of the world. The scorpion has nipping claws in front and a long jointed tail that ends in a poisonous stinger. The sting of the scorpion, while sometimes fatal, usually just makes adults sick.

COMMON MEANING: your power; power that can sting; power that can poison you or others; score beyond.

TRICKSTER MEANING: reference to the sign of Scorpio; a person who likes to be perverse.

TRANSCENDENT MEANING: a gift of power in the dream state, one that must be handled cautiously, it can sting if it is used before it is understood.

Sea Gull

KEY WORDS: OMNIPRESENT; SCAVENGING; ADAPTABLE; INDISCRIMINATE; SLOVENLY; NOISY; ANNOYING; INSPIRING; GRACE; PEACE.

DESCRIPTION: Sea gulls, birds with webbed feet and long wings, are probably one of the most omnipresent birds in the United States today. Once sea gulls mainly ate fish and what they could scavenge along the shores. Now many species have come inland to feast off the garbage left by humans. Sea gulls are noisy, scrappy, and not very discriminating in their eating patterns. However, their flight and their presence reminds many people, some who would otherwise forget, of the beauty of the Earth Mother and the freedom of the bird nations.

COMMON MEANING: a part of you that will pick up anything without discrimination; the need to set limits; the need to practice silence.

TRICKSTER MEANING: see gull, or see gal; see all.

TRANSCENDENT MEANING: a gift of inspiration and freedom.

Seal

KEY WORDS: PLAYFUL; INTELLIGENT; QUICK.

DESCRIPTION: Seals are sea mammals with a long, slender body and a doglike head. They have four webbed feet, commonly called flippers, that they can use to play and throw objects. Seals are quick carnivores, able to swim at twenty-five miles per hour, and they have a sonic device for underwater guidance. They are vocal, making a characteristic barking sound. They like to throw objects and catch them on their noses, and they seem to applaud themselves with their flippers.

COMMON MEANING: the ability to play and communicate; giving yourself approval.

TRICKSTER MEANING: a signature; a mark or approval; a guarantee; to close.

TRANSCENDENT MEANING: giving a dream your "seal" of approval; a gift of acceptance and play.

Serpentine

KEY WORDS: PROLIFIC; FOUNDATION; HEALING; SERPENT; MALLEABLE; MYSTERY; SHAWNODESE, SPIRIT KEEPER OF THE SOUTH.

DESCRIPTION: Serpentine, the mineral associated with Shawnodese and the South, is magnesium silicate. It is a stone that rests beneath much of

North America. It comes in both greasy and waxy textures, and in colors that range from olive to white and combinations of all the shades in between. Serpentine got its name both because it was thought to heal a serpent's bite and because it can resemble the skin of a serpent.

COMMON MEANING: snakes or serpents; the feminine; sexuality; something of mystery; the foundation of your feminine sexuality.

TRICKSTER MEANING: serpent in; serpent inn.

TRANSCENDENT MEANING: increased ability in prophecy; deep understanding of all the serpent means to you.

Shark

KEY WORDS: ANCIENT; SURVIVORS; PREDATORY; HUNGRY.

DESCRIPTION: Sharks are ancient sea beings magnificently suited for their own survival. They have slender, streamlined bodies, thick fleshy tails, and a large mouth on the underside of the body, filled with sharp and efficient teeth. Most sharks eat fish; larger ones, if hungry, will attack man. While sharks often inspire fear in humans, they are only aggressive when they are hungry and are particularly aggressive when in groups.

COMMON MEANING: what you fear; your power to protect yourself; a vicious part of your nature.

TRICKSTER MEANING: someone who cheats others; in slang, a person who is an expert in a field; also in slang, a warrior.

TRANSCENDENT MEANING: a dream statement of what you should be eating, or what is eating you.

Shawnodese, Spirit Keeper of the South

KEY WORDS: COYOTE; PARADOX; VULNERABILITY; THE PLACE OF THE HEART; TRUST; HUMOR; SEXUALITY.

DESCRIPTION: In Sun Bear's vision of the Medicine Wheel, Shawnodese is the name given to the Spirit Keeper of the South. The South is the direction of exploration, seeking vision, acceptance of life, mystery, rapid change, learning about nurturing, gullibility, and sensuality. In human life, this is the time of adolescence and young adulthood. In earth life, it is the time of summer and of midday. The element associated with Shawnodese is water; the mineral, serpentine; the plant, sagebrush; the animal, the coyote; the colors, yellow and green.

COMMON MEANING: understanding of your path in life; increasing acceptance of yourself as a person; learning how to nurture yourself and others; finding out about your sexual nature; exploration of life.

TRICKSTER MEANING: Shawn (name); a direct current.

TRANSCENDENT MEANING: a gift from the South.

SEE ALSO: *Cardinal Directions—South.*

Sheep

KEY WORDS: CONFORMITY; HERD; HELPLESSNESS; VULNERABILITY; SERVICE.

DESCRIPTION: Sheep, ruminant animals related to goats, have heavy woolly fleece and edible flesh. Found both wild and domesticated in many parts of the world, all kinds of sheep have been used by man both for food and clothing. Fleece provides wool, and sheepskin has been used as the raw material to make leather and parchment. Sheep are considered easy to care for because they are herd animals, which makes them vulnerable to man's direction as well as to victimization by other animals. The male sheep, the ram, often has long horns, which are associated with power. A female sheep is called a ewe. A baby sheep, a lamb, is considered to be particularly helpless and vulnerable, and has become, for many people, a symbol of peace and innocence.

COMMON MEANING: a part of you that goes along with the herd; a part of you that feels vulnerable and helpless; a part of you that wishes to serve.

TRICKSTER MEANING: a thoughtless follower; a silly person; a term used to refer to humans who are under the protection of a religion or church, a church official, or God; lamb is a term of endearment; sudden or hurried flight, as in "on the lam."

TRANSCENDENT MEANING: a revelation about your own conformity or your own vulnerability.

Shell

KEY WORDS: COVERING; SEA CONNECTION.

DESCRIPTION: A shell once provided the mollusk, a sea creature, with a home. Shells were valued by Earth people. They were used as utensils, ornaments, in ceremonies, and as a measure of value similar to money.

COMMON MEANING: your connection with the ocean; tools you have; what you value.

TRICKSTER MEANING: any hard outside covering; to bomb; to separate from the cob or ear, as in corn; to remove from a shell; shell out; shill; chill.

TRANSCENDENT MEANING: a clear understanding of your own hard, external covering.

Shields

KEY WORDS: PROTECTION; HEALING; CLAN; SOCIETY; ALLIANCES; STORYTELLING; EVENT RECORDER.

DESCRIPTION: A shield was an object that was used either for protection or for identification. Shields were used in various battles by Earth people, but they were also used to identify the clan or society from which you came, to tell of any alliances you had made, to tell your life story, or to record events that were considered noteworthy by the people. Shields were considered protectors on all levels of being, mental, emotional, spiritual as well as physical. They were considered to bring spiritual protection to a person, a home, a family, a tribe.

COMMON MEANING: a time when you feel the need for protection, or when you feel that you are giving protection to yourself or something or someone else; a desire to tell your own story; recording a journey you have taken, or embarking upon a new path.

TRICKSTER MEANING: a person who shields others; a cover; warriors in armor; panty shields.

TRANSCENDENT MEANING: a gift of protection.

Silver (color)

KEY WORDS: VALUE; MAGIC; INTUITION; MOON CONNECTION; REST AND CLEANSING MOON.

DESCRIPTION: Silver is the color associated with Grandmother Moon, as well as with the Rest and Cleansing Moon (Otter). Silver, being the color of one of the minerals most valued by society, is consequently considered a color of value. This valuing seems to extend back through the ages, where in older times silver was valued because it looked like the light of the moon, and therefore was thought to represent magic, intuition, and spiritual powers.

COMMON MEANING: moon connection; purifying your spirit; increased psychic abilities.

TRICKSTER MEANING: a mineral; a name; "Heigh ho, Silver!"; sliver.

TRANSCENDENT MEANING: a revelation about what will purify your spiritual life; increased psychic and dream abilities.

Silver (mineral)

KEY WORDS: VALUE; MALLEABILITY; MAGIC; MOON; REST AND CLEANSING MOON.

DESCRIPTION: Silver is the mineral totem for those born during the Rest and Cleansing Moon (January 20–February 18). Silver has long been a measure of value and wealth. It is also a very malleable mineral.

COMMON MEANING: adaptation; being adaptable; coming to value yourself; realizing others value you; magical abilities; moon connection.

TRICKSTER MEANING: a name; a color.

TRANSCENDENT MEANING: silver can bring energy or a message from other realms into the physical realm.

Skullcap

KEY WORDS: CALM; PEACE; SLEEP.

DESCRIPTION: Skullcap, or *Scutellaria laterifloria,* is a plant that is native to North America. Skullcap is a perennial with blue flowers. The whole plant was considered a very important medicine for nervous conditions. It was said to promote calmness and sleep while strengthening the entire system.
COMMON MEANING: your desire for calm and peace; a willingness to release excitable or irritable aspects of your nature.
TRICKSTER MEANING: a hat; a head covering worn by Jewish men; bandage; skull and crossbones.
TRANSCENDENT MEANING: peaceful sleep that will allow you to dream deeply and fully.

Skunk

KEY WORDS: REPELLING; SCENT; SIGHT; MESSENGER.
DESCRIPTION: The skunk is a black animal with white stripes and a scent gland that enables it to repel the advances of other beings by squirting a smelly liquid for up to fifteen feet. After being squirted once by skunk, most creatures, no matter how aggressive, will give a wide berth to any skunk in the future. The skunk's spray not only smells bad but burns the eyes, making its victim temporarily blind. The skunk will spray when surprised or feels a need to protect itself or its young. Skunks move slowly, preferring the night to the day. They often remain underground. The skunk, in our experience, is a messenger animal, one who observes what is happening between the different kingdoms of creation and lets the other animal beings know of any changes in a situation.
COMMON MEANING: what you do to repel other people; what you do that repels other people; your defensive tactics.
TRICKSTER MEANING: a deceitful or disreputable person; to defeat someone in a game; a "stinker."
TRANSCENDENT MEANING: skunk brings a direct message from Creator, or from the animal kingdom.

Smoke

KEY WORDS: CEREMONIAL; SACRED; CENTERING; PRAYING; PURIFYING; CLEANSING.
DESCRIPTION: Smoke is an etheric substance that comes from the transformation of plant material by fire. Smoking is a sacred ceremony to many Earth peoples, whether it is smoking tobacco in a pipe or smudging a person with the smoke from burning herbs.
COMMON MEANING: sending prayers to the Creator; being healed by obtaining greater focus, clarity, and purification.
TRICKSTER MEANING: to smoke cigarettes; to give up smoking; to smoke out or drive into the open; to season something with smoke flavoring.

TRANSCENDENT MEANING: a healing in the dreamtime; a chance to step through the crack between the worlds.

Smudging

KEY WORDS: CLEANSING; RENEWING; PURIFYING; FOCUSING; HEALING; BEGINNING CEREMONY.

DESCRIPTION: Smudging is a universally used process of clearing and focusing energy through the element of smoke. The smoke comes from a plant substance being burned. Native people often used sage, sweet grass, cedar, and tobacco in their natural form; Earth people in the Orient used crushed herbs formed into incense sticks; European people used frankincense; Central and South American people used copal.

COMMON MEANING: cleansing yourself; focusing yourself.

TRICKSTER MEANING: a spot of dirt; a small stain.

TRANSCENDENT MEANING: preparation for a dream ceremony; an indication that you need to prepare for a ceremony in your waking life.

Snake

KEY WORDS: MYSTERIOUS; COLD-BLOODED; GLIDING; FORKED TONGUE; EXQUISITE SENSITIVITY; ANCIENT POWERS; SECRETIVE; MESSENGER; LIFE-GIVING; SEXUAL; VITAL; BALANCING; TRANSFORMING; SLOW TO ANGER; FREEZE UP MOON.

DESCRIPTION: The snake, the animal totem for the Freeze Up Moon (October 24–November 21), is a limbless reptile that contains many vertebrae with loosely attached ribs, allowing the snake to loop itself around objects. Snakes also have a large row of belly scales called scutes, which overlap and allow the snake to slither and glide. The tongue of the snake enables the animal to both taste and smell. There are close to twenty-five hundred species of snakes worldwide. The snake has been on the earth since the Cretaceous period, when the dinosaurs were ready to leave.

During most of the years when man has cohabited the planet with the snake, the snake has been misunderstood, and sometimes feared. Snakes, though cold-blooded, are very adaptable to their environment, exquisitely sensitive to touch and vibration. They can change their coloration to blend with their environment, and they can hiss.

COMMON MEANING: exploring your vital and sexual energies; exploring the feminine aspects of your being; an understanding of your connection with the earth; a dream of increasing balance.

TRICKSTER MEANING: a double-crossing person; a way of moving; Eve and the apple.

TRANSCENDENT MEANING: a revelation of transformation; a direct message from Spirit.

FOSTERS' TEACHING: sexuality, especially female sexuality.

Snipe

KEY WORDS: WADING; LONG-BILLED; SERVING.

DESCRIPTION: A snipe is a wading bird with a long, slender bill and no feathers on his lower legs. Snipes live by streams or marshes and use their beaks to dig for insect food. By digging in the soil they help to aerate it, and they also get rid of some worms that could otherwise be harmful. The migration behavior of the snipe shows a balance between individualism and service to the flock. Snipes spend the day apart feeding, but come together at dusk to continue their migration.

COMMON MEANING: your instinct for digging under the surface; what you are hiding or finding.

TRICKSTER MEANING: to snipe is to shoot from a hidden position, either literally or figuratively; a simpleton; guttersnipe, a person of the lowest moral or economic station.

TRANSCENDENT MEANING: a gift of unexpected knowledge.

WOLF CLAN TEACHING: service; clan animal for August.

Snow Goose

KEY WORDS: TRADITION; AUTHORITY; COOPERATION; CEREMONY; EARTH RENEWAL MOON.

DESCRIPTION: The snow goose is the animal totem for people born during the Earth Renewal Moon (December 22–January 19). The snow goose is a traveler who goes from the far north to the far south each year, bringing knowledge of those two areas of the world with them. The snow goose is able to survive in part because of his ability to cooperate with the rest of the flock, and because of his respect for authority and tradition.

COMMON MEANING: an understanding of how you view authority, community, and tradition; an opening to the wilder aspect of your imagination or creativity.

TRICKSTER MEANING: to pinch the behind; snow, or no; no goosing.

TRANSCENDENT MEANING: an understanding of the real purpose and meaning of ceremony.

SEE ALSO: *Goose*

Snowy Owl

KEY WORDS: MAGIC; ALLY; LIGHT; GOOD.

DESCRIPTION: Snowy owl is a large owl with white feathers and yellow eyes that flies during the day. They are usually silent. Many contemporary women are drawn to the snowy owl as a symbol of feminine magic.

COMMON MEANING: good magic; the part of you that can work with the supernatural while still keeping within the light of the Creator.

TRICKSTER MEANING: snowy howl; a white-haired intellectual with glasses.

TRANSCENDENT MEANING : a gift of good feminine magic.
WOLF CLAN TEACHING : the North, or wisdom.
SEE ALSO : *Owl*

Soapstone

KEY WORDS : SOAPY; CARVED; CLEANSING; ENHANCING; STRENGTHENING; MUDJE-KEEWIS, SPIRIT KEEPER OF THE WEST.

DESCRIPTION : Soapstone is the mineral associated with Mudjekeewis, the Spirit Keeper of the West. Soapstone is known as steatite and is composed largely of talc. The stone is soft but can feel greasy, like soap. The stone varies from pale green to black or white and is sometimes found with a reddish tint. It is very malleable and has been used for bath products, powders, and for carving.

COMMON MEANING : cleansing that strengthens you on all levels of being; helping you find the root cause that allows for true cleansing, particularly in relationship to disease.

TRICKSTER MEANING : a stone that seems soapy.

TRANSCENDENT MEANING : understanding of cleansing; a gift of power and maturity that only comes when cleansing of childish ways is completed.

Sodalite

KEY WORDS : CLEANSING; TRUTH; PROBLEM-SOLVING.

DESCRIPTION : The mineral associated with cleansing and the first Spirit Path Stone of the North, sodalite, is sodium aluminum silicate with chlorine. Sodalite comes in color variations with blue, white, gray, translucent, and green. It is named for its sodium content.

COMMON MEANING : cleansing on all levels of being.

TRICKSTER MEANING : a light soda, or a diet soda; so delight!

TRANSCENDENT MEANING : a gift of cleansing.

Songbirds

KEY WORDS : JOY; FREEDOM; ECSTASY; HARMONY.

DESCRIPTION : There are many varieties of songbirds that grace the Earth Mother both with their beauty of plumage and their beauty of song. These mostly small birds have a large job in the world. They help flowers grow, they help keep insect populations under control, they provide food for larger birds and small four-leggeds, and they are often most responsible for calling human interest back to nature. Songbirds are found in the city as well as the country. Many people who otherwise seem not to notice nature put out feeders to attract these feathered ones to come and sing for them, bringing their message of oneness with nature and hope for life.

Many Native people consider small songbirds to be messengers. If you encounter a small bird in the woods, you should follow it, as it might be leading you in the direction you should go. If you encounter a songbird in your dream, you should also follow it, as the bird might be taking you on your proper path.

COMMON MEANING: beauty; joy; nature.

TRICKSTER MEANING: a woman singer.

TRANSCENDENT MEANING: in dreams, messages can be encoded within the song of the bird, so listen closely. Also observe the color of the songbird.

Sparrow

KEY WORDS: FAMILIAR; MUSICAL; LINK.

DESCRIPTION: The sparrow is a weaver finch that was introduced into the United States from Europe. They took well to this country and are now found in cities and countryside all across the United States.

COMMON MEANING: beauty in the familiar.

TRICKSTER MEANING: spa; row, as in to row a boat, to plant a row, or to fight; spar as in verbal sparring.

TRANSCENDENT MEANING: a gift of spiritual power in something that seems common.

Sparrow Hawk

KEY WORDS: ENLARGING VISION; INCREASING CLARITY.

DESCRIPTION: The sparrow hawk, little brother to the larger hawks, is also called the American kestrel. These birds are not as good at hunting as their larger relations. They subsist on grasshoppers, mice, and sometimes birds. While the sparrow hawk cannot fly as high as the larger hawks, he does have keen sight.

COMMON MEANING: enlarging your vision; moving toward a place of greater clarity.

TRICKSTER MEANING: hawk or sell a sparrow; see *Sparrow*.

TRANSCENDENT MEANING: a deep understanding of your vision; a deep understanding of your place in the web of life.

SEE ALSO: *Sparrow* and *Hawk*.

Spider

KEY WORDS: WEAVING; WEB; ANCIENT; INTERCONNECTED; FEMININE; PROTECTOR; DUALITY; UNITY.

DESCRIPTION: The spider's body is made up of two almost circular segments, and it has eight legs. Spiders weave webs of durability and complexity. In many Native legends, Spider Woman is associated with the First Woman, the Spirit Woman, who weaves all of creation. Spider Woman has the ability to create. She also has the ability to destroy. Through understanding this duality, one can come to understand the unity of all creation that is embodied in the endless web that Spider weaves.

COMMON MEANING: the enduring part of your nature; the enduring aspects of the circle of life; your feminine nature, your creativity, your intuition; getting your attention, as when a spider drops from above.

TRICKSTER MEANING: spied her, or saw her; despite her.

TRANSCENDENT MEANING: a clear revelation about your place in the web of life; an indication of how you should be weaving yourself with the life web at this particular point of your life.

Spring

KEY WORDS: NEW GROWTH; ENTHUSIASM; ENERGY; NEW BEGINNINGS; THE EAST.

DESCRIPTION: Spring is the time of year when the energy of the earth turns from the internal to the external. It is the time of new growth, new beginnings. It is the time when everything seems to come alive again. It is a time that brings a lot of energy, enthusiasm, and joy.

COMMON MEANING: a new beginning; joy, enthusiasm; renewed energy and hope.

TRICKSTER MEANING: a person's name; to jump out; a source of water; let someone out of captivity; sparing.

TRANSCENDENT MEANING: the opportunity to take a new spiritual path; a gift of renewed energy and enthusiasm.

SEE ALSO: *Cardinal Directions—East* and *Wabun.*

Squash

KEY WORDS: FRUIT; HARVEST; THREE SISTERS.

DESCRIPTION: Squash is the fruit of a viny member of the gourd family. There are many varieties of squash. Some resemble pumpkins; others, like zucchini, are more similar to a cucumber. To Native peoples the squash was one of the three sister plants, along with corn and beans. These three provided a major part of the food supply, as well as a nutritionally balanced diet.

COMMON MEANING: thanksgiving, or harvest; the end point of a project; something that can grow prolifically.

TRICKSTER MEANING: to crush or silence or suppress; a game; Sasquatch.

TRANSCENDENT MEANING: understanding of what is nurturing you.

SEE ALSO: *Corn* and *Beans.*

Squirrel

KEY WORDS: BUSY; PREPARED; CHATTERING; ADAPTABLE; ACROBATIC.

DESCRIPTION: Squirrel is a familiar figure to people in most parts of the country. Squirrels are adaptable, acrobatic rodents who easily climb the highest trees, scurry along the road, over roofs, down drain pipes, and back into the trees again. The squirrel always seems to be busy, and is often chattering. Squirrels weigh just over a pound. Their long tails, which can reach almost ten inches in length, are said to protect them if they fall out of trees. The squirrel prepares during good times for lean times that might follow, and thus can teach the gift of preparation. Most squirrels are active all day long, obtaining and burying food. While the squirrel does not remember where it buried acorns or nuts, it can smell them, even when thick layers of snow cover the ground.

COMMON MEANING: the chattering part of your mental process; the mind vampire that is difficult to quiet; the busy aspect of your nature; an ungrounded part of your being.

TRICKSTER MEANING: to hide or to hoard something; squirrelly (odd, crazy).

TRANSCENDENT MEANING: a clear view of the strength, intensity, and busyness of your mind; can be a warning to prepare for problematic times that might follow.

Staff

KEY WORDS: POWER; GUIDE; PATH; SUPPORT.

DESCRIPTION: A staff is a stick or pole, either carved or natural, usually used for support in walking. Sometimes staffs are also used as weapons or as symbols of authority.

COMMON MEANING: what supports you; what or who you support; the path that you are taking, or the path that you should take.

TRICKSTER MEANING: a group of people who help the boss to accomplish her or his aims; a support; staph infection.

TRANSCENDENT MEANING: a gift that will support you in your dreamtime work.

Stars

KEY WORDS: DISTANT SUNS; POINTS OF LIGHT; WARMTH; GUIDANCE; A MARKER.

DESCRIPTION: Stars are distant suns that we see during the night as small points of light. The stars in the night sky both gave direction to ancient cultures and told much about the people who lived in them. Different groupings of stars in the sky were given names and associated with stories that made these incomprehensible points of light understandable to humans here on earth. Some Native people speak of the stars as the Star Nations. Sun Bear would often see stars in his visions as points of light that would enliven the earth during this time of earth changes.

COMMON MEANING: your relationship to the infinite mystery of the universe; turning your vision beyond the mundane. In dreams of stars, always note any shapes, constellations, or other points of reference, as these will help you understand your dream.

TRICKSTER MEANING: a person who is famous for his or her performance, usually as a musician or actor; something influencing your destiny, as in astrology; brilliant or outstanding; a shape; a name.

TRANSCENDENT MEANING: guidance in the overworld; a gift from the Star Nations.

Starlings

KEY WORDS: GREGARIOUS; GARRULOUS; INVADERS.

DESCRIPTION: Starlings are brown to black birds with somewhat iridescent plumage; they originally came from Europe and were introduced into the United States. In some parts of the country, they have transplanted so well that they've become flocks of invaders who push out all the other birds who once were native to the area. Flocks of starlings are often seen flying overhead in cities, making their not particularly musical noise and causing problems for humans.

COMMON MEANING: someone invading your territory; you're invading someone else's territory.

TRICKSTER MEANING: Star (name); staring; sterling.

TRANSCENDENT MEANING: knowledge of the part of you willing to fight for whatever it is you desire; the part of you willing to protect yourself from invasion by others.

Stinging Insects

KEY WORDS: ATTENTION; ANNOYANCE; PAIN.

DESCRIPTION: A stinging insect is one that is capable of inflicting pain on humans or other animals by either inserting its stinger and releasing some venom, or by biting. People tend to say they have been stung even by insects that actually bite, like flies.

COMMON MEANING: something trying to get your attention; something causing you pain. It's very important to note all the circumstances that preceded your being stung. There is probably something in that part of the dream that is important but has escaped your attention.

TRICKSTER MEANING: insects are contemptible people; to sting is to take advantage of; a badge of cowardice.

TRANSCENDENT MEANING: Spirit trying to wake you up to see clearly what is around you.

Strength

KEY WORDS: STAMINA; STEADINESS; POWER; ENDURANCE; DISCIPLINE; COURAGE; DETERMINATION; CONCENTRATION; BALANCE; CONVICTION; WESTERN SPIRIT PATH.

DESCRIPTION: Strength is the inner Spirit Path Stone of the West in the Medicine Wheel. The mineral associated with strength is amber; plant, nettle; animal, ant; color, golden yellow. To dream of strength tells you that you have learned the lessons of endurance, steadfastness, and courage. Strength is the quality of power or vigor that can resist stress. This quality can be on the physical, mental, emotional, or spiritual level.

COMMON MEANING: what your strengths are on all levels of your being; knowledge about your true abilities.

TRICKSTER MEANING: inability to surrender; superiority masking feelings of inferiority.

TRANSCENDENT MEANING: a gift of power, stamina, endurance.

Sturgeon

KEY WORDS: REGAL; ANCIENT; ARMORED; DEPTH; STRENGTH; DOMINANT; SEXUAL ENERGIES; RIPE BERRIES MOON.

DESCRIPTION: Sturgeon is the animal totem for people born during the Ripe Berries Moon (July 23–August 22). The sturgeon is a primitive fish that has probably existed since the time of the dinosaurs. The sturgeon comes in a variety of sizes and can reach twelve-foot lengths and three-hundred-pound weights. The fish has a row of bony plates and a long snout. It lives in the mud bottoms off coasts, and doesn't reach sexual maturity until about twenty years of age. The sturgeon is considered the king of the fish. The roe of the sturgeon is called caviar.

COMMON MEANING: the primitive parts of your being; that which armors you; a time of life to explore your own leadership abilities; a time when you will be thought of as regal and sexual.

TRICKSTER MEANING: a surgeon.

TRANSCENDENT MEANING: the ability to go to the depths of the underworld in your dreaming.

Summer

KEY WORDS: RAPID GROWTH; FRUITION; FERTILITY.

DESCRIPTION: Summer is the time when the earth and all her children undergo rapid growth. It is the time when the flowers of spring begin to become the fruits of summer, a time when things go from a tentative to a definite form. It is a fecund, fertile time of birth and growth.

COMMON MEANING: rapid growth; a fertile part of your life; the ability to reach your goals.

TRICKSTER MEANING: sum her; or her sum, meaning her total, her bill.

TRANSCENDENT MEANING: a revelation about the results of the spiritual work you have done.

SEE ALSO: *Cardinal Directions—South* and *Shawnodese.*

Sun

KEY WORDS: THE CENTER OF A SOLAR SYSTEM; THE MASCULINE; HEAT; WARMTH; LIGHT.

DESCRIPTION: A sun is an incandescent heavenly body around which planets turn. The sun furnishes planets with energy, light, and heat and is necessary for their continuation. To Earth peoples the sun was considered the father of life, as the earth was the mother of life. Both were needed for life to continue. It was the sun god of the Earth religions that became the son of god in many modern religions.

COMMON MEANING: seeing what is central to your life; understanding what gives you energy; knowledge about the masculine.

TRICKSTER MEANING: son; Sun Bear.

TRANSCENDENT MEANING: traveling in your dream state to the source of energy for your life.

HUICHOL TEACHING: a dream of going to the sun means taking light into your life to be happy.

Sunflower

KEY WORDS: TALL; DEEP-ROOTED; NUTRITIOUS; HEALING; BRIGHT; FATHER SUN.

DESCRIPTION: The Father Sun position in the Center Circle of the Medicine Wheel is associated with the sunflower, the common plant that bears the name of the star most important to life on Earth Mother. With its brilliant yellow flower, the sunflower resembles the star we know as Father Sun and grows tall reaching toward his light. The seed of the plant provides vitamins and nutrients. Oil made from the seeds has medicinal as well as culinary purposes. It also brings softness and shine to skin and hair.

COMMON MEANING: your connection with the sun; your connection with your masculine energy; a willingness to redefine what a man is; something that is bringing increasing softness to your masculine nature; a flowery part of you that shines.

TRICKSTER MEANING: a flower of the sun; a flower from the sun; yellow flour.

TRANSCENDENT MEANING: an examination of the volatile part of your nature that yearns for communion with the creative force; a gift of understanding from Father Sun.

Swan

KEY WORDS: GRACE; BEAUTY; TRANSFORMATION; IMAGINATION; TRAVEL BETWEEN THE REALMS; LOVE.

DESCRIPTION: The swan is a web-footed water bird that has a plump body, a long neck, and short legs. All except two swan species known in the world have white plumage as adults. Swans are graceful swimmers and strong fliers who float through the symbology of many peoples around the globe. Some believe that a swan boat takes you from this earth into the next realm. Others believe that the swan, and not just the butterfly, has the medicine of transformation. Looking at the beauty of the swan evokes both a sense of beauty and an appreciation of mystery in many of the earth's two-legged children. There are several common legends about the swan. One says that it sings a beautiful song just before dying; the other tells about the ugly duckling who turns into a swan.

COMMON MEANING: surrendering to beauty; transformation and rebirth.

TRICKSTER MEANING: a swan song is an exit; a person who sings or composes exceptional poetry.

TRANSCENDENT MEANING: the swan is a messenger between different realms of reality, ergo a wonderful ally to help take you farther into the dreamtime.

Sweet Flag

KEY WORDS: CALMING; STRENGTHENS THE VOICE; IMPROVES DIGESTION.

DESCRIPTION: Sweet flag, or calamus, is a perennial that grows near water. It has been used medicinally throughout the world, largely to cure heartburn. Native people of the United States are purported to have chewed calamus to cure a hoarse or sore throat. It was also used by singers to allow them to sing more strongly and for a longer period of time.

COMMON MEANING: allowing your true voice to come forth; an unwillingness to choke back anything you know to be the truth; a need to relax in order to improve your digestion.

TRICKSTER MEANING: a flag on which you are sweet; a flag of which you are proud.

TRANSCENDENT MEANING: a strong gift of song.

Sweet Grass

KEY WORDS: RESPECT; EARTH CONNECTION; WISDOM; PERENNIAL; REEDLIKE; LONG; SWEET; GIVEAWAY; PREPARATION; UNDERSTANDING; HAIR OF THE EARTH MOTHER; WABOOSE, SPIRIT KEEPER OF THE NORTH.

DESCRIPTION: Sweet grass is the plant associated with the Northern position in the Medicine Wheel, the position named for Waboose, Spirit Keeper of the North. Sweet grass, or *Hierochloe odorata,* is a perennial that grows near wet areas. It used to be found all over the North American continent, but much of it was destroyed during European settlement of the Americas. For a period of time it mainly came from Canada, but now many people are trying to reinstate this perennial in various parts of the country. Sweet grass was usually braided before being picked, and was referred to as "the hair of the Mother." It was most often used as a smudge, and it was said that the sweet smell of the plant burning would draw good energies, good spirits, to a ceremony.

COMMON MEANING: the state of your relationship with the Earth Mother; the level of your respect for the earth.

TRICKSTER MEANING: a grass that tastes or smells sweet; in slang, marijuana that is good.

TRANSCENDENT MEANING: drawing good spirits and energies to you in the dream state.

Tarantula

KEY WORDS: DANCER; PET; SOMEWHAT POISONOUS.

DESCRIPTION: A tarantula is a large, hairy spider whose bite is poisonous although not fatal. They are found in the southern part of Europe, the United States, and in Central and South America. Some people today keep tarantulas as pets.

COMMON MEANING: a frightening part of you; a part of you that is poisonous or poisoned; an aspect of you that, while powerful, is dependent on someone else for nurturance and praise.

TRICKSTER MEANING: a dance; a town in Italy.

TRANSCENDENT MEANING: an ally to help you move through your fears.

Teenager, see Adolescence.

Tepee

KEY WORDS: HOME; EARTH ENERGY; NATURAL; PHYSICAL WORLD; PART OF EARTH MOTHER.

DESCRIPTION: The tepee is used in the earth stone form of the Medicine Wheel. It appears in the northern quadrant, and it represents your home and your relationship with all that is physical in the world. The tepee was a form of home used by the plains and Western Native people of the United States. In the old days tepees were made of hide, which was stretched in a conical shape over lodge poles. Today most tepees are made of canvas. The tepee provides a home that gives you a way of living very close to the earth.

COMMON MEANING: your attitude toward your home; your attitude toward the earth; your connection with your home life.

TRICKSTER MEANING: in slang, t.p. is an abbreviation for toilet paper, or something that cleans your waste away.

TRANSCENDENT MEANING: your attitude toward the physical world. The appearance of a tepee can also bring you back home into your body in situations where you have wandered too far away in your dream work.

Tern

KEY WORDS : GRACE; OCEAN; DIVING.

DESCRIPTION : Terns are water birds that resemble gulls but are much more graceful and slender. They hover and dive for their fish. They normally do not swim as gulls do.

COMMON MEANING : a part of you that can gracefully explore the waters of your own life, whether figurative or literal.

TRICKSTER MEANING : turn; turn on.

TRANSCENDENT MEANING : a gift from the ocean.

Thirteenth Moon

KEY WORDS : TRANSITION; CHANGE; NEW WAYS; INDECISIVE; RESTLESS; CHAOS; GREAT POTENTIAL FOR GROWTH; THE SHADOW; FEAR OF CHANGE; DEALING WITH CONTROL; DEALING WITH FEAR OF DEATH; LOVE; RELATIONSHIP; THE MOON.

DESCRIPTION : Some years there are thirteen moons because a lunar month consists of the twenty-nine days, twelve hours, forty-four minutes, and two and seven-tenths seconds it takes to pass from one new moon to the next. We live in a twelve-moon society governed by calendars that would not work well if they were forced to make room for a thirteenth moon that only appeared intermittently. The thirteenth moon concept, which is an important part of the Medicine Wheel, is difficult to explain to people used to the time tracking of mainstream Western society. Consequently, the thirteenth moon is the invisible moon that heralds change in the life of a person.

COMMON MEANING : a time of intense change, with a possibility for intense growth and progress; living through a chaotic or confusing time of life; feeling indecisive.

TRICKSTER MEANING : to expose your posterior thirteen times; to get to the bottom of some situation.

TRANSCENDENT MEANING : the ability to deal with all the shadows in your personality and in your life that have heretofore hid both from the full light of Father Sun and the dimmer light of Grandmother Moon.

SEE ALSO : *Moon, Full Moon, Crescent Moon, Half Moon, Dark of Moon,* and *Menstruation.*

Thistle

KEY WORDS : EDIBLE; MEDICINAL; RICH; MINERAL-LADEN; INCREASES NURTURING; STRENGTHENER; HOLY; BLESSED; FREEZE UP MOON.

DESCRIPTION : Thistle is the plant totem for people born under the Freeze Up Moon (October 24–November 21). The thistle, sometimes called the holy thistle or blessed thistle, is a tall, sharp-spined plant that grows both in urban and country areas. It has red, purple, or white flowers in loose clusters. All parts of the plant are covered with very sharp, prickly hairs and a bristly down, making thistle a difficult plant to either ignore or pick. The thistle was used for both food and medicine, as all parts of the plant are rich in minerals. The thistle is said to aid in digestive problems, to reduce fever, and to increase milk. Thistle was sometimes considered to be an all-purpose herb capable of healing most maladies, and strengthening the body.

COMMON MEANING: a healing; increased ability to nurture or be nurtured.

TRICKSTER MEANING: this old.

TRANSCENDENT MEANING: a gift of healing, either of your dream state or of your life.

Thunder Beings

KEY WORDS: POWER; RAIN; WATER; MESSENGERS.

DESCRIPTION: The thunder beings are the spirit forces behind the clouds that bring rain, thunder, and lightning to the earth. The thunder beings help life to continue by bringing the life-giving rains. They can also cause change through the power of fire if lightning strikes land during a dry season. The thunder beings are very powerful elemental forces.

COMMON MEANING: your connection with these elementals; the need to bring more water into your life; a desire to work with your emotions.

TRICKSTER MEANING: gods; strength; frightening; loud.

TRANSCENDENT MEANING: indication of a gift for working with the thunder beings. In some Native traditions to dream of the thunder beings was to dream that you would be a contrary one who did things opposite from the way in which they were normally done. The thunder beings bring strong messages from Spirit.

Thunderbird

KEY WORDS: RADIANT; PURIFYING; BURNING; CHANGING; INNER FIRE; BRILLIANCE; QUICK FLASHING; DIRECT; BRIGHT; ENERGETIC; PENETRATING; LIGHTNING; TRANSMUTATION; FIRE BIRD; PHOENIX; FIRE CLAN.

DESCRIPTION: The Thunderbird Clan in Sun Bear's vision of the Medicine Wheel is the clan associated with fire. People of the Budding Trees Moon (Red Hawk), the Ripe Berries Moon (Sturgeon), and the Long Snows Moon (Elk) are all members of the Thunderbird Clan. Lightning flashes from Thunderbird's eyes, and thunder comes from the beating of its wings. The Fire Clan is composed of people with a lot of radiant energy and the capacity to purify themselves and things they touch. These people are active, always looking for new things. They are often leaders who depend upon their strong intuitive energy. People of the Fire Clan tend to be charming and witty; consequently they make friends quickly. Sometimes they speak before they think, and they can have a tendency toward arrogance.

COMMON MEANING: a time when you are strongly connected to all those qualities associated with the Thunderbird Clan; a time when you're ready to take center stage.

TRICKSTER MEANING: bird, meaning woman; woman who thunders; hot rodders; Thunderbird, the car.

TRANSCENDENT MEANING: a powerful message of transformation.

SEE ALSO: *Fire.*

Tick

KEY WORDS: DEPLETING; BLOODSUCKING; PARASITIC.

DESCRIPTION: A tick is a wingless insect that sucks the blood of man and other animals.

COMMON MEANING: something that is eroding your vital essence or depleting you.

TRICKSTER MEANING: an unplanned movement of the face; an encasement for a mattress or pillow; a light touch; the sound made by a clock; angry, "ticked off."

TRANSCENDENT MEANING: a warning of something that is eating off of you in the dream state.

Tobacco

KEY WORDS: SACRED; CLARITY; CAN POISON; DISCRIMINATION; HELPER; HEALER; WABUN, SPIRIT KEEPER OF THE EAST.

DESCRIPTION: Tobacco is the plant associated with the East and with Wabun, Spirit Keeper of the East. Tobacco was cultivated by Native people in the Americas for use in the pipe and in making offerings. Tobacco was a very sacred plant to many Earth peoples in the Americas and was used in a sacramental way. Tobacco was often the ritual sacrifice in pipe ceremonies, or other smoke ceremonies, the plant that gave itself to transformation so that healing smoke could be released. See *Corn* for a legend that tells how tobacco came as a gift of First Woman to the people.

It is said that smoking tobacco calls the spirit people to come and be with you. Sun Bear taught that this is one of the reasons recreational smoking is harmful for people; it calls spirits when you don't really want them. Consequently, they don't know when you really do need them.

COMMON MEANING: searching for ways to allow the sacred to permeate your life; being drawn to the ways of Native people or to spirits that are part of this continent; clarity asked for or received; a time of new beginnings; a time when you can release negativity; the need for discrimination, or the gift of discrimination; time to reconsider a recreational smoking habit.

TRICKSTER MEANING: to back, oh; back hoe.

TRANSCENDENT MEANING: tobacco in a dream draws spirit forces to you, or indicates that spirit forces have come.

SEE ALSO: *Cardinal Directions—East* and *Wabun.*

Tortoise

KEY WORDS: TURTLE; SERVICE; SACRIFICE; ANCIENT; ENDURANCE; STABILITY; EARTH MOTHER.

DESCRIPTION: Tortoise is the animal associated with the Earth Mother position in the Center Circle of the Medicine Wheel. A tortoise is a member of the reptile family that frequently lives on land. Tortoise is a very long living creature who can reach a hundred and fifty years of age or more. Native people of the Americas honored the tortoise by referring to the northern part of the continent as Turtle Island. In part, this is because of a variety of legends that say that it was the turtle or tortoise who offered its back for the foundation for the land that is now known as North America. This was at a time after the earth had been cleansed by the power of the waters. A spirit woman, First Woman, came from the heavens, found a morsel of earth, spread it around the tortoise's back, and breathed life into the earth so that the tortoise was able to go back and live among its own kind. In honor of the sacrifice turtle was willing to make, this land was named in turtle's honor.

COMMON MEANING: your deep connection with the earth; your willingness to give of yourself to others.

TRICKSTER MEANING: tort is a term having to do with the legal system; torte is a rich cake.

TRANSCENDENT MEANING: a gift of ancient wisdom.

Totem Pole

KEY WORDS: HISTORY; MESSAGES; FAMILY; TOTEMS; SYMBOLS.

DESCRIPTION: The totem pole is a carved column of wood, often cedar, that shows figures with important symbolic meaning. Totem poles come from tribes of the northwest and Alaska, and often show clan, totem, animals, fish, birds, or mythological creatures. Totem poles tell a story, often the story of a family, a clan, or a tribe.

COMMON MEANING: your own history; a message about your family; symbols important to your life. It is important to observe the figures on the totem pole, as these can tell you much about what has gone before in your life or the life of your family.

TRICKSTER MEANING: tote, or carry them; a Polish man; poll.
TRANSCENDENT MEANING: an understanding of your life story.

Traveling

KEY WORDS: WAY OF GOING THROUGH LIFE; METHOD OF REACHING GOALS; EARTH PATH; CONNECTION TO THE EARTH.
HORSE: primitive; powerful; connected; animal nature; intensity; emotions; sexuality.
BIKE: ecological; close to earth; demonstrates own strength.
CARRIAGE: speed, separation from earth, utilizing horse; technology.
CAR: speed; technology; disconnected; mainstream; in control or out of control.
MASS TRANSIT: out of control; part of the crowd; lacking individual direction and vision.
DESCRIPTION: Traveling means going from one place to another.
COMMON MEANING: Traveling dreams can help you understand where you are now in life and where you wish to be going. The mode of travel is indicative of your way of doing things in life. To dream of walking means you feel strongly connected both with the earth and with your own path. To dream of riding a bicycle means you are still feeling a strong earth connection but have the desire to utilize some of the methods of technology in order to reach your destination more quickly. To dream of riding in a carriage takes you one step farther from your connection with the earth, and possibly from your own path. It indicates greater desire for speed.

To dream of driving a car means you are feeling very much a part of modern society, and in a hurry to do whatever it is you are about to do. Such a dream indicates a lack of connection with the energies of the earth. If you dream that you are riding in a car with someone else driving, this means that you feel somewhat out of control in your own life.

To dream of riding a bus, a train, a boat, or some other surface mode of mass transportation means you feel quite out of control of your life. This indicates a feeling that someone else is taking you where you need to go, and telling you how to get there. Such dreams can also indicate a serious lack of connection with the Earth Mother and with your own sacred path.

To dream of riding in an airplane means you greatly desire to obtain your goal as quickly as you can. Because a plane is also a method of mass transportation, it can mean that you feel out of control in regard to this goal. A dream of being in a plane is also a flying dream. Flying does not necessarily mean a lack of connection with the earth. Note whether you are paying any attention to what is below you as well as what is around you. Sometimes such a dream can give you a broader view of your earth connection.

To dream of traveling means that you are preparing to, or are in the process of, moving to a different place on the Medicine Wheel. It is important to note the details of such dreams, as they can give you indications as to where you have been and where you may be moving on the Wheel. For example, if you had a dream with raspberries in it, it might indicate that you were moving to the sturgeon position. If you dreamt that you were traveling on a train and noticed you had on a copper bracelet, it might indicate that you are moving to the snake position.

TRICKSTER MEANING: travailing, or experiencing intense work, pain, or agony; vacation or exploration.

TRANSCENDENT MEANING: understanding your goals and how you are working to reach them.

Tree

KEY WORDS: SACRED SPIRITS; DANCING BEINGS; CONNECTOR OF EARTH AND SKY; ROOTEDNESS; SKY-REACHING; POWERFUL; MYSTERIOUS.

DESCRIPTION: Trees are woody plants that have a trunk and branches. Most of them are taller than bushes or shrubs. There are many varieties of trees worldwide. Ancient peoples considered the tree to be a conductor of the energy of both the earth and the sky. They considered trees as very important beings who had very specific missions to fulfill upon the earth. Some Earth people considered the trees to be very sacred, while all Earth people acknowledged that they were strong and respected beings.

COMMON MEANING: exploring your connection with the energy of earth and sky; exploring the roots of your life.

TRICKSTER MEANING: to trap or corner.

TRANSCENDENT MEANING: a gift from the tree people; understanding or an experience of the energy of trees.

Trillium

KEY WORDS: DELICATE; PRISTINE; ENDANGERED; HEALING; CONNECTED TO FEMININE; PURIFYING; ANTISEPTIC; CLEANSING.

DESCRIPTION: Trillium is the plant associated with the third Spirit Path position of the North, purity. Trillium is now a rare herb that loves the deep woods and the rain forest. It is a delicate plant, and one of the many species that have been grossly hurt by the destruction of the earth's rain forests. Trillium is now an endangered species. In older times, when the earth was in a more balanced state, trillium root was used as a healer for many ills. It had a particularly auspicious effect on problems of women.

Today trillium should not be used at all by humans until we come to a time again when we have ceased destroying its ecosystem and allowed this plant to regenerate itself.

COMMON MEANING: the primitive parts of your nature that have been untouched by external events; the still, quiet center within; your deep roots in the earth.

TRICKSTER MEANING: to trill in music is to quickly alternate two notes that are close together; trill, to vibrate the tongue or uvula rapidly as a means of pronouncing letters in some languages; to sing or speak with this rapid vibration.

TRANSCENDENT MEANING: a revelation about the core of your being.

Trout

KEY WORDS: AT HOME IN THE WATER; STRONG-SWIMMING.

DESCRIPTION: Trout is the name given to a number of fish of the salmon family that are used for sport and food. One kind of trout wears the rainbow and takes it from the world's streams into the world's lakes.

COMMON MEANING: a part of you comfortable in the water; a part of you comfortable with your emotions; a part of you that is nurtured by water.

TRICKSTER MEANING: drought; try out.

TRANSCENDENT MEANING: messages about the world's streams and lakes; a blessing from the water beings.

Trust

KEY WORDS: CONFIDENCE; ACCEPTANCE; STRONG BELIEF; FAITH; SOUTHERN SPIRIT PATH.

DESCRIPTION: In the Medicine Wheel, trust is the middle Spirit Path Stone of the South. The mineral associated with trust is lepidolite; plant, borage; animal, salmon; color, lavender.

COMMON MEANING: gaining more assurance, acceptance, and strength; a willingness to explore your own vulnerability.

TRICKSTER MEANING: something that is managed by someone other than its true owner; custody; responsibility; a combination of businesses; trussed, or tied up.

TRANSCENDENT MEANING: a willingness to surrender to life. This is not the surrender of weakness; it is the surrender of strength that allows you to truly know the Creator.

Turkey

KEY WORDS: ABUNDANT; POWERFUL; SACRED; STUPID; EARTH CONNECTION; BLOCKING.

DESCRIPTION: A turkey is a large bird with a small, featherless head. There were once large numbers of wild turkeys that spread across the United States. Like many animals, they were overhunted when European immigration exploded here, and they almost became extinct. The turkey was sacred to many Native people and was respected by the early Europeans. In fact, the symbol of the United States was almost the wild turkey instead of the eagle. Some Native people felt that while the eagle represented the sky, the turkey represented the earth. Turkeys have long been easy to domesticate, in part because of their desire to remain in flocks. While domestic turkeys are said to lack intelligence (a fact substantiated by the vast numbers of baby turkeys who drown in their own water dishes), wild turkeys were quite intelligent birds with the ability to fly for short distances and to roost high in trees.

COMMON MEANING: abundance in your life; understanding of the depth of your connection with the earth; an indication of your feelings about community.

TRICKSTER MEANING: a failure; a dumb or foolish person; turn key.

TRANSCENDENT MEANING: a gift of abundance.

Turquoise (color)

KEY WORDS: HEALING; CONNECTING; BALANCING; BIG WINDS MOON.

DESCRIPTION: Turquoise is the color associated with the Big Winds Moon (Cougar). Turquoise is a shade of blue that is often found in the sky, most often over desert areas or during times when the sun is rising or setting. It is a brilliant mixture of blue and green that is generally healing both to the eye and to the soul. There is a stone often found in this color that is named for the color.

COMMON MEANING: a healing from reconnecting with the energies of the sky; a reminder to look skyward.
TRICKSTER MEANING: see *Turquoise (stone)*.
TRANSCENDENT MEANING: balance with whatever realms you are currently working.
SEE ALSO: *Turquoise (stone)*

Turquoise (stone)

KEY WORDS: SKY STONE; CONSTANCY; PROTECTION; BIG WINDS MOON.
DESCRIPTION: Turquoise is the mineral totem for people born during the Big Winds Moon (February 19–March 20). Turquoise was often referred to as the "sky stone." Earth peoples believed wearing turquoise would keep bones from breaking, provide protection from weapons, and keep lovers constant with each other. Another belief about turquoise was that a turquoise bead on a bow or arrow would make the arrow always hit its target.
COMMON MEANING: a reminder to look skyward; a warning of possible danger; the possibility of a steady relationship.
TRICKSTER MEANING: a Turk is someone from Turkey; it also refers to someone who is fierce or unkind.
TRANSCENDENT MEANING: an indication that you are exactly on target about whatever material you were working with in your dream.

Turtle

KEY WORDS: EARTH; SUSTENANCE; STABILITY; FOUNDATION; CONSTANCY; HARDNESS; STUBBORN; SLOW; CLOSE TO THE EARTH; TENACITY; LONGEVITY; EARTH CLAN.
DESCRIPTION: Turtle is the animal associated with the element of earth. In the Medicine Wheel, people of the Earth Renewal Moon (Snow Goose), the Frogs Return Moon (Beaver), and the Harvest Moon (Brown Bear) are all members of the Turtle Clan. The turtle is associated with the earth because it is said that the turtle offered her back to become the foundation for what is now called the United States but was known to Native people as Turtle Island. People associated with the Earth Clan are stable and constant in their opinions, ideals, and ideas. They are dependable and loyal, but with a tendency to sometimes become too rigid or stubborn. This is the clan associated with the physical aspects of being.
COMMON MEANING: seeing the foundation of your life, or of your philosophies or ideas; perceiving what you feel rooted to; experiencing your connection both with the planet Earth and the element of earth; exploring your loyalties, opinions, and ideals; can be an indication that you need to spend more time with the earth.
TRICKSTER MEANING: chortle; hurdle.

TRANSCENDENT MEANING: a gift of earth energy; deeper understanding of your connection with the earth.
WOLF CLAN TEACHING: work; clan animal for October.
SEE ALSO: *Tortoise*

Uva-Ursi, see Bearberry.

Violet

KEY WORDS: SHADOW; SHADE; DELICATE; THICKENING; PENETRATING; HEALING; SENTIMENTAL; RETIRING; HARVEST MOON.
DESCRIPTION: Violet, the plant totem for people born during the Harvest Moon (August 23–September 22), is found in forests and meadows throughout the world. There are four hundred species. Violets grow close to the ground and have dark green, rounded leaves and delicate violet flowers. Leaves and flowers have both been used medicinally as an antiseptic and expectorant. Violet, particularly the variety known as wild okra, has been used to thicken soups and stews. The violet is purported to have a property that allows it to reach places normally only penetrated by the blood and the lymphatic fluids, and then to dissolve toxic materials. It is a general tonic, and has been said to aid with difficulties in breathing and with sore throats.
COMMON MEANING: being shy; a delicate part of your being; an aspect of you that desires to penetrate and heal; the sentimental part of your nature; the part of you that would just as soon keep away from other people.
TRICKSTER MEANING: a name; a color; a word to describe a very sweet, shy, and retiring person, as in "a shrinking violet"; violent; file it.
TRANSCENDENT MEANING: a revelation about your own sentimentality.

Vision

KEY WORDS: PURPOSE; DESTINY; FULFILLMENT.
DESCRIPTION: The vision, according to Sun Bear, is what gives meaning and purpose to a person's life. It is the vision that drives you forward each day, and enables you to do whatever it is that Spirit has told you is your destiny, your goal in life. Each person's vision is different, each person's vision needs to be respected. In Earth societies, children were prepared to seek vision from the time of their youth. In today's world, it is only the lucky few who even know that vision is possible for them.
COMMON MEANING: seeing something clearly; getting a direction in your life.
TRICKSTER MEANING: your eyesight; fission; envision.
TRANSCENDENT MEANING: can be a literal dream indicating it is time for you to go out on a vision quest.

Vision Quest

KEY WORDS : THRESHOLD; DIRECTION; CONNECTION WITH CREATOR AND THE EARTH.

DESCRIPTION : In the ancient Earth cultures, the vision quest was a time when a person would put aside the things of everyday life and go into the sacred time, the dreamtime. Such vision quests would often provide the direction for a person's life. An increasing number of contemporary people are also choosing to go seek their vision, praying that they might be blessed with a clear direction and a good way in which they can serve their people.

COMMON MEANING : great receptivity to messages from other realms. Be very careful to remember anything that comes after such an image in your dreamtime.

TRICKSTER MEANING : a quest for better sight; or a quest for a better site; question.

TRANSCENDENT MEANING : a visionary dream; an indication that it is time for you to go out and seek your vision.

Vulture

KEY WORDS : PEACE EAGLE; ADAPTABLE; SERVICE; CLEANING; PATIENCE; WATCHFULNESS.

DESCRIPTION : Vultures are large birds with wingspans that can reach twelve feet, and an ability to perform elaborate aerial acrobatics. In flight, vultures can often be mistaken for hawks or eagles; on closer examination, you can recognize the flying vulture by its small head and the shape of its tail. Vultures also tend to fly in groups. They are useful animals because they get rid of dead things that would otherwise take much longer to decompose. Some Earth people call them the "peace eagles" because they never kill in order to eat.

COMMON MEANING : something that needs to be cleaned up; a bigger picture of such situations, and the knowledge of how you got into them, as well as a clear view of how to correct them.

TRICKSTER MEANING : a person who preys upon others.

TRANSCENDENT MEANING : a deep understanding of death, rebirth, and the circle of life.

Waboose, Spirit Keeper of the North

KEY WORDS : WHITE BUFFALO; ACCEPTANCE; PEACE; POWER; FORGIVENESS; SURRENDER; ENDING; BEGINNING; GIVEAWAY OF WHAT WE HAVE LEARNED AS WE JOURNEY THROUGH LIFE; CONTEMPLATION OF PARADOXES.

DESCRIPTION : In Sun Bear's vision of the Medicine Wheel, Waboose is the name given to the Spirit Keeper of the North. The North is the time of winter, the time of night, the time when we humans are either elders or newborn babies, and the period that lies between. The element associated with Waboose is the earth; the mineral, alabaster; the plant, sweet grass; the animal, the white buffalo; the color, white.

COMMON MEANING: how you will be when you become an elder; what you were like as a newborn.

TRICKSTER MEANING: "wah," a cry; caboose; "boo," an exclamation.

TRANSCENDENT MEANING: revelation about the giveaway; understanding of life's paradoxes.

SEE ALSO: *Cardinal Directions—North* and *Winter*.

Wabun, Spirit Keeper of the East

KEY WORDS: GOLDEN EAGLE; ENTHUSIASM; BURSTING THROUGH; REBIRTH; INNOCENCE; ETERNAL SPRING; SPONTANEITY; WONDER; INQUISITIVENESS; EXPLORATION; CURIOSITY; MESSENGER OF TRUTH; OBSERVANT; PASSIONATE.

DESCRIPTION: Wabun is the name given to the Spirit Keeper of the East in Sun Bear's system of the Medicine Wheel. This is the time of youth, of new beginnings, of spring, of the dawn. The element associated with Wabun is air; the mineral, pipestone; the plant, tobacco; the animal, the golden eagle; the colors gold and red.

COMMON MEANING: a time of new beginnings; enthusiasm; fresh, vital energy.

TRICKSTER MEANING: robin; woe; buns; a bun.

TRANSCENDENT MEANING: a rebirth.

SEE ALSO: *Cardinal Directions—East* and *Spring*.

Wand

KEY WORDS: POWER; SPIRITUALITY; DIRECT CONNECTION; SHARING; GENEROSITY; UNDERSTANDING TRUTH; BALANCING.

DESCRIPTION: A wand is a slender piece of wood or other material. A musician's baton is a wand, as is a staff of authority like a scepter. There are many stories of magic wands used by fairies and other entities of the old Earth religions.

COMMON MEANING: a time of deep connection with the powers of creation; being given a tool that will allow you to use your energy more powerfully. It is important to note the kind of wand and its composition, to note any stones or parts of plants or animals that are on the wand, to note the colors of the wand, to note whether you are holding it, to note what you are touching with it. All of these will indicate the kind of gift that you are being given.

TRICKSTER MEANING: slang for male genitals; Wanda (name); want.

TRANSCENDENT MEANING: a gift of magic.

• • •

Water

KEY WORDS : CLEANSING; CHANGING; EMOTIONS; SENSUALITY; SEXUALITY; MOON EN-
ERGY.

DESCRIPTION : Water is a transparent liquid composed of hydrogen and oxygen. As a liquid, it fills the earth's rivers, lakes, streams, and oceans. Frozen, it becomes ice. If boiled, it becomes steam.

COMMON MEANING : your emotional being and your connection with the element of water; your sensuality, your sexuality; the feminine aspect of your nature; your connection with the energy of the moon.

A dream of still water indicates that you are at a placid, tranquil period of life. Moving water, as in a stream, indicates that you are at a time of change in your emotional life. Quickly moving water, as a waterfall or the ocean, indicates that you are in a time of rapid change, that you have come to a time of life in which you need to let go of control and enjoy the flow of the life force around you.

Dreaming of waves crashing on the beach means that you are seeing how your emotions interface with your physical reality. Dreaming of large waves coming to the beach can be dreams of major emotional happenings coming to you. How you feel about waves coming to the beach indicates whether you are in a time of happiness, fear, or apprehension. Dreams of large waves can also indicate remembrances of past existences, other worlds that may have been cleansed by the power of water.

TRICKSTER MEANING: to cry or to sprinkle; thirst; life-giving; emotions, Aquarius (Water Bearer).

TRANSCENDENT MEANING: an initiatory dream, particularly one that has to do with your emotional life.

HUICHOL TEACHING: white foam on the ocean means love, creation; walking on water means trying to re-create something.

SEE ALSO: *Frog Clan.*

Weasel

KEY WORDS: ADAPTABLE; FAST; LONG AND THIN; POWERFUL; TRICKY.

DESCRIPTION: Weasels are courageous, small, carnivorous hunters brave enough to attack animals several times their size. The weasel is very adaptable. In many species the fur will change from brown to white as a means of camouflaging itself during the winter.

COMMON MEANING: a part of you that has the courage to act quickly; an adaptable part of you; the trickster in you.

TRICKSTER MEANING: a person who is cunning or sly; to equivocate; to escape from an obligation or responsibility.

TRANSCENDENT MEANING: a revelation about what is at the heart of any matter or situation.

Whale

KEY WORDS: ANCIENT; LARGE; POWERFUL; STRONG; LONG-LIVED; HARMONIOUS WITH THE ENVIRONMENT; EXPERIENCE.

DESCRIPTION: Whale, the animal that represents experience, the first Spirit Path position of the West, is a large mammal that breathes air, bears its young live, and is found in all the seas of the world. There are two main types of whales: the baleen whales, which are toothless and have a massive fringe of long bony plates that strains food from the water; and the toothed whales, which include orcas, dolphins, and porpoises. Whales are still in jeopardy today because, although almost taken to the point of extinction, some of the world's nations still allow them to be hunted. Some Earth people feel that whales have the capacity to communicate with humans, and that one of their messages and lessons is that we must come back into a more harmonious relationship with all of creation. Other people believe that whales have psychic powers and can directly communicate with humans.

COMMON MEANING: your connection with all that is ancient upon the earth and within the waters; how ancient knowledge ties into contemporary emotional life; aspiring to greater harmony with the environment; your own strength or power.

TRICKSTER MEANING: to hit hard; to cry; something that is very large and exceptional, as in "a whale of a tale."

TRANSCENDENT MEANING: a direct message about how you can help to heal the Earth Mother as a whole, and the waters of the earth specifically.

White

KEY WORDS: PURITY; INNOCENCE; BALANCE; TRANSFORMATION; PERFECTION; TRANQUILLITY; HARMONY; WABOOSE; EARTH RENEWAL MOON; GRANDMOTHER MOON; CORNPLANTING MOON.

DESCRIPTION: White is associated, along with silver, with the Grandmother Moon position of the Medicine Wheel; with the northern position of Waboose, Spirit Keeper of the North; and with the Earth Renewal Moon (Snow Goose). Along with green, it is a color for the Cornplanting Moon (Deer). In a translucent shade, it is the color associated with the purity stone in the Spirit Path of the North.

White, which is the absence of color, is considered by many to be the most powerful color. In many spiritual paths it represents purity, virginity, innocence, spiritual power, connection with spirit, transformation, perfection.

COMMON MEANING: your purest spiritual desires; transformation; striving for perfection; the innocent aspect of your being; a tranquil and harmonious person.

TRICKSTER MEANING: the color used to describe the skin of people of northern European heritage; one of the four races of humans; a virgin; a harmless idea or action, as in "white magic" or "a white lie"; whitey; fearful, as in white with fear.

TRANSCENDENT MEANING: to see yourself surrounded with white light is to see yourself spiritually transformed, at least for the duration of the dream.

White Buffalo

KEY WORDS: SACRED; FEMININE; MYSTERIOUS; MESSENGER; CEREMONY; TEACHING; EARTH CONNECTION; WABOOSE.

DESCRIPTION: White buffalo is the animal associated with the North, and with Waboose, the Spirit Keeper of the North. A white buffalo is very rare and was greatly valued both in reality and in the mythology of Native people. The Lakota people say it was White Buffalo Calf Woman who brought the pipe to their people. White Buffalo Woman was also considered to be the bringer of many other ceremonies and mysteries. Today, it is reported that White Buffalo Woman is appearing frequently in the dreams and visions of women, who are finding once again their deep connection with the earth, and with all of life.

COMMON MEANING: your own connection with the earth and with life.

TRICKSTER MEANING: to buff is to polish; for trick meanings of white, see *White;* to be buffaloed or tricked.

TRANSCENDENT MEANING: a powerful female spirit who can bring ceremony and sacred knowledge to humans in the dreamtime.

MEDICINE EAGLE'S TEACHING: White Buffalo Woman is the mystical teacher who came to the Lakota people with teachings of unity, wholeness, and sacred ecology. She represents the feminine, nurturing renewal of the world, global harmony, and working with All Our Relations.

SEE ALSO: *Waboose* and *Cardinal Directions—North.*

Wild American Ginseng

KEY WORDS: FLUORESCENT; ALMOST EXTINCT; OVERUSED; DELICIOUS; HEALING; PREVENTATIVE; REGENERATING; CALMING; ILLUMINATION.

DESCRIPTION: Wild American ginseng is the plant associated with the third Spirit Path position of the East, illumination. The plant can grow to eighteen feet in height and can reach an age of fifty years, although it is rare these days to find either old or large plants because so many have been picked by those trying to profit by providing this strong healing herb to manufacturers of herbal preparations. At night, ginseng is slightly fluorescent. The root of the plant has been used for cooking as well as for medicine. It was considered to be one of the most delicious wild plants, as well as a strong healer.

Wild American ginseng has become very rare, and should never be picked. If you ever find it, you should make prayers for its continuation and leave the plant. There are now farmers who are cultivating American ginseng, usually on a small scale and/or as a home industry. Support them, as well as the plant, by always knowing the source of any herb you use.

COMMON MEANING: a deeply healing part of your being; where you need strong healing; an aspect of you that could disappear if not explored; a part of you capable of regenerating.

TRICKSTER MEANING: a wild American.

TRANSCENDENT MEANING: a revelation about your own inner light. In the dreamtime, ginseng can illuminate your path through any darkness that you are experiencing.

Willow

KEY WORDS: WATER-LOVING; GROUNDED; VARIETY; HEALING.

DESCRIPTION: There are many species of willow found throughout the world. Perhaps most familiar to people are pussy willow, red willow, golden willow, and weeping willow. Willow bark has been used medicinally for a variety of cures. Willow bark contains salicylic acid. Bark containing this has been used for untold years to help with fever and as tonics and astringents. Aspirin, commonly used for many problems, is acetylsalicylic acid. Earth peoples used willow to weave baskets and other containers. It was also used to make frames for some dwellings and sweat lodges. Willow switches were also used as dowsing wands.

COMMON MEANING: the feelings that connect you to Earth Mother; what you need to do to heal your connection with the planet, and with all of life.

TRICKSTER MEANING: willowy, slender; a name; a low will; a badge of sorrow; something used to hit or punish; will o' the wisp; we'll owe.

TRANSCENDENT MEANING: a gift of healing from the Earth.

Winter

KEY WORDS: COLD; SILENT; SLOW; WISDOM; DEATH; REBIRTH, INTENSE INNER WORK; WABOOSE; THE NORTH.

DESCRIPTION: Winter is the season in temperate zones when things of the earth appear to be in their least active state. While this is true on the surface, it is the time when, in apparent rest, all of Earth Mother's children draw upon their most essential inner resources to prepare themselves for the times of rapid growth that follow. Winter is the most paradoxical season. While things appear calm on the surface, it is the time for intense inner workings. Winter is the time associated both with elderhood, death, and preparation for rebirth.

COMMON MEANING: a period of your life when you can slow down and relax; a time of wisdom; the willingness to endure a small death that will contribute to rebirth; the need for rest and renewal; a lesson about your physical body; an event occurring in that season; foreseeing how you will be as an elder.

TRICKSTER MEANING: winner.

TRANSCENDENT MEANING: a literal death and rebirth experience, either within the dream or one that has or will be happening in life.

SEE ALSO: *Cardinal Directions—North* and *Waboose.*

Wisdom

KEY WORDS: UNDERSTANDING; ACTING ON KNOWLEDGE; DISCERNMENT; MATURITY; STABILITY; THE SAGE; EASTERN SPIRIT PATH.

DESCRIPTION: To be wise is to show good judgment, usually judgment that is gleaned from experience of life. Wisdom is the middle Spirit Path Stone of the East. The mineral associated with wisdom is jade; plant, sage; animal, owl; color, jade green.

COMMON MEANING: a realization of maturity and stability; showing discernment, discrimination, and good judgment; a part of you is a sagacious person; recognizing and accepting limitations and boundaries; understanding your place in the sacred web of life.
TRICKSTER MEANING: a "wise guy" is someone who is annoyingly self-assured; wise/dumb.
TRANSCENDENT MEANING: a gift of wisdom.

Witch Hazel

KEY WORDS: WATER; HEALING; DIVINING; ASTRINGENT.
DESCRIPTION: Witch hazel, or *Hamamelis virginiana,* is also known as spotted alder and winter bloom. Witch hazel is either a shrub or a small tree found in woods where there is sufficient water. The tree is very fragrant and has flowers that bloom in November and December. Twigs from the witch hazel have long been used as divining rods. The bark and leaves make a very powerful astringent that also has sedative and tonic properties. It is used today largely to heal and stimulate the skin.
COMMON MEANING: a part of you with ancient healing knowledge; a part that can find water, either literally or figuratively.
TRICKSTER MEANING: witch, a wise woman; witch, as stereotyped in patriarchal society; Hazel (name or color); which one; witching hour (time to leave).
TRANSCENDENT MEANING: wisdom from your emotions.

Wolf

KEY WORDS: LOVING; POWERFUL; CUNNING; ELUSIVE; PROTECTIVE; DISCRIMINATING; COMPASSIONATE; LOYALTY; FIDELITY; PERSEVERANCE; GUARDIANSHIP; PATH FINDER.
DESCRIPTION: The animal that represents love, the third Spirit Path position of the South, is the wolf. The wolf is a very social animal who lives in packs that have firm traditions and boundaries. Wolves also generally mate for life. The wolf has long entered man's imagination, often being represented as a loner and often symbolizing the wilderness and the wild parts of human nature. Although wolves were once found worldwide, they have become almost extinct, although they are making a comeback. Earth peoples had great respect for the wolf because of his love for family and because the wolf always showed discrimination in only hunting weak or sick members of other species.
COMMON MEANING: your relationship to your family or your community; the loving side of your nature; your feelings about intimacy.
TRICKSTER MEANING: an aggressive male who flirts a lot; to eat ravenously.

TRANSCENDENT MEANING: a protector animal who can teach you about love and about family.
WOLF CLAN TEACHING: sharing; clan animal for November.

Wolverine

KEY WORDS: AGGRESSIVE; VICIOUS; FEARED; COURAGEOUS; SOLITARY; AVOIDED; PROTECTOR.

DESCRIPTION: Wolverine is also known as the skunk bear. It does look somewhat bearlike, with dark brown fur and hands that are broad and yellowish. Wolverines are about two and a half feet long, yet despite their small size they are very successful at hunting. The wolverine is a very aggressive animal that will take on animals many times its size. Wolverines are feared because of their sharp teeth, their claws, and their aggression. They are said to be so tough that bears or cougars will flee from them. While wolverines like carrion, they will eat whatever they can, sometimes gluttonously.

COMMON MEANING: the most aggressive and vicious parts of your nature, often the parts of you filled with deep rage; the part of you that will fight to protect; a deep well of courage within you; your willingness to take on something bigger than you are.

TRICKSTER MEANING: wool; voracious; wavering.

TRANSCENDENT MEANING: deep understanding of parts of your nature you might ordinarily fear; a strong protector animal.

Yarrow

KEY WORDS: USEFUL; VERSATILE; ASTRINGENT; SOOTHING; STRENGTHENING; CLEANSING; CORNPLANTING MOON.

DESCRIPTION: Yarrow is the plant totem for those born during the Cornplanting Moon (May 21–June 20). It looks like a fuzzy fern on a stem with white or sometimes pink or yellow flowers that grow on the top of the stalk in small, numerous heads. It is also called *Achillea millefolium,* after Achilles, who is said to have discovered the value of the plant. The whole plant can be used medicinally, as a tonic, to help the digestive tract, to help you rid yourself of toxins. Yarrow is useful for colds, flu, and related diseases. It will also work as a diuretic. Yarrow can be found anywhere. Its strong scent and sharp taste come from the tannic and achilleine acid it contains.

COMMON MEANING: a sharp aspect of your nature that is willing to help you get rid of anything that is detrimental to your full healing.

TRICKSTER MEANING: a name; yeah, a row; arrow.

TRANSCENDENT MEANING: a gift of cleansing and/or healing.

Yellow

KEY WORDS: WARMTH; SUN; TRUST; GOOD NATURE; HAPPINESS; ENCOURAGEMENT; FUN; MENTAL REALITY; INTELLECT; SHAWNODESE; BUDDING TREES MOON; STRENGTH.

DESCRIPTION: Yellow is the color, along with green, associated with the South and with Shawnodese, Spirit Keeper of the South. It is also the color of the Budding Trees Moon (Red Hawk) and, in a golden shade, of strength, one of the Western Spirit Path positions on the Wheel.

Yellow is a color often associated with the sun as it is high in the sky. Yellow is a color that tends to coax new and rapid growth. It is a color of warmth and a color that penetrates, often bringing feelings of humor and cheer.

COMMON MEANING: parts of your world that are experiencing rapid growth.

TRICKSTER MEANING: someone who is cowardly; mellow; Jell-O; yell.

TRANSCENDENT MEANING: help with penetrating into new realms.

Yerba Santa

KEY WORDS: HEALING; BLESSED; BREATHING.

DESCRIPTION: Yerba santa (*Eriodictyon californicum*), also called mountain balm and bear's weed, is an evergreen shrub that grows mainly in the Sierra Nevadas. It has been used to help cure all forms of respiratory problems and was given the name yerba santa or holy herb, blessed herb, by a Spanish priest who found the plant to be helpful in curing such problems.

COMMON MEANING: a part of you that wishes to breathe easily and freely; warning about possible respiratory problems.

TRICKSTER MEANING: Spanish Santa; Santa's herb; saint's herb.

TRANSCENDENT MEANING: a revelation about the sacred energy within you, and ways that you can allow it to come fully into your breath and being.

Yew Tree

KEY WORDS: DEEPLY HEALING; EVERGREEN; REVITALIZING.

DESCRIPTION: The yew tree is an evergreen that has red berries and bears cones. In old times it was used particularly for making archer's bows. Today's modern medicine has found that it has extremely potent healing abilities. It is purported to be able to cure advanced forms of cancer. However, it takes a large number of trees to prepare the cure for one person.

COMMON MEANING: a healing that is coming; a deepening understanding of your vital energy.

TRICKSTER MEANING: you, tree; you treat.

TRANSCENDENT MEANING: a gift of deep healing.

• • •

Yucca

KEY WORDS: HEALING; CLEANSING.

DESCRIPTION: Yucca is a plant belonging to the lily family; it has stiff, almost sword-shaped leaves and white flower clusters in the center. It is found in the southwest of the United States and in Central and South America. It was used by Earth peoples as a detergent and also as a cleanser that could heal external skin irritations. Modern researchers are finding that the powder of the leaves contains a potential precursor for cortisone.

COMMON MEANING: exploring a semiarid or ignored part of your being; preparing for a cleansing; healing something that is on the surface of your being or personality.

TRICKSTER MEANING: yuck; Yucatan.

TRANSCENDENT MEANING: a revelation about what covers you.

Appendix

CHAPTER 1, PAGE 25

Exercise One: Using a Talking Stick or Bowl

What you will need: A stick of any kind, either taken as it is from nature or decorated with beadwork, fur, leather, or feathers. You also need two or more people who wish to honestly talk and listen to one another.

Estimated time: One minute to several hours.

1. Either pick up a stick that you find in nature, after leaving a prayer or offering of thanksgiving, or obtain a stick that has been decorated for this purpose from a craftsperson. You can also get a stick from nature and then decorate it yourself by wrapping it with leather or fur, or beading around the handle of the stick, or attaching some feathers to the end of the stick. You may use your creativity in decorating a talking stick, but remember to make the end of it easy for a person to hold. People who wish to come in closer contact with their feminine energy can use a bowl rather than a stick to pass between people. It is felt that the bowl represents the womb and the feminine. The bowl, like the stick, can be either plain or decorated and can be made of any natural material. It is good to use a

bowl instead of a stick in women's circles or in any councils or situations where the people present feel that it is important for them to be in deepest contact with their feminine energy.

2. The purpose of the talking stick is to encourage the person holding it to feel free to say whatever is in their heart at the time they are holding the stick.

3. Only the person holding the talking stick has the right to speak.

4. Everyone else present should listen to the person speaking with as much of an open mind and heart as they possibly can.

5. Using a talking stick is a good way to encourage otherwise shy people to speak whatever their truth is. It is also a good exercise for talkative people who have not yet learned the gift of actively listening to others.

CHAPTER 2, PAGE 37

Exercise Two: Using Senoi Dream Work Techniques with Children

What you will need: Yourself, a child or children, time, patience, and a pleasant, nonjudgmental manner.

Estimated time: Five minutes to a half hour.

1. Encourage your child or children to remember their dreams. The best way to do this is to set the example of remembering and valuing dreams by discussing your dreams both with the child and with other adults in your household each morning.

2. Teach your child to complete his or her dreams.

3. If the children have a dream that is frightening, encourage them to relax and enjoy whatever dream situation they have encountered. Let them know that there is a gift for them and for their family at the conclusion of whatever the dream situation is. A common example of a frightening dream is to dream of falling. If children have this dream, tell them to relax and enjoy falling, knowing that there will be a gift for them when they come to the bottom.

4. Another way to deal with a dream of falling is to encourage children to start flying at some point during the fall, and to keep flying until they come to someone or something that has a gift for them or their people.

5. If children dream of a monster or something else they perceive as frightening, tell them that they should not run away but should stand there, look at the monster, and ask the monster what gift the monster has for them or their people. People we know have reported that their children

tell them that the monster always has a present, candy, or something nice to give them.

6. Be willing to play-act the gifts or instructions that children receive in the dream state. For example, if the monster sings a song, encourage the children to sing the song, and then sing along with them. Or if they learn a dance, ask them to show you how to do the dance.

CHAPTER 4, PAGE 53

Exercise Three: Sun Bear's Suggestions for Having Good Dreams

Technique I

What you will need: A dream object, such as a crystal, a stone, a mask, or a dream net.

Estimated time: To place the objects, five minutes. For using the objects, however long you normally sleep at night.

1. Obtain a crystal, a stone, a mask, or some other personal power object that you will use only for dreams. Make sure this is a power object that feels comfortable and safe for you to use, and be sure that your dream object is cleansed before you use it. (See following exercises.)

2. Put the object near your bed, hold it in your hand, or put it by you on the pillow or bed.

3. Take a few minutes to think about the day that has passed. Touching your dream power object, pray for a strong and powerful dream. In this prayer, ask the Creator and the spirits to help you to know all you need to about your life path and going in the proper direction upon your path.

4. Fall asleep, and enjoy your good dreams.

Technique II

What you will need: A dream net, which is a net woven from some sort of thread on a small willow frame. Dream nets have a hole in the middle that allows bad dreams to escape. The web of the dream net catches the good dreams.

Estimated time: The time it takes you to obtain a dream net and to place it in your room, and the time you normally spend each night asleep.

1. Obtain a dream net, making sure it feels safe and comfortable for you to use.

2. Cleanse your dream net.

3. Sit in your bedroom with the dream net until you are certain of the proper place near your bed to put it. Commonly, dream nets were placed above the baby's cradle or the child's bed.

4. Before you go to sleep each evening, take a moment to think about, look at, or touch your dream net, knowing that this net will draw good dreams to you and allow any bad dreams to go quickly away.

5. Enjoy your sleep and the dreams that the dream net helps to bring you.

Technique III

What you will need: A quart of water, preferably pure water from a good spring, or a quart of herbal tea.

Estimated time: Ten minutes before going to sleep.

1. When you are almost ready to go to bed for the evening, get a quart jar of either good spring water or a calming herbal tea.

2. Take this with you to your bedroom.

3. Sit and sip the water or tea while you think about the day that has passed and make prayers for good dreams that night.

4. When you have finished drinking the water or tea, lie down and go gently to sleep.

5. It is likely that your bladder will wake you in the middle of the night because of the water or tea you have ingested. Because of waking up, your dream cycle will be disturbed and you will be more likely to go into the level of sleep that allows you to have more than one powerful dream during the night.

6. Drinking and dreaming in this way is usually particularly effective for people who have had problems remembering their dreams.

CHAPTER 4, PAGE 54

Exercise Four: Purifying a Person or Space

Technique I: Smudging

What you will need: Sage, sweet grass, cedar, juniper, or tobacco, either singly or in combination; a shell or a heatproof bowl; a fan or feathers from a domestically raised bird, either chicken, turkey, pheasant, or duck; matches.

Estimated time: Five minutes if you are alone, more if you are with other people.

1. Place the herbs in a shell or in a sturdy, heatproof bowl. Using the matches, light the herbs until they begin to burn.

2. When the surface area of the herbs is burning well, use your fan or feather to put out the flame. As the ceremony continues, you may need to intermittently fan the herbs to keep them smoldering.

3. When the herbs are smoldering and producing smoke, draw this smoke to your heart, over your head, down your arms, down the front of your body, then down the back of your body. If some part of your body needs healing or balancing, wash this part with extra smoke.

4. In most instances, it is your responsibility to cleanse your own energy field. Remember that the smoke from the plants helps to do this but does not do it for you.

5. You may offer smoke to the six directions, first upward to the Creator, then down to the Earth Mother, then northward, eastward, southward, and westward.

6. After you have smudged yourself and offered the smudge, you may hold the bowl while other people present smudge.

7. You can then walk around the room in which you sleep, wafting the smoke in all directions and paying particular attention to the corners of the room.

8. You may also smudge any dream crystals, stones, pillows, or nets that you use to help you in dreaming.

Technique II: Cleansing Through Water

What you will need: A bowl or shell with water. You may also use a feather.

Estimated time: Five minutes if alone, more if you are with a group of people.

1. You may cleanse yourself with a small amount of water in much the same way as you wash yourself with the smoke in the smudging ceremony.

2. You would begin by dipping your fingers into the water and washing your hands, then bringing a few drops of water to your heart, up over your head, down your arms, down the front of your body, then the back of your body. If you have an area that needs special healing or balancing, you would put extra water there.

3. You would then offer the water to the six directions by taking a drop on your fingertips and flinging it in those directions.

4. Remember, as with the smoke, it is your responsibility to cleanse yourself. The water helps, but it cannot do it for you.

5. After you have smudged yourself with water, you can hold the bowl while other people present do the same. You may then walk around your bedroom flinging drops of water to cleanse it—pay particular attention to the corners.

6. You may use a feather instead of your fingertips to cleanse yourself, others, or an area with water.

7. Remember to cleanse any dream tools you will be using.

Technique III: Cleansing with Salt

What you will need: A shell or bowl with salt; seawater, or salt water.

Estimated time: Five minutes alone, more if you're with a group.

1. You would use the salt, saltwater, or sea water in the same way you would use the smoke from the smudge or the water in the previous exercises.

2. Follow the same order as in the previous exercises, cleansing yourself first, offering your cleansing material to the six directions, cleansing anyone else present, cleansing the area you will be using, and then cleansing any dream tools.

Technique IV: Cleansing with Sound

What you will need: A rattle or drum.

Estimated time: Five minutes alone, more if you're with a group.

1. Begin rattling or drumming until you have established a rhythm that feels cleansing to you.

2. Begin smudging yourself with the sound from the rattle or drum, starting at your head and going to your feet.

3. Next, offer the rattling or drumming to the six directions.

4. After you have cleansed yourself with sound and made your offering, you may then cleanse any other people present.

5. You then walk around the area where you will be sleeping while drumming or rattling and paying particular attention to the corners.

6. You would then cleanse any dream tools you would be using.

Technique V: Cleansing with Prayer

What you will need: Your focused attention and a quiet space in which to pray.

Estimated time: A minute to an hour.

1. Center yourself, generally by paying attention to your breathing.

2. When you feel centered, ask the Creator to help you to cleanse, purify, focus, and center yourself.

3. Ask the Creator to cleanse the space in which you are, and any dream tools you will be using.

4. Ask the Creator to help you with dreaming and to bring you any messages you need to learn through your dreams.

5. Thank the Creator for the day you have had, taking time to review the activities of the day.

6. Complete your prayer by thanking the Creator for the many blessings you have been given. Be as specific as you wish to be.

CHAPTER 4, PAGE 54

Exercise Five: Luke Blue Eagle on Working with Herkimer Diamonds

What you will need: A Herkimer diamond, which is a crystal from Herkimer County in upper New York State; salt water.

Estimated time: Five to fifteen minutes to prepare yourself; however long you sleep at night.

1. Luke Blue Eagle recommends Herkimer diamonds as a dream stone because they protect in the dreamtime and help you to remember your dreams clearly.

2. He cautions that they can be difficult to work with because they will send you to "the opposite of what your normal habits are." This means that if you have a good ability to remember dreams, at first you might forget your dreams when working with the Herkimer diamond. However, if you normally don't remember dreams, the Herkimer will help you to do so.

3. Purify the Herkimer in salt water or seawater for a week.

4. After the initial purification, purify the Herkimer diamond after every use.

5. As you prepare for sleep, hold the Herkimer diamond in your hand. You do this because it allows the Herkimer to have a direct influence on your brain. If you let go of the Herkimer during the night, that's not important.

6. As you fall asleep holding the Herkimer diamond, tell yourself that you will allow the Herkimer to bring you whatever good dreams it can help draw to you that night.

7. When you awaken in the morning, find the Herkimer if you have let go of it.

8. Remember to purify the Herkimer diamond so it will be ready to use the next time you wish to use it.

CHAPTER 4 PAGE 56

Exercise Six: Meditation to Remember Your Dreams

What you will need: Cleansing materials; notebook and pen/pencil or tape recorder.

Estimated time: Prior to sleeping, thirty minutes; however many hours you normally sleep at night; fifteen to thirty minutes to record your dreams in the morning.

1. Place a pad of paper and a pen or pencil by your bed where you can easily reach it. If you would prefer to record your dreams, place a tape recorder with a blank tape already in it by your bed.

2. Have a light source readily available so you can see to write or record at any time of the night.

3. Prepare yourself for sleep and get into bed. Lie in a position that is comfortable but not "too comfortable." To complete the exercise successfully you need to be in a state of relaxed awareness, but you do not want to fall asleep too soon. If your position is too uncomfortable, you won't relax. If your position is too comfortable, you may fall asleep.

4. If you are already relaxed, skip this step. If you perceive any tension, use an exercise of progressive relaxation. For example, tense and relax the muscles of your feet, breathe relaxation into them, then tense and relax your legs, breathe relaxation into them, and so on. Work your way up your body, remembering your hands, your arms, the muscles of your face. It is particularly important that the muscles of your feet, hands, stomach, and face, especially the jaw, be relaxed. Once you have achieved a reasonable state of relaxation, move on to the next step.

5. You may use the visualization as a self-directed meditation or as a guided meditation. If you are using it as a guided meditation, a friend or partner can read it to you, or you can record the visualization and play it back before going to sleep.

6. Imagine there is an old stone well in a meadow. It's a beautiful day, and you are resting beside the well.

7. You notice that written on the rim of the well is: "The well of _____'s unconscious." Put your name in the blank.

8. Take a few moments to relax into the scene of the meadow, the well, and the beauty of the day.

9. Imagine you have a pad of paper and a pen or pencil.

10. Write the following statements: "I, _____ (fill in your name), now release whatever I need to release and accept whatever I need to accept to remember my dreams now. You, _____, now release whatever you need to release and accept whatever you need to accept to remember your dreams now. He (or she), _____, now releases whatever he (or she) needs to release and accepts whatever he (or she) needs to accept to remember his (or her) dreams now."

11. Sign the note you've just written as you would sign a check and date it. Be sure you use the correct date, which means you will need to know the date before you go to bed.

12. Fold the note up into a small square and drop it into the well of your unconscious.

13. Watch the note as it floats down into the well, getting smaller and smaller until it disappears into the darkness of your unconscious.

14. After the note has disappeared imagine you are in bed sleeping. It is a peaceful and restful night. Imagine yourself sleeping, then imagine yourself beginning to experience a dream. Make it a simple dream, perhaps a rainbow after a summer storm.

15. Become acutely aware of the vividness of the colors of the rainbow and your surroundings. Let the smell of the air after the storm come into your awareness. Hear clearly the sounds of birds singing. Run your hand through the wet grass. Become keenly aware of the texture and feel of the grass. Use each of your senses within the dream as vividly as possible.

16. Imagine yourself waking up from the dream, feeling excitement and success at having recalled a dream.

17. Imagine yourself recording the dream in as much detail as you can immediately upon awakening. See yourself recalling the shapes, textures, and colors of the rainbow scene. Remember the smell of the air and the feel of the wet grass.

18. Having seen in your mind's eye that you recorded the dream, now allow yourself to feel a sense of pride and exaltation at having accomplished the goal you set out to achieve.

19. Let that feeling flow through you, and then allow yourself to drift off into a natural sleep.

20. If you have difficulty completing the visualization before falling asleep, do the exercise sitting up in a chair. Go through the entire visualization all the way to the part where you are feeling success at having recorded a dream. At this point, get up and go to bed.

CHAPTER 4, PAGE 61

Exercise Seven: Modifying Your Sleep Pattern

What you will need: Initially, an alarm clock.

Estimated time: Fifteen minutes prior to sleeping; however many hours you normally sleep; five to fifteen minutes upon awakening.

1. You can modify the meditation to remember your dreams so as to help you arise at your chosen time without the need for an alarm clock.

2. Let's take the example that your usual time of awakening is 6:00 A.M.; however, you have determined that you would like to have ten minutes

before you get out of bed to experience the postsleep state.

3. Go through the relaxation techniques given in the Meditation to Remember Your Dreams.

4. Use the visualization given in the meditation so that you see yourself in the meadow with the well of your unconscious.

5. Instead of writing about remembering your dreams, you would write the following: "I,_____ (fill in your name), will awaken at 5:50 A.M. tomorrow. You, _____, will awaken at 5:50 A.M. tomorrow. She (or he), _____, will awaken at 5:50 A.M. tomorrow."

6. Sign the piece of paper as you would a check, date it, drop it into the well of your subconscious, and see it disappear just as you did with the other note.

7. Imagine yourself falling asleep.

8. Imagine that it is 5:50 in the morning and you awaken peacefully, naturally.

9. You look at your alarm clock and see it is 5:50.

10. You feel happy you were able to awaken early enough to spend some quality time alone in bed before the alarm goes off.

11. After you have worked with this for a number of weeks, you'll find that your body rhythm has you awakening naturally at the time you desire.

12. At this point you might consider advancing your alarm just one minute. Practice getting up and shutting off the alarm before it goes off. In this way you can avoid the jarring effects of the morning alarm entirely.

13. By only setting your alarm one minute past your usual waking time, you won't be late even if you sleep in while your body adjusts to its new rhythm.

CHAPTER 4, PAGE 62

Exercise Eight: Making a Dream Pillow

What you will need: Cleansing materials; cloth (soft cottons, calico, velvet, or any other soft, pleasant material works well for dream pillows), scissors, needle, thread, dried herbs.

Estimated time: Time for obtaining the herbs, plus one hour to make the pillow.

1. Cleanse yourself and all materials to be used.

2. Fold the material in half, mark a square about eight by five inches, then cut out the square. If the material allows, cut through both layers together.

3. Turn the material inside out and pin together.

4. Sew three sides together, sewing across the top, down one side, and then across the bottom, so that you leave the last side open.

5. Assemble the herbs and any other materials you wish to place in the dream pillow. If you want to remember your dreams, the pillow should contain: mugwort, lavender, rose petals, and/or chamomile flowers. If you wish protection during your dream state, your pillow should contain one or more of these: mugwort, sage, cedar. If you are trying to recall some specific elements into your dreams, your dream pillow should include any or all of the following: lavender, mugwort, chamomile, and/or rose petals.

6. In addition, you can add something to symbolize the element of creation you wish to contact through your dreams. For example, if you want to contact the spirit of the deer, you might include a small deer dew claw in the dream pillow.

7. Fill the pillow with the herbs and any other materials until it is quite fluffy.

8. Sew the remaining side closed.

9. Before going to sleep, cleanse yourself and your dream pillow. Then place it under your regular pillow, and say a prayer to remember your dreams.

CHAPTER 5, PAGE 72

Exercise Nine: Working with Nightmares

Note: These techniques are not to be considered a cure for the type of nightmare that accompanies, and is a hallmark of, post–traumatic stress disorder. If you have recurrent nightmares, we encourage you to seek professional help.

Technique 1

What you will need: Time upon awakening to examine your dream experience.

Estimated time: Fifteen minutes to an hour.

1. When you wake up, either from the nightmare or in the morning, carefully examine the nightmare. Pay attention to all of the elements within it, particularly the most frightening aspect.

2. Look at that aspect as a symbol.

3. Examine the day preceding the nightmare.

4. Look for any unpleasant or unhappy situation that might have reflected into the dream world as some frightening symbol.

5. Try and understand the experience, and how and why it came into your dreamtime.

6. Whenever possible, correct the situation in waking time.

Technique II

What you will need. Time, either just before you go to sleep the night after a nightmare, or the first few minutes upon waking up after having a nightmare.

Estimated time: Five minutes.

1. Preferably in the first few minutes upon waking up in the morning after having had a nightmare, take the time to replay the dream and give it a happy ending.

2. If you cannot make the time in the morning, utilize the period just before you go to sleep the following night to replay your dream and give it a happy ending.

For example, if you dream of being chased by someone with murderous intent, go back into the dream and dream of that person being apprehended, disarmed, and imprisoned. If you don't like that ending, try another. For example, have the person with murderous intent realize that the wrong they perceive never occurred, making their murderous intent dissolve. You can even dream yourself befriending the person who had murderous intent.

Technique III

What you will need: Cleansing materials; knowledge of the Medicine Wheel Meditation described in Exercise Sixteen.

Estimated time: Fifteen minutes to a half hour.

1. Using the Medicine Wheel Meditation described in Exercise Sixteen, call the frightening element of the nightmare that is chasing you, and ask him who he is and what he wants.

2. Listen to the reply.

3. If possible, correct any situations that can be corrected in the waking time.

Using the example of John to illustrate this technique, a Medicine Wheel Meditation would involve him cleansing and centering, then going within his mind's eye to the center of the Medicine Wheel. Once there, he would call the tiger of his dream to him. Then he would ask the tiger, "Who are you?" The tiger would respond, "I am your brother Bill." John would ask, "What is it that you want? Why are you chasing me?," and Bill might reply, "I would like you to respect my opinions a little more regarding how you raise your children."

4. Use this technique as a guided meditation, taking someone else

through the process of confronting a nightmare aspect of a dream and having this aspect reveal its true nature and true desire.

5. If you learn the true nature and desire of the nightmare aspects, the nightmare usually ceases.

CHAPTER 5, PAGE 73

Exercise Ten: Enfolding Yourself Within Your Dream

What you will need: A focused state before drifting off to sleep.
Estimated time: One to five minutes.

1. If you have a dream that you wish to continue, try and elicit within yourself the sensation of wrapping the dream around you as you drift off to sleep.

2. To do this, replay the dream up to the point where you were awakened and the dream stopped.

3. Hold that spot in your mind as you drift off to sleep.

4. Particularly with dreams that were interrupted by telephone calls, a baby's cry, or other noises, you may have very good success with reentering and continuing a dream. It is possible to go back into the same dream more than once.

CHAPTER 5, PAGE 74

Exercise Eleven: Protecting Your Dream Space

What you will need: Cleansing materials.
Estimated time: Fifteen to thirty minutes.

1. Cleanse your sleeping space before going to bed.

2. Prior to going to sleep, place yourself in a meditative state.

3. Call out for a spirit of protection to come and stand beside your bed. You can summon four spirits, one for each cardinal point on the compass.

4. Envision these guardians standing facing away from you at each of the four cardinal points around your bed.

5. Or, imagine yourself facing east and saying within your mind and heart, "I ask now for a protector to come from the East, a guardian to stand at the east of my bed to guard and protect my dreams this night."

6. Facing south, in heart and mind you would again call out, "I ask for a protector to come from the South, a guardian to stand at my bed

and protect my dreams and sleep this night."

7. Repeat the process to the west and north.

8. Imagine these guardians standing at the four points of the bed.

9. Having called the four guardians, come out of the meditative state and then fall asleep.

CHAPTER 6, PAGE 81

Exercise Twelve: Working with Your Dreams

What you will need: A notebook or paper and a pen or pencil and/or a tape recorder; time upon awakening to both record your dream and to work with the elements of it.

Estimated time: Thirty minutes.

1. Write down a short dream that you've had during the night.

2. Write down how you see that dream reflecting your present.

3. Write down how that dream reflects your near past.

4. Write down how that dream reflects your far past.

5. Write down how that dream reflects your future.

6. Write down how that dream reflects where you are physically.

7. Write down how that dream reflects where you are mentally.

8. Write down how that dream reflects where you are emotionally.

9. Write down how that dream reflects where you are spiritually.

10. If you have others with whom you can share your dream, you will sometimes gain more information about yourself and your dream if you share the material you have written with someone else and allow them to comment.

CHAPTER 6, PAGE 81

Exercise Thirteen: Perspective in Dreams

What you will need: Paper and pen/pencil or a tape recorder.

Estimated time: Thirty minutes.

1. When interpreting a dream, it's important to note how removed you are from the dream content. The further removed you are, the more repressed the dream content is.

2. There are three perspectives common in dreams. The first is that you are taking part in whatever scenario the dream is presenting. This kind of dream represents something close to your consciousness.

The more dissimilar the dream you is from the real you, the more removed from your waking consciousness the content of the dream is. For example, if you dream of yourself as much older or younger, that dream content is removed from your conscious life.

3. The second dream perspective we refer to is the point of awareness. In this kind of dream, you are not aware of yourself as a participant or a nonparticipant. You seem to be a point of awareness within the dream, observing but not directly experiencing. Point of awareness dreams deal with something we are not quite so willing to look at in our conscious life.

4. A third dream perspective is where we are aware of ourselves as existing separate from the dream. You might be watching the dream as you would watch a movie, so that the dream is taking place in front of or behind you. We distance the dream from us as we distance the content from our conscious awareness. Such material is quite removed from your conscious awareness.

5. Some people dream they are dreaming. The material in the dream just before you wake up is much more accessible to you than the material in the dream in which you dreamed you were dreaming.

6. When you have a dream where you question whether you were asleep, the content of that dream is very close to the conscious surface of your mind.

7. To differentiate between your different perspectives in dreaming, it is critical that you record your dreams and then take the time to go over them and compare the different perspectives you experienced.

CHAPTER 6, PAGE 83

Exercise Fourteen: Luke Blue Eagle on Types of Dreams

What you will need: Material to record and review your dreams.

Estimated time: Fifteen to thirty minutes upon awakening, and thirty to sixty minutes or more once a week to review your dream content for that week.

1. The first level of dreams Luke Blue Eagle has identified are digestive dreams, or dreams that are doing things on a physical level, processing things on a physical level. These are dreams where the images are of no importance and don't have any particular meaning.

2. Another kind of dream is one where you're mentally processing things that happened during the day or during the previous days. These dreams

also don't have much importance. They're not of a level where you should sit down and work with them. They're just about daily stuff that hasn't been done and needs to get done.

3. Another reason for the aforementioned type of dream is that we live lives where there's too much information, so we have to process a lot of it in the nighttime. These kinds of dreams are good to practice remembering your dreams.

4. Another type of dream talks about the person's psychology. It's a spiritual type of dream that speaks symbolically to the dreamer of the way he is, what's happening in his life, how he's reacting, and how he is in a general way. This kind of dream makes it easier to evolve and perfect your being. This type of dream never offers solutions, all it does is just show in a symbolic way how you're living your life.

5. On this level of dreaming are the fun dreams, dreams in which you're flying, experimenting, having a pleasant time, but on a level that's very spiritual. Luke feels this is one of the higher levels of dreams.

6. The final level of dreaming is what in French is called *le songe*. This is a dream that is very particular, clear, and contained. You remember everything in it so very clearly that it seems more real than real life. This kind of dream sticks with you because it is a straight message from the spirit world, meant to be shared with other people.

7. The only way to begin to differentiate between your own dreams is to take the time to record them, and then to take the time to reflect upon them when you have enough dreams that you have a basis for comparison.

CHAPTER 7, PAGE 97

Exercise Fifteen: Working with a Dream Council

What you will need: A group willing to meet regularly to discuss their dreams as a way of experiencing personal growth. You will also need cleansing materials and a talking stick.

Estimated time: One to three hours, depending upon the size of the group.

1. You might meet with your family, with a group of individuals living together, or with a group of individuals who get together regularly for personal growth and have decided to meet to discuss their dreams.

2. The individuals involved would begin the dream council by some method of cleansing themselves.

3. The talking stick is also cleansed, and then given to the person upon whose dream the council is going to focus.

4. That person, while holding the talking stick, tells the circle the story of his or her dream.

5. The person then passes the talking stick to the person sitting to the immediate left.

6. That person, and each person in their turn, is allowed to question the dreamer on the finer points of the dream—colors, qualities, feelings, nuances—that may have been missed in the first telling.

7. The talking stick can pass around the circle of the dream council up to three times, or until no one else has any more questions about the actual content of the dream.

8. The dreamer then tells the council what he or she feels the dream means.

9. In their turn, each member of the council, as they hold the talking stick, tells the dreamer what he or she feels the dream means.

10. When the stick returns to the dreamer, the person may elect to say again what he or she feels the dream means if it has changed at all after the input of the other people.

11. It is important to understand that each person's interpretation of the dream is true and correct for that person, and not necessarily for the dreamer. Each person interprets the dream from their own frame of reference, even when they are using information they have about the dreamer.

12. By sharing the dream in the dream council, the dream becomes a dream of that council. In effect, every person participating gets to have more dreams.

CHAPTER 7, PAGE 98

Exercise Sixteen: Owning Your Dream

What you will need: Materials for recording and interpreting your dream. This exercise can be done alone, with one other person, or with a circle of people.

Estimated time: A half hour to two hours, depending on the size of the group involved.

1. This technique, at least initially, works best with short dreams.

2. The dreamer writes out the dream in as much detail as possible.

3. The dreamer then owns each element in the dream.

4. Owning the dream always begins with the following statement: "I am dreaming, and the dreaming part of me is a _____" (fill in the blank). Every aspect of the dream is brought into the present tense, first person, and described as a part of the dreamer.

5. When this first round of owning is completed, the dreamer says, "And I am awake," to indicate the end of the round.

6. It is possible that speaking the dream in this way will trigger insight that makes the meaning and intent of the dream clearer to the person speaking.

7. If that is not the case, or if particular parts of the dream are difficult to understand, or if you want to get at other levels of interpretation, then the dreamer takes the time to write down lists of words he or she associates with the words used to describe the dream.

8. If people are helping the dreamer, they also take the time to write down such a list. For example, if you used the term yellow rose, you would say, "I am dreaming, and the dreaming part of me is a yellow part of me, which is a cowardly part of me, which is a hopeful part of me, which is a fearful part of me, which is a denying part of me, which is a spiritually powerful part of me." You would go on from there, describing all of the things you associate with the color yellow. Then you would take the word rose and do the same thing.

9. As you go through and process each part of the dream this way, you will get additional insights.

10. When you have finished this round, you would say, "And I am awake."

11. Be sure to record any insights you gain from this method of owning all elements of your dream.

CHAPTER 7, PAGE 100

Exercise Seventeen: Medicine Wheel Dream Meditation

What you will need: Access to a Medicine Wheel, if possible, otherwise a calm and conducive place to sit in meditation; cleansing materials; a drum or rattle; materials to write or record your dream; optional, a drumming tape.

Estimated time: Thirty minutes.

1. If you have constructed a Medicine Wheel, whether large or small, go to it and sit at whatever place feels right to you. If you are not familiar with the Medicine Wheel, the best place to start is with the position

that corresponds with your birth. If you were born in the spring, sit in the East; in the summer, the South; in the autumn, the West; in the winter, the North.

2. If you don't have a Medicine Wheel or if it is impractical to sit at it, sit anyplace that is calm and conducive to meditation.

3. Once you're sitting comfortably, cleanse yourself.

4. If you wish, you can chant or drum for a few minutes to get yourself more centered and focused.

5. It is possible to do this entire meditation drumming or listening to a drumming tape, and some people find this to be a very powerful method.

6. Once you've cleansed and centered yourself, close your eyes and imagine the Medicine Wheel in front of you.

7. In your mind's eye, get up and walk to the center of the Medicine Wheel.

8. As you stand in the center of the Medicine Wheel, begin by saying something like this: "Creator, I come with honor and respect for those who have gone before me, with honor and respect for those who walk beside me in this earth walk, and with honor and respect for those who have yet to come, the great grandchildren of my children's grandchildren. I come seeking truth and understanding about the dream I have had. I ask only that which is of the light and love and truth and life. All else, all negativity be banned from this circle."

9. You would then state your entire dream within this inner circle.

10. You would end by inviting your own internal dream council to come and share with you. You might do this in the following manner: "I now invite the members of my sacred dream council to come and sit with me in the circle of the ancient Medicine Wheel. I call my child, male and female, from the East; I call my adolescent, male and female, from the South; I call my adult, male and female, from the West; I call my elder, male and female, from the North."

11. Imagine these eight figures stepping into the Medicine Wheel, and sitting down with you in a circle.

12. Address each one, one at a time. Begin with the child that is of the same sex, and say something like: "I ask from you the gift of understanding of this dream. Tell me what it means to you."

13. Be peaceful, quiet, and listen to the response from that still, small voice within you.

14. As each member of the Medicine Wheel circle finishes speaking, thank them for the gifts they have shared with you. You may use the words: "Thank you for the wisdom you have shared with me. I ask that I use this wisdom in a good and wise way."

15. When the last of these eight teachers have spoken to you and you

have thanked them, thank them as a group before you leave the circle. You could use the following words: "I give thanks to you, my dream circle, thanks to you and thanks to all of my relations. It is good."

16. If you haven't done so already, imagine these teachers leaving you.

17. Imagine yourself getting back up from the center of the Medicine Wheel and returning to where you were sitting.

18. Gently become aware of your surroundings.

19. Stretch, open your eyes, feel the earth beneath you and the sky above you.

20. Give thanks for the wisdom that has been shared with you.

21. It is good to take the time to record what your dream council has told you.

CHAPTER 7, PAGE 102

Exercise Eighteen: Concentration/Meditation

What you will need: A comfortable place to sit, a clock within easy view; optional, a Tibetan bowl, bells, or cymbals.

Estimated time: Five minutes to an hour.

1. This technique, which is used to help you understand a dream symbol that does not make sense to you, no matter how you work with it, has two phases, the concentration phase and the meditation phase. The concentration phase can be from one to ten minutes long, and the meditation phase can be equal to or up to four times longer than the concentration phase.

2. Sit in a comfortable position, with a body attitude that is closed.— that is, your ankles are gently crossed, and your hands are folded or lying on your thighs, palms down.

3. Begin to concentrate on one thing. You can use any single sense for this focus of concentration—for example, sight, where you focus on a burning candle or on a picture. You can focus on sound, either a mantra or the sound produced by a Tibetan bowl, bells, or cymbals, struck once. Listen, and focus all your attention on that sound as it slowly fades into silence. It is possible that you may have to strike the instrument several times during the period of your concentration to renew the sound on which you are focused. Eventually you'll be able to strike the instrument once, and the sound will carry throughout the concentration phase. You may also use incense or smudge as a focus for the sense of smell. You can also use the sense of taste, or the flow of your breath. It really doesn't matter what you concentrate on, as long as you concentrate.

4. While concentration sounds easy, it might be more difficult than you imagine. If you find your mind wandering, bring it back without recrimination. It is important not to change the sense with which you've decided to concentrate in the middle of the process. Stick with it through one concentration period, and preferably through five more, before you select another point of focus.

5. We recommend five minutes the first few times you try concentration/meditation. Have a watch or a clock easily within view so you can open your eyes and see what time it is.

6. At the end of your concentration phase, uncross your feet and turn your palms face upwards to the sky.

7. At that moment, ask within your inner being, "What is the meaning of this symbol?"

8. Then meditate or observe. You might find this just as difficult as focusing.

9. When you find yourself in a daydream, remove yourself from it and return to the position of observer.

10. This technique may require many attempts, but if you use the technique of concentration for five minutes, asking the question "What does this particular symbol mean?" and then allowing yourself to be open for an answer to that question for the next five minutes, without hanging onto thoughts, eventually an answer will come to you.

11. It is very important that you don't ask about another symbol before you have the answer to the first one.

12. The answer may not come to you within the observation phase. It may come later in the day, or it may come within another dream. It may come out of the mouth of a friend, or it may come from a book you open intentionally or by accident.

13. As you get better at using the technique, the answers about a symbol may come more and more quickly, until you get to the point where you merely have to think of asking "What does this symbol mean?" and the answer will come clearly into your mind.

CHAPTER 8, PAGE 112

Exercise Nineteen: Dreaming Together

Technique I

What you will need: A group of people who wish to dream together; optional, dream pillows or pouches for everyone in the group.

Estimated time: For preparation, thirty minutes.

1. It is possible for a group of people to dream together simply by sitting and praying together.

2. The focus and prayer should take about thirty minutes.

3. Another thing that can help a group of people to dream together is for each person to make a dream pillow or pouch, which they would pass around the circle, with each person holding every item for a moment and then passing it on until the pillow or pouch returns to its owner.

4. Everyone would then sleep with a pillow or pouch under their pillow or beside their bed as preparation and focus for the group dream.

Technique II

What you will need: A large room, and a group of people who wish to dream together.

Estimated time: Eight to ten hours.

1. Everyone in the group cleanses, concentrates, and focuses.

2. Then people form a wide circle with their heads directed toward the center so that they sleep as if each were a petal of a large daisy.

3. After sleeping, the group gets together and reports the dreams they've had to see whether this method produced results.

CHAPTER 8, PAGE 114

Exercise Twenty: Meditation to Dream Together

What you will need: Desire on both people's part to dream together; a realization that dreaming together can change the nature of a relationship; a dream pillow made as instructed below; time to meditate; drums, rattles, or chanting tapes.

Estimated time: Preparation phase (making the dream pillow), one hour; meditating together, one to two hours; reporting the results, one to two hours.

1. Remember that this meditation can only be done with the conscious permission of the other people involved. Discuss with each other your desire to dream together and become clear on your reasons. The clearer your reasons, the more likely you are to have a pleasant and successful experience.

2. Each participant makes a dream pillow. Be very focused while you are doing so. See the instructions for making a dream pillow in Exercise Eight. Include one or more of the following herbs: mugwort, lavender, rose petals, and chamomile. Also put in a picture of yourself or, in your own handwriting, your name, date of birth, place of birth, and the address

where you are currently living. All this is done with the thought that you are giving this pillow to the other person as a gift so you might share dreams together. Sew the dream pillow closed.

3. Go to a Medicine Wheel, or some other place where you can sit together in meditation.

4. Cleanse yourselves and the dream pillows.

5. Sit side by side at a point on the Wheel that feels comfortable, and center yourselves by meditation, chanting, drumming, or by listening to a tape.

6. When you feel centered, reach out with the hand closest to the other person. Hold hands joined palm to palm, while you are doing the meditation.

7. You can continue doing this as a guided meditation, with one of you being the guide, or you can do it with each of you doing the visualization in your own heart and mind.

8. In your heart and mind's eye, with your hands joined together, get up and walk to the center of the Medicine Wheel circle. When in the center, ask the Creator to bring each of you into harmony, so that you might walk together in the dreamtime.

9. Imagine the Creator and the forces of the center of the circle playing through you, making adjustments in the frequency of your vibrations so that, from head to toe, there becomes a harmony between the two of you.

10. When harmony has been achieved, return to the place where your bodies are sitting in meditation.

11. Gently squeeze the hand of your partner, release it, and stretch.

12. Become aware of your surroundings.

13. If you are doing this silently, you might cue each other with gentle hand pressures. A first pressure would indicate you are ready to go into the center of the circle. The second pressure would indicate you are ready to leave and are waiting for a response from your partner.

14. When you are back in normal time, give each other the dream pillows you have made and agree upon a day and time the shared dream is to take place.

15. On the night of the shared dream, prepare as you always would for remembering your dreams. Be sure to have the paper and pencil, or tape recorder with tape in it, by your bed ready to go.

16. Place the dream pillow under your own pillow, beside your head, or underneath your head, and allow yourself to drift off to sleep.

17. Make a point of recording all the dreams you remember from that night.

18. Get together with your dream companion the next day, if possible, and compare dreams.

19. It may take several attempts before you succeed in having a shared dream. Continue with the guided meditation on a daily basis until you have success with the shared dream.

20. After your first success, continue with the shared meditation for a period of time until the pattern of dreaming together is firmly established. Once it is established, all you need to do to dream with the other person on any given night is to take out the dream pillow and sleep with it.

CHAPTER 9: PAGE 119

Exercise Twenty-one: Taking a Mini-Walkabout

What you will need: A wild area or a park; a day when you are fasting at least from solid foods; a method of cleansing yourself; a notebook or journal and pen or pencil, or a tape recorder.

Estimated time: One to four hours.

1. Set aside the time to go into the country or into the park.

2. Fast, at least from solid foods, prior to and during your mini-walkabout.

3. Be sure to go to an area you have scouted out ahead of time, one in which you feel safe and comfortable.

4. Begin by cleansing yourself if you have access to a sauna or a sweat lodge. If that is not the case, smudge or cleanse yourself.

5. When you arrive at your chosen area, begin to walk.

6. Open yourself up consciously by observing every aspect of nature.

7. Note the physical surroundings, the plants and animals, changes within the sky, the wind, the temperature, everything.

8. At the completion of the time you have scheduled, take your journal and write down everything you have seen, everything that happened, as if it were a dream.

9. After you write things down, work with them. Work with all the symbols that came to you as if they were from a dream, coming from your subconscious, speaking to you. The events of the mini-walkabout need to be interpreted just as if they were visionary dreams.

10. Interpreting them this way clearly reveals the person and the path you are walking in life. It will also help you to understand your dream language.

Bibliography

Andrews, Lynn V. *The Power Deck: The Cards of Wisdom*. San Francisco: Harper San Francisco, 1991.

Bach, Edward, and F. J. Wheeler. *The Bach Flower Remedies*. New Canaan, Conn.: Keith Publishing Company, 1931, 1933, 1952, 1979.

Bouerkens, Beth. *By the Light of Your Dreams*. (no information available; library does not list book)

Bro, Dr. Harmon Hartzell, under the editorship of Hugh Lynn Cayce. *Edgar Cayce on Dreams*. New York: Warner Communications Company, 1968.

Brown, Tom, Jr. *Tom Brown's Field Guide to Wilderness Survival*. New York: Berkley Books, 1983.

Bryant, Dorothy. *The Kin of Ata Are Waiting for You* (formerly published as *The Comforter*). New York: Moon Books, 1971.

Bryant, Page. *The Aquarian Guide to Native American Mythology*. London: The Aquarian Press, 1991.

Campbell, Dan, under the editorship of Charles Thomas Cayce. *Edgar Cayce on the Power of Colors, Stones, and Crystals*. New York: Warner Books, 1989.

Caras, Roger. *The Endless Migrations*. New York: E. P. Dutton, 1985.

Castaneda, Carlos. *Journey to Ixtlán*. New York: Simon & Schuster, 1972.

Chesterman, Charles W. *The Audubon Society Field Guide to North American Rocks and Minerals.* New York: Alfred A. Knopf, 1979.

Door, Gary. "The New Shamans." *The Foundation for Shamanic Studies Newsletter,* vol. 3, no. 3. Westport, Conn., 1991. First appeared in *Yoga Journal,* 1989.

Eaton, Evelyn (Mahad'yuni). *I Send a Voice.* Wheaton, Ill.: Theosophical Publishing House, 1978.

———. *Snowy Earth Comes Gliding.* Spokane, Wash.: Bear Tribe Publishing, 1974.

———. *The Shaman and the Medicine Wheel.* Wheaton, Ill.: Theosophical Publishing House, 1982.

Faughan-Lee, Llewellyn. *The Lover and the Serpent.* Dorset, England: Element Books, 1990.

Fay, Marie. *The Dream Guide.* Los Angeles: Center for the Healing Arts, 1978.

Fontana, David. *Dream Life: Understanding and Using Your Dreams.* Dorset, England: Element Books, 1990.

Foster, Steven, with Meredith Little. *The Book of the Vision Quest.* New York: Prentice-Hall Press, 1987.

———. *The Roaring of the Sacred River.* New York: Prentice-Hall Press, 1989.

Freud, Sigmund. *The Interpretation of Dreams.* First published New York: Carlton House, 1931. Reissued: New York: Modern Library, 1978.

Garfield, Patricia. *The Healing Power of Dreams.* New York: Simon & Schuster, 1991.

Gonzales, Magda Weck (Star Spider Woman), and J. A. Gonzales (Rattling Bear). *Star Spider Speaks: The Teachings of the Native American Tarot.* Stanford, Conn. U.S Game Systems, Inc., 1990.

Halifax, Joan. *Shamanic Voices.* New York: E. P. Dutton, 1979.

Hamilton, A. Tyler. *Pueblo Birds and Myths.* Flagstaff, Ariz.: Northland Publishing Company, 1991.

Hausman, Gerald. *Turtle Island Alphabet: A Lexicon of Native American Symbols and Culture.* New York: St. Martin's Press, 1992.

Hendricks, Gay, and Russel Wills. *The Centering Book.* Inglewood Cliffs, NJ: Prentice-Hall, Inc., 1975.

Hutchens, Alma R. *Indian Herbology of North America.* Ontario, Canada: Merko, 1973.

Hylpon, William H. *The Rodale Herb Book.* Emmaus, Pa.: Rodale Press, 1974.

Johnston, Basil. *Ojibwa Heritage.* Toronto, Canada: McClellan and Stewart, 1976.

Jung, Karl G. *Man and His Symbols.* Garden City, N.Y.: Doubleday, 1964.

Kaplan-Williams, Strephon. *Dream Cards*. New York: Simon & Schuster, 1991.

Krieger, Louis C. C. *The Mushroom Handbook*. New York: Dover Publications, 1967.

Medicine Eagle, Brooke. *Buffalo Woman Comes Singing*. New York: Ballantine Books, 1991.

Medicine Story. *Return to Creation*. Spokane, Wash.: Bear Tribe Publishing, 1991.

Miller, Gustavus Hindeman. *The Dictionary of Dreams*. New York: Simon & Schuster, 1992.

Moony, James. *The Ghost Dance Religion: Smohalla and His Doctrine, Extract from the Bureau of American Ethnology*. Seattle, Wash.: The Shorey Bookstore, 1972.

Neihardt, John G. *Black Elk Speaks*. Lincoln, Nebraska: University of Nebraska Press, 1961.

Nitsch, Twylah. *Entering into the Silence: The Seneca Way*. Irving, N.Y.: Wolf Clan Teaching Society Publications, 1976.

———. *Wisdom of the Seneca*. Irving, N.Y.: Wolf Clan Teaching Society Publications, 1979.

Orien. *Dreams, Hidden Meanings, and Secrets*. New York: Simon & Schuster, 1987.

Ott, Jonathan. *Hallucinogenic Plants of North America*. Berkley, Calif.: Rainbow Press, 1976.

Perry, Francis, ed. *Simon & Schuster's Complete Guide to Plants and Flowers*. New York: Simon & Schuster, 1974.

Peterson, Lee Allen. *A Field Guide to Edible Wild Plants, Eastern and Central North America*. Boston: Houghton Mifflin Company, 1977.

Peterson, Roger Tory. *A Field Guide to the Birds East of the Rockies*. Boston: Houghton Mifflin Company, 1980.

Reed, Anderson. *Shouting at the Wolf: A Guide to Identifying and Warding Off Evil in Everyday Life*. New York: Carroll Publishing Group, 1990.

Relander, Click. *Drummers and Dreamers*. Caldwell, Id.: The Caxton Printers, Ltd., 1956.

Sams, Jamie. *Sacred Path Cards*. San Francisco: Harper San Francisco, 1990.

Sams, Jamie, and David Carson. *Medicine Cards*. Santa Fe, N.M.: Bear & Company, 1988.

Schultes, Richard Evans, and Elbert Hofmann. *Plants of the Gods: Origins of Hallucinogenic Use*. New York: McGraw Hill Book Company, 1979.

Scully, Nicki. *The Golden Cauldron*. Santa Fe, N.M.: Bear & Company, 1991.

Sechrist, Elsie. *Dreams—Your Magic Mirror*. New York: Warner Books, 1974.

Sun Bear. *At Home in the Wilderness*. Happy Camp, Calif.: Naturegraph Publishers, 1968.

———. *Buffalo Hearts*. Spokane, Wash.: Bear Tribe Publishing, 1976.

———. *The Path of Power*. As told to Wabun and to Barry Weinstock. New York: Prentice Hall Press, 1986.

Sun Bear, Crysalis Mulligan, Peter Nufer, and Wabun. *Walk in Balance: The Path to Healthy, Happy, Harmonious Living*. New York: Prentice-Hall Press, 1989.

Sun Bear, with Wabun Wind. *Black Dawn, Bright Day*. New York: Simon & Schuster, 1992.

Sun Bear and Wabun. *The Medicine Wheel: Earth Astrology*. New York: Simon & Schuster, 1980.

Sun Bear, Wabun, Nimimosha, and the Tribe. *The Bear Tribe's Self-Reliance Book*. New York: Simon & Schuster, 1987.

Sun Bear, Wabun Wind, and Crysalis Mulligan. *Dancing with the Wheel: The Medicine Wheel Workbook*. New York: Prentice-Hall Press, 1991.

Whittaker, John O., Jr. *The Audubon Society Field Guide to North American Mammals*. New York: Alfred A. Knopf, 1980

Wind, Wabun. *Woman of the Dawn*. New York: Berkley Books, 1989.

Wind, Wabun, and Anderson Reed. *Lightseeds: A Compendium of Ancient and Contemporary Crystal Knowledge*. New York: Prentice-Hall Press, 1988.

Wren, R. W. *Potter's New Cyclopaedia of Medicinal Herbs and Preparations*. New York: Harper New York, 1972.

Ywahoo, Dhyani. *Voices of Our Ancestors*. Boston: Shambhala, 1987.

Zolar. *Book of Dreams, Numbers, and Lucky Days*. New York: Prentice-Hall Press, 1985.

———. *Encyclopedia and Dictionary of Dreams*. New York: Simon & Schuster, 1963.

The Dream Council

Luke Blue Eagle
C.P. 85
Loretteville, Quebec, Canada, G2B 3W6
   Luke Blue Eagle is a healer and teacher who has studied with teachers from the Apache, Cherokee, and Mohawk nations. He worked with Sun Bear for ten years. He is a pipe carrier who has been empowered by Sun Bear to awaken pipes. Luke has an apprentice program and does a lot of work with the Native people of Quebec. He is the author of two books: *The Use of Crystals in Therapy* and *The Sacred Heritage of the Amerindian People,* both available in French. Luke teaches in both French and English.

Brooke Medicine Eagle
P.O. Box 121
Ovando, Montana 59854
   Brooke Medicine Eagle is an American Native Earthkeeper, teacher, healer, songwriter, ceremonial leader, sacred ecologist, and author of *Buffalo Woman Comes Singing*. She is dedicated to bringing forward the ancient truths concerning how to live a fully human life in harmony with all

of our relations. At home in the Montana forest, Brooke is the creator of EagleSong, a series of spiritually oriented wilderness camps and is the founder of FlowerSong Project, which promotes a sustainable, ecologically sound beauty path upon the Mother Earth.

Steven Foster and Meredith Little
The School of Lost Borders
Rites of Passage Press
Box 55
Big Pine, California 93513

The School of Lost Borders is a training facility for wilderness rites and ceremonies of initiatory passage. The facility trains others in the form and process of conducting people in life transition through these ceremonies. Candidates for training may apply for regimens two weeks to two months in length. Training involves personal experience with fasting, solitude, and exposure in natural places. Teachings include the four shields of initiation, the vision fast, earth lodge and purpose circle, the mythos of life story, "Mirroring," initiatory archetypes and allegory, deep ecology, no-trace camping, safety, emergency and first-aid procedures, and intense self-study. Enrollment is open to people of any heritage, ethnicity, sex, or sexual preference. Candidates may be required to pledge their intent as far in advance as a year.

The codirectors, Dr. Steven Foster and Meredith Little, have conducted wilderness passage rites for over twenty years. The fruits of their experience and apprenticeship to a variety of teachers (among whom was Sun Bear) are set forth in several books: *The Book of the Vision Quest: Personal Transformation in the Wilderness, The Trail Ahead: A Course Book for Graduating Seniors, The Sacred Mountain: A Vision Fast Handbook for Adults, The Roaring of the Sacred River: The Wilderness Quest for Vision and Healing,* and *Betwixt and Between: Patterns of Masculine and Feminine Initiation,* edited with Louise Mahdi. Dr. Foster, who has worked with people in initiatory work since 1971, is currently working on a book entitled *The Four Shields of Initiation: The Foundations of Eco-Psychology.* This book will be available in 1994.

Page Bryant Guynup
707 Brunswick Drive
Waynesville, North Carolina 28786

Page is an internationally recognized author, teacher, lecturer, and psychic counselor. She and her husband, new-age visionary artist Scott Guynup, have traveled extensively throughout the United States for the past twenty-one years and in England for the past three years, conduct-

ing lectures, workshops, and seminars on planetary changes and awareness, sacred sites, ceremony, astronomy, ancient wisdom, and earth energy. Page is the author of *The Ancient Starwalkers, Terravision,
Awakening Arthur, The Aquarian Guide to Native American Mythology,
The Earth Changes Survival Handbook, Crystals and Their Use, The Magic
of Minerals,* as well as others.

*Twylah Nitsch
12199 Brant Reservation Road
Irving, New York 14081*

   Grandmother Twylah Nitsch is the guiding energy behind the Seneca
Indian Historical Society and the Elder of the Wolf Clan Teaching Lodge.
Many decades ago she was designated to preserve the Wolf Clan Teachings by her maternal grandfather, Moses Shongo, the last of the practic-
ing Seneca medicine men. Twylah is also a direct descendant of the Seneca
peace chief Red Jacket. Grandmother Twylah is an author, lecturer, teacher,
and advocate of the need to preserve the teachings and wisdom of Native
Peoples.

Index

About the Authors

Shawnodese
16149 Redmond Way, Suite 308
Redmond, Washington 98052

Shawnodese has worked with Sun Bear and the Bear Tribe since 1979, creating and developing much of the course work for Sun Bear's apprenticeship program. He is a healer of both mind and body.

Sun Bear

Sun Bear, a sacred teacher of Chippewa descent, was the founder and medicine chief of the Bear Tribe, a multiracial educational society. He was a world-renowned lecturer and teacher, and the author or coauthor of eight books. He was the creator and publisher of the magazine *Wildfire,* and founder of the World Earth Fund. Sun Bear passed into spirit in 1992.

Wabun and the Bear Tribe
P.O. Box 9167
Spokane, Washington 99209-9167

Wabun Wind, Sun Bear's named successor as director of the Bear Tribe and publisher of *Wildfire,* is the author or coauthor of nine books, a lecturer, ceremonialist, transpersonal practitioner, wife, and mother. She holds an M.S. from the Columbia School of Journalism and has written for a wide variety of publications. She is on the board of advisors for *Women of Power Magazine* and the World Earth Fund. She teaches professionals how to give Medicine Wheel and Earthstone consultations.